5 3 8
Five-Thirty-Eight

5 3 8
Five-Thirty-Eight

**The One Hundred Year Electoral College Disaster
How Can America Achieve "One Person, One Vote"**

Joe Albanese

Library of Congress Control Number: 2024915389
ISBN: Hardcover   979-8-3694-2618-0
               Softcover   979-8-3694-2617-3
               eBook   979-8-3694-2616-6

Exterior Design done by Michele Hoffman
Tables and Interior Graphics done by Derek Albanese

Print information available on the last page.

Rev. date: 10/02/2024

To order additional copies of this book, contact:
Xlibris
844-714-8691
www.Xlibris.com
Orders@Xlibris.com
844673

Contents

INTRODUCTION

The process of election affords a moral certainty, that the office of President will never fall to the lot of any man who is not in an eminent degree endowed with the requisite qualifications. Talents for low intrigue, and the little arts of popularity, may alone suffice to elevate a man to the first honors in a single State; but it will require other talents, and a different kind of merit, to establish him in the esteem and confidence of the whole Union, or of so considerable a portion of it as would be necessary to make him a successful candidate for the distinguished office of President of the United States.
—Alexander Hamilton, Federalist Paper No. 68
(March 14, 1788)

Do you remember voting for the president of the United States in a mock classroom election in your elementary, middle school, junior high, or high school days? It became a regular practice whenever we studied American history or government during a presidential election year. Although your vote did not count because you were not old enough to vote. Plus, many of us did not follow any of the candidates and what their policies were for or against. The fact is most of us at our early age get most of our political information listening to our parents and sometimes other relatives at the dinner table or watching national news on the television. It was a regular exercise that showed us, as students, the value of exercising our right to vote while also making us aware of what the historical importance was of choosing the most powerful person in the free world— the president of the United States.

Now we are older, wiser, and have hopefully registered to vote. Every four years on the Tuesday after the first Monday of November, hundreds of millions of US citizens who are registered to vote will place their ballots. Then when the polls close that evening, the votes are counted, and a winner is usually declared—or maybe not? Why? Because we do not directly vote to elect the president. We are really voting for the electors committed to a specific presidential candidate, according to the rules of the very confusing Electoral College system. Also, the national media networks who declare "projected winners" on election night are the final decision makers.

This method makes voters feel less important and totally disenfranchised, resulting in low voter turnouts because they stay home or do not vote at all, or even worse, never register to vote. The problem is the 236-year-old Electoral College system. There are several opinions whether we should reform or abolish this antique election system that was written into the Constitution in 1787 because of limited knowledge that our framers had about the people of America.

In this book, I will give you the historical details and events relating to the many pros and cons of the Electoral College versus the one person, one vote concept. Remember there were no political parties in 1787 or no daily newspapers. Other newspapers took days or weeks to reach the public. Also, we had no radio or television, and of course, no social media networks. Remember we were a new country that finally obtained its independence through a brutally fought long war that finally released us from the stranglehold of the British.

The book will demonstrate how our original framers could have dealt with these consequences as early as 1796. There is always the ever-present danger of "wrong winners," or the looming possibility of a "no winner" situations causing Congress to choose the president, which our framers vehemently opposed. And they had that part correct. Unchallenged gerrymandering, voter suppression, and simple favorite son bias also became corrupt political partisanship.

There are many valuable studies of significant alternative reforms that could offer satisfactory solutions to these inadequacies of the present electoral system. Also, there are possibilities of completely reforming or abolishing the present Electoral College that can work nationally. These studies and how they will work will be presented in detail. The solutions will demonstrate how the current Electoral College runs contrary to principles of an equal democratic government.

The reasoning that residents of the so-called "least populated and least represented small states" lead people to believe their votes are not worth very much compared to those voting in "larger more populated states." However, there is sufficient data and evidence that we can argue does the complete opposite, making misrepresentation another partisan talking point.

The presidency is the grand prize and crown jewel of American politics, so it is not surprising to find partisanship has played a significant role in the debate about how we should best choose our chief executive. For decades, Americans have protested tirelessly for true election bipartisan reform of the presidential election process. Consequently, there have been no less than 700 challenges to the system without any success, making it a major objective to describe and analyze later.

At the time of this publication, there is unfortunate dissension among the political leadership of both parties who refuse to work as a bipartisan team to reform or abolish this electoral system. Political differences continue to stand in the way of assuring the American people directly choose its president as the Constitution states, and that we are "of and for the people" and not indebted to any political party or their personal agendas. These concerns and problems directly influence terribly low voter turnouts as only two times in our history has 60 percent of registered voters in presidential elections showed up to vote due to them being disenfranchised. If free and fair elections are to become the norm of our democracy, the integrity of the voting system must be undaunted.

This book is unique in focusing closely on the procedural problems of our electoral system and the potential corrections that can solve many distinct types of voting systems. The contents will recommend several reforms that will safeguard our democracy and ensure that the voice of the people, not the voice of politicians, is heard loud and clear. The book enlightens issues to the pure values that are vital to our democracy. All these issues are directly tied to an insufficient electoral system that we have.

History shows the primary factors in success, longevity and integrity have been the development of procedures for peaceful and orderly transfers of political power from one generation to the next. History has been messed up by nations that collapsed not because of external threats, but rather under the strains of internal rivalries who use political powers instead of people power. This political power has become far more important to ensuring future leaders are righteous, fair, competent, and acceptable. As far back as the Roman Empire, internal rivalries for political power were shredded from inside due to the incompetence of political leaders that ultimately caused other democracies to fall.

There is a need to challenge us to increase our civic engagement that will cause a compelling case for reforms that will keep American elections democratic (with a small *d*) and give more of the electable powers to the people. There are many analyses in the relationship to individual state populations versus equal votes for everyone. We offer a strong debate of how the impact of political affiliations, money, and lobbyists have on American elections.

Disastrous elections will be dealt with in great length when we argue clear proof it should never happen again, especially with the technological advancements of this twenty-first century. We explore the difference between voter issues today and access to nearly all forms of information to help us make intelligent choices on our own versus those who had no access to what was needed to make those important decisions in earlier centuries. We will raise substantial and reasonable debate whether "one person one vote" really exists in the present election system. We will uncover false narratives that the opposite is true due to antiquated laws backing a system that could be easily considered violations of many constitutional rights and laws.

There are a lot of historical events and the future proposals for and against the Electoral College and the pros and cons will be discussed at great length. However, there is one important note to consider as you begin reading this book, and that is the issue that if the Electoral College system is the best way to choose a president, why would we have tried to reform or abolish it more than 700 times?

CHAPTER 1
How the Electoral College Was Created

The functions of our Electoral College and how it chooses our president is sometimes traced all the way back to the Centurial Assembly system used by the Roman Republic. It gave what the government leaders who were considered the most knowledgeable and informed individuals to select leaders based on the merits. The system allowed only adult male Roman citizens to be divided into groups of one hundred (which were called Centuries) according to their wealth. Each group of one hundred was entitled to only casting one vote either in favor or against the proposals submitted to them by the Roman Senate.[1]

That would be comparable to our Electoral College that uses a state population size to determine how many representatives that state has in Congress and consequently would be the number of electors designated for that state. Our original system only allowed white male landowners twenty-one years or older the right to vote which caused discrepancies in determining populations of states. These electors would vote as a single state for the winner of that state. The two systems have similar designs because they share some of the advantages and disadvantages. These similarities between our Electoral College and the ancient classical institutions is not an accident, because our Founding Fathers were knowledgeable about ancient history.[2]

Before a national leader, or president, could be chosen delegations of our various colonies (that later became state legislatures), the First (1774) and Second (1775–1781) Continental Congress were tasked with creating our first functioning provisional federal government. In 1777, the Articles of Confederation became our first informal constitution drafted by the Second Continental Congress. It made decisions and modifications but lacked enforcement powers needed because it required unanimous approval and ratification from all thirteen state legislatures.[3]

As the Revolutionary War ended, the country was still without an official governing body. Finally, the Second Continental Congress became the Confederation Congress (1781–1788). A group of men formed an assembly of representatives from all 13 colonies, many of which were Founding Fathers who signed the Declaration of Independence, creating a temporary government. This Congress appointed temporary leaders each year to preside over and serve the country. The delegates established an acceptable national government, known as the Articles of Confederation, that became the framework for the Constitution.[4] However, they did not establish a separate executive branch, the president. Those congressional committees under congressional direction.

To understand where the United States was headed under this Articles of Confederation reflected the individual state constitutions between 1776 and 1787, the government was dominated by state legislatures in favor of a federal government with a single stronger executive. We must think in terms of what the political climate was led to the idea of an executive holding substantial unstated, unenumerated, or residual rights because this executive power would avoid against potentially oppressive authorities.[5]

As we know, George Washington became America's first President after the Articles of Confederation in 1789 when the Constitution became the official framework for the United States of America. Washington was elected unanimously.[6]

In 1787, the Constitutional Convention began framing our US Constitution that appointed George Washington President by that convention. The framers deliberated with the first order of business to draft an effective central government that had a wide range of power that replaced the Articles of Confederation. Two plans of a federal government arose from the convention.[7]

The most debated and disputed questions that would be the most difficult to be resolved by the delegates in 1787 was how to choose an executive branch, a president. Because our nation just completed a fight to get out from under a tyrannical king or authoritarian governors created a deep-rooted mistrust of executive power complicated. After several months, a Committee of the Whole set forward a plan for electing the president. Our Framers to choose a leader that would eliminate the authoritative consequences as dictated by the British.

The first idea introduced by Edmund Randolph of Virginia, from the most populated state at that time. The plan was called the Virginia Plan, which in many ways mirrors our Congress and executive branch today. It would create a bicameral legislature allocated proportionately by population. The upper house would be nominated by individual state legislatures while the lower house would be proportioned by population and directly elected by the people.[8] The Virginia Plan called for Congress to choose the president the same way the Virginia state legislature chose its governors. That plan was too divisive as our constitutional framers felt Congress should not have anything to do with picking the president because it would give too much opportunity for favorite son[1] candidates causing corruption between the executive and legislative branches. They believed it would lead to political partisanship and unfair representation and put us back where we were with the British. This corruption would also invite political bargaining and perhaps interference from foreign powers. This agreement would upset the balance of power between the legislative and executive branches of the new federal government.[9]

After discussion, James Madison and James Wilson also drafted and presented a plan proposing a strong central government composed of three branches: legislative, executive, and judicial, which seemed more favorable to highly populated states.[10]

Another plan, the New Jersey Plan, was proposed by the less populated states who feared the Virginia Plan would result in these lesser populated states being overwhelmed by

---

[1] A favorite son is a political term used by political parties of a state delegation that sometimes nominates and votes for a candidate from their state or region.

larger states. The plan was introduced by William Paterson and used by the English Whigs. It proposed a unicameral (one body) legislative department of one body with one vote per state, regardless of population, creating equality for the lesser populated states. This group believed states were independent entities.[11] Proponents of this plan argued that it left the Articles of Confederation in place with amendments allowing Congress similar powers to our current Senate.[12] However, the argument against for this type was the fact the population in the south and west was growing more rapidly than the north.

The next proposal was like the Virginia Plan; however, rather than having Congress choose the president it would instead have the individual state legislatures select the president. This idea was vehemently rejected because of fears that a president would become beholden to that state legislature that elected him and that may erode any federal authority over the executive branch and further undermine the idea of a federation.[13]

Another idea was presented by three prominent delegates—James Wilson, James Madison, and Gouverneur Morris. Their proposal called for the president to be elected by a direct popular vote giving the people the power of "one person one vote" because it would be a true indication of the people's choice. James Wilson explained the essential idea of "popular sovereignty, establishing a national government that ought to flow from the people at large." He said "no government could exist without the confidence of the people."[14]

This direct election was rejected because the framers had serious doubts that the public had the knowledge or understanding about the candidates from outside their own state, leading to continuous favorite son candidates. Also, a direct vote might make a large number of candidates attempting to be elected president with no candidate emerging with a majority of the popular vote across the whole country. This would allow the choice of president to always be from the largest most populous states with little or no regard to the smaller states.[15] Cities such as Philadelphia and Boston had the ability to get voters sufficient data, whereas the rural southern states had less access to the information necessary for intellectual decisions. Others feared democratic mob rule as no country at that time directly elected its chief executives. It also gave too much executive power after the nation just fought its way out from under this form of authoritarian leadership.

Another factor that needed consideration was the fact that states like Virginia had a 60 percent slave population that was not counted, so either a direct popular vote or a delegate vote (like electors) would not work in the south. The fact is in 1787 African American slaves made up 40 percent of the south's total population, so their delegates wanted them counted as part of their population. Northern states argued slaves were property, not people, and therefore did not deserve representation, which divided slave-owner and non-slave-owner states. The debate got ugly but finally was resolved with the Three-Fifths Compromise allowing blacks to count as only three-fifths of a person without any right to vote. The Three-Fifths Compromise is outlined in Article 1, Section 2, Clause 3 of the US Constitution and affected how the nation would elect its presidents.[16]

While Madison acknowledged a popular vote would be ideal, he also knew it would be difficult to get consensus on that proposal given the prevalence of all the slavery in the south. His proposal also consisted of two houses in Congress, one a state-based legislature choosing the Senate and the other a population-based House of Representatives elected by the people and the president elected by a mixture of both. The right of suffrage was significant in the north versus south, as the latter had a larger influence on election decisions decided by a large population of African Americans counting as only three-fifths of a person. Madison acknowledged that "the great danger is the southern and northern interests opposed each other which stood more divided by the geography than the size of the states."[17]

Alexander Hamilton the use of a group of designated electors directly elected by the people in each state. He explained elections taking place in each state would alleviate corruption tainting the integrity of the people. He also argued that majority rule is critical to the principles of a republic. This is as close to what we have today as Hamilton was always ahead of his times. This substitution of electors helped change Madison's opinion and seemed to be less liable to objections. Hamilton wrote in the *Federalist Papers Number 68* that the electors (the Electoral College), could "prevent cabal, intrigue, and corruption, which could be deadly adversaries of a republican government. Moreover, it was a moral certainty the system would prevent the election of any man who is not an eminent degree endowed with the requisite qualifications."[18]

This group of electors' method was approved by several delegates (including Mason, Butler, Morris, Wilson, Madison, and Hamilton) who openly recognized its ability to protect the election process from secret political cliques or factions, corruption, and intrigue. James Wilson, referred to as the Father of the Electoral College,[19] said choosing the president indirectly would give each group of a state's electors to be proportioned equal to the number of representatives and senators. They agreed these electors would be chosen by each state in a way that each individual state legislature directed. Committee member Gouverneur Morris explained the reasons for the changes were "fears of potential secret plans of choosing the president by a small group of men who met together regularly, as well as concerns for the independence of the president if he were elected by the Congress."[20]

Finally, the Committee of Eleven developed the Great Compromise at the Constitutional Convention that worked out a compromise related to the representation in a federal legislative branch and the indirect election of the president by delegates, to be called electors, and what that would look like. They agreed a republican form of federal government representing the people was needed in their states. For the legislature, this Great Compromise proposed representation for seats in the House of Representatives allowed the people voting directly for these representatives. It also called for equal representation for each state to have two members of what would be our Senate, with each state's legislators choosing those respective senators. This Great Compromise ended the stalemate between patriots and nationalists and led to numerous other accommodating compromises. All that remained were sectional interests to be balanced by the Three-Fifths Compromise.[21]

Next, the committee dealt with the details of the mode of electing the president, including final recommendations using electors from each state. This original Electoral College was most comparable to the Centurial Assembly of the Roman Empire, which gave groups of one hundred people the ability to vote as one to select a leader, the president. States would be compared to these Centuries with the electors voting as single groups based on their popular vote choice in that individual state. The only difference from the Roman Empire was the number of electors would be determined by state congressional delegations being proportioned by population.[22]

The Great Compromise would ultimately decide the final selection of the president, how long that term would be, what would be the executive powers and finally how to deal with the powers of jurisdiction of the third branch, a federal judiciary branch. The convention approved the proposal that electors be represented equal to the legislative branch, with minor modifications. This important outcome ensured that southern states would ratify the Constitution by giving Virginia's 200,000 slaves more than 25 percent of the total electors required to win the presidency. The compromise provided how a runoff among the top five candidates in the case of no one candidate getting a majority would be handled by the legislative branch. If a candidate did not get the majority of electors, it would require a contingent election in the legislative body (House of Representatives) where each state would cast only one vote per state. Although it did not meet all the demands of smaller states, they went along and agreed with this proposal.[23] This gave smaller populated states equal authority because the philosophy was the greater the number of candidates the better chance a contingent election would become the deciding factor giving each state one vote or equal power to elect the president.[24]

The final draft was presented to the Convention on September 17, 1787, that included a preamble, seven articles, and a closing endorsement to eventually become our Constitution. There was twenty-nine signers and Benjamin Franklin addressed the convention saying, "I confess there are several parts of this constitution which I do not at present approve, but I am not sure I shall never approve because I expect no better and because I am not sure that it is not the best". He went on to say, "It's a **Republic** (or as many believe he said it's a **Democracy)** if you can keep it."[25] The two versions have been debated for over 200 years based on partisanship. The advocates finally accepted a formula with the closing endorsement unanimously adopted by all the states.[26]

By the end of July 1788, eleven states ratified the process of the new government. The Continental Congress passed a resolution on September 13, 1788, putting the new constitution into operation. On March 4, 1789, the new federal government began operations of the new federal government.[27]

Article 2 became the Executive Branch describing the powers and how we would choose our presidents. The Constitution still needed to deal with the balance of certain sectional interests. But it did set forth the presidential qualifications, terms, powers, and most importantly the method of selecting our president. This first design of the original Electoral College addresses the electors themselves and how they shall be chosen and vote. Each state was allocated electors that would be equal to the number of US Senators and Representatives from that state. The states' representatives would be represented according to the size of each state population, while the Senate would have two per state and be chosen by their states legislative body. It addressed all the needs of the larger and smaller state populations.[28]

Based on that allocation the manner of choosing these electors was left up to the individual state legislatures, who would appoint independent electors to cast the actual ballots for the presidency, alleviating suspicions of a central national government interference. It prohibited members of Congress and the employees of the federal government from serving as electors to maintain a balance of power between the legislative and executive branch. These electors were required to meet in their respective states to prevent any possible bribery, corruption, secret deals, and foreign influence.[29]

The first design gave each elector two votes, without designation of which one was for president or vice president. However, these electors had to vote for at least one candidate not from their home state. This would alleviate favorite son candidates and create a winner that at the very least be each elector second favorite choice. The ballots would be submitted to the Senate president, who would read the results. The Senate President is the vice president, which could be the one who was defeated in the election. Article 2 specifies that the candidate elected president must have a majority of the total electors. Whoever received the second most votes with or without majority would become the vice president. At that time, the only purpose of the vice president was to serve as a future guarantee in the event of a possible situation where the president becomes incapable or dies. Later it was determined that the vice president would be the president of the Senate serving as a presiding officer who only voted if there was a tie.[30]

Finally, it explains how the House of Representatives would conduct a contingent election in the case where no candidate received a majority or in case of a tie. The contingent election gave state one vote each and the candidate would have to obtain an absolute majority to become the president with the vice president being the one with the second most votes. Originally, prior to our Twelfth Amendment, the top five candidates would be taken up by the House of Representatives.

Although the United States Constitution refers to the voters choosing the president through a system known as electors, the actual phrase "Electoral College"[2] nor any other form of that name is used to describe the electors collectively. It was not until the 1845 Presidential Election Day Act that the use of the term "College of Electors" came into general usage

---

[2] An electoral college is a set of electors, often from different organizations or political parties, selected to elect a candidate to a particular office with their votes weighted in a particular way

as the collective designation for the electors selected to cast votes for president and vice president.[31] Clause 3 is the one that describes who the electors are.[32] Here is the text from the Constitution of that very important Article 2, Section 1, explaining the choosing of our president by the electors:

Article 2, Section 1

Clause 1: *The executive power shall be vested in a president of the United States of America. He shall hold office during the term of four years and, together with the vice president, chosen for the same term, be elected as follows:*

Clause 2: *Each state shall appoint, in such manner as the legislature thereof may direct, a number of electors equal to the whole number of senators and representatives to which the state may be entitled in the Congress, but no senator or representative or person holding an Office of Trust or Profit under the United States shall be appointed an Elector.*

Clause 3: *The electors shall meet in their respective states and vote by ballot for two persons of whom one at least shall not be an inhabitant of the same state with themselves. And they shall make a list of all the persons voted for and of the number of notes for each, which list they shall sign and certify and transmit sealed to the Seat of the Government of the*

United States, directed to the president of the Senate. The president of the Senate shall, in the presence of the Senate and House of Representatives, open all the certificates, and the votes shall then be counted. The person having the greatest number of votes shall be the president. If such number be a majority of the whole number of electors appointed and if there be more than one who have such majority and have an equal number of votes, then the House of Representatives shall immediately choose by ballot one of them for president. And if no person have a majority, then from the five highest on the list the said House shall in like manner choose the president. But in choosing the president, the votes shall be taken by States, the representation from each state having one vote; a quorum for this purpose shall consist of a member or members from two thirds of the States, and a majority of all the states shall be necessary to a choice. In every case, after the choice of the president, the person having the greatest number of votes of the electors shall be the vice president. But if there should remain two or more who have equal votes, the Senate shall choose from them by ballot the vice president.

Clause 4: *The Congress may determine the time of choosing the electors and the day on which they shall give their votes, which Day shall be the same throughout the United States.*

Clause 5: *No person except a natural born citizen or a citizen of the United States, at the time of the adoption of this Constitution, shall be eligible to the Office of President, neither shall any person be eligible to that office who shall not have attained to the age of thirty-five years and been fourteen years a resident within the United States.*

Clause 7: *The president shall, at stated times, receive for his services a compensation, which shall neither be increased nor diminished during the period for which he shall have been elected, and he shall not receive within that period any other emolument from the United States, or any of them.*

Clause 6: *In case of the removal of the president from office or of his death, resignation, or inability to discharge the powers and duties of the said office. The same shall devolve on the vice president, and the Congress may by law provide for the case of removal, death, resignation, or inability, both of the president and vice president, declaring what officer shall then act as president, and such officer shall act accordingly until the disability be removed or a president shall be elected.*

Clause 8: *Before he enters the execution of his office, he shall take the following oath or affirmation: "I do solemnly swear (or affirm) that I will faithfully execute the Office of President of the United States, and will to* *the best of my ability, preserve, protect, and defend the Constitution of the United States.*

Source: The National Constitution Center: Interactive Constitution, Executive Branch, Article 2: https://constitutioncenter.org/interactive-constitution/article/article-ii

This was a very elaborate and clever design. This whole electoral operation was supposed to work without political parties and without national campaigns. To appreciate the reasons for this Electoral College in its original form, it is essential to understand the historical context and the problems that our founding fathers actually faced in 1788:[33]

- There were only thirteen states, some with significantly larger populations than others, having their own rights and powers causing suspicions of a centralized national government.
- Our nation had only 4,000,000 people spread up and down a thousand miles along the Atlantic seaboard barely connected by transportation or communication.
- There were no political parties, and the drafters of the Constitution assumed that electors would vote according to their individual independence and discretion and not be dictated to by voting law pressures or state or national party.

- After being under the influence of British political power the people feared political parties would become mischievous and downright evil.[34]

From this earliest version of the Constitution, the presidency became a powerful institution with powers over law execution, foreign policy, and executive officers. In particular, the president would control all correspondence with foreign countries, direct American ambassadors, oust foreign ambassadors, execute federal laws, direct prosecutors, and regularly command and remove executive officers. There is no statute authorizing these actions, but their common foundation arose from the Constitution, which granted the president "the executive power of the United States," all without statutory warrant.[35]

Most of the Founding Fathers' assumptions about the origination of this electoral system proved unsuitable. The reason why this Electoral College is what it is because usually the party in power typically benefits the most while the minority party has little chance of changing it because constitutional amendments require a two-thirds super majority in Congress plus ratification by three-fourths of the states.[36] However, the term "Electoral College" does not appear anywhere in the US Constitution. Article 2 of the Constitution and the Twelfth Amendment simply refer to the electors but not the Electoral College.[37]

This brings us to the question, If the electors were to be chosen by how each individual state determined, how are the state legislators chosen? To get this answer, we have to go back up to Article 1, Section 2 of the original signed and ratified Constitution in 1788. This established the US House of Representatives which provided for the direct election of the House members "by the people of the several states." Under the previously mentioned Articles of Confederation, delegates to the Confederation Congress were selected as state legislatures directed. However, the influential members James Madison and James Wilson successfully argued that direct elections were necessary to connect the national government to the people.[38] The House of Representatives also set the benchmark for the largest portion of our Electoral College.

Here is that complete text of Article 1, Section 2 of the Constitution:

Article 1, Section 2

The House of Representatives shall be composed of members chosen every second year by the people of the several states, and the electors in each state shall have the qualifications requisite for electors of the most numerous branches of the State Legislature.

No person shall be a representative who shall not have attained to the age of twenty-five years and been seven years a citizen of the United States and who shall not, when elected, be an inhabitant of that state in which he shall be chosen.

Representatives and direct taxes shall be apportioned among the several states which may be included within this union, according to their respective numbers, which shall be determined by adding to the whole number of free persons, including those bound to service for a term of years and excluding Indians not taxed, three fifths of all other persons. The actual enumeration shall be made within three years after the first Meeting of the Congress of the United States, and within every subsequent term of ten years, in such manner as they shall by law direct. The number of representatives shall not exceed one for every thirty thousand, but each state shall have at least one representative; and until such enumeration shall be made, the state of New Hampshire shall be entitled to choose three; Massachusetts, eight; Rhode-Island and Providence Plantations, one; Connecticut, five; New York, six; New Jersey, four; Pennsylvania, eight; Delaware, one; Maryland, six; Virginia, ten; North Carolina, five; South Carolina, five; and Georgia, three.

When vacancies happen in the representation from any state, the Executive Authority thereof shall issue writs of election to fill such vacancies.

The House of Representatives shall choose their speaker and other officers and shall have the sole power of impeachment.

Source: The National Constitution Center: Interactive Constitution, Executive Branch, Article 2: https://constitutioncenter.org/interactive-constitution/article/article-i

It is obvious our framers never mentioned a right to vote. They did not forget but rather intentionally left it out because the founders did not trust ordinary citizens endorsing the rights of others. They were attempting to create an experiment of self-government paired with the protection of individual rights often resented by the majority at the time. As a result, they never laid out an inherent right to vote because of fear that the masses were not knowledgeable, and this would cause destruction of all the other rights awarded in the Constitution and Bill of Rights. What they emphasized put highlights on the other core rights over voting which is still a creation of tension that still remains today.[39]

Not all of the people were eligible to vote at the time of the Constitution's ratification. Article 1, Section 2 made the qualifications for voting the same as those in the larger branch of the state legislature. It gave only white men who had property ownership that were over the age of twenty-one the right to vote. It excluded women, free African Americans and Native Americans and some white men who did not have property ownership requirements. Ben Franklin reminded them that many common people who were part of the fight for independence deserved to vote. This uniform suffrage requirement was ultimately rejected because of fear that it would lead some states to reject the Constitution.[40]

Ultimately a compromise took place tying qualifications for voting in US House elections to the qualifications for voting in state legislative elections, allowing roughly two-thirds of white men who were property owners and over the age of twenty-one to vote. At the time of the first presidential election in 1789, only 6 percent of our nation's population were property-owning tax-paying white males. That practice started to change during the early nineteenth century when states extended voting rights to wider segments of the population, and by 1832, only South Carolina had not transitioned to popular election. It was not until 1880 that the electors in every state were chosen on a basis of the popular vote election for president on Election Day.[41] These popular elections for electors mean the president and vice president are chosen through a separate indirect election by the citizens.[42]

CHAPTER 2
Early Electoral College Failures and the Twelfth Amendment

The first design and creation of the Electoral College adopted in our Constitution only lasted through two presidential elections without any issues. Initially there was only sixty-nine electors that existed following the ratification of the United States Constitution. Eight weeks after the ratification on April 30, 1789, the first United States presidential selection took place and the great general of the Revolutionary War and the "father of our country," George Washington, was chosen unanimously and John Adams became the first vice president.[43] Then again in the 1792 election the same unanimous vote of 132 electors (due to population growth and addition of new states). In 1796, Washington set a precedent that is now the law of the land today. He decided that two terms were sufficient for a president to serve and therefore decided he would not seek a third term.[44]

Article 2 of our Constitution along with our framers granted each elector two votes for president without having the elector designate a separate vote for vice president. The framers thought it would make it simple awarding the candidate with a clear majority of electors as president, with the person receiving the second most votes (with no majority required) became the vice president. That original plan of the electoral system was based upon those several assumptions discussed in the last chapter at that time in our history. The most problematic assumption was we would not have political parties.[45]

The electors were mostly chosen by their state legislatures and were not elected officials and should be independent in their judgement without partisan influence or corruption from other outside sources. According to the text of Article 2, each state government was free to have its own plan for selecting their state electors as the original Constitution did not require states to conduct a popular vote of these electors. The framers intensions were to secure the election of the president would reflect the ideals of all the people at a particular time and should not be based on desires of factions of preestablished bodies, such as Congress or state legislatures, and be independent of the influence of outside foreign powers. When citizens cast their ballots for a president in the popular vote, they are selecting the slate of electors committed to that certain candidate. That is still true today. Electors will then meet later to cast the actual votes that decide who becomes president of the United States. Usually, electoral votes align with the popular vote in an election.[46]

Another issue surfaced quickly about how could we choose presidents without political parties or national campaigns without upsetting the carefully designed balance of power between the presidency, Congress, and individual states? It did not take exceptionally long for this issue to create problems for this Electoral College system with the emergence of political parties and nationally coordinated campaigns.[47]

After 1792 our nation's first two political parties formed, the Federalists and the Democratic-Republicans. The people who had previously condemned them publicly started to build on them privately. The major political philosophers, Edmund Burke, James Madison, and Alexander Hamilton began writing their support for political parties that allowed them to gain respectability.

Political parties were organized by people divided into separate groups based on their different political philosophies. Burke, Madison, and Hamilton became believers because as framers they figured that without political parties many future elections would cause a significant number of candidates dividing the electoral votes into tiny chunks, causing most elections to be decided in contingent elections by Congress picking the president. This was exactly what the framers argued vehemently that they did not want. Their strategy was as national political parties formed; the number of presidential candidates would shrink in most elections.[48]

1796: John Adams vs. Thomas Jefferson — "Faithless Electors" and "Different Parties"

The political parties began causing controversial outcomes in the first actual contested election as they played a dominant role. Also, Article 2 does not discuss political parties and therefore never addressed the possibility of electing a president and vice president from the same political party. This made some problems evident since the two-party system revealed different views which would result in a strain on power in the executive branch.[49]

The election of 1796 became the only election in our history that elected a president and vice president from opposing parties. Washington did not seek a third term, leaving the election to his Federalist vice president John Adams and Governor Thomas Pinckney of South Carolina. The new Democratic-Republican Party congressional caucus chose Secretary of State Thomas Jefferson of Virginia and Senator Aaron Burr of New York as their choices for president and vice president.[50]

The candidates were still technically running as four separate individuals as electors made no designation of whom they were choosing for president or vice president. This election was historic in a sense as it also conducted the first but unofficial popular votes in five states where voters chose the electors of the presidential candidate of their choice.[51] Most voters and electors were confused, as they were unable to determine what specific candidate was the preferred president or vice president. Other confusions were the two Adams, Vice President John Adams and Governor Samuel Adams of Massachusetts, on the ballot along with two Pinckney's, Thomas and Charles, who were also both from South Carolina.[52]

There were thirteen candidates, eight electors representing Federalist candidates, and four representing Democratic-Republicans. This caused concern of a potential nightmare where no candidate could attain the necessary majority to be elected president, causing a contingent election in the House of Representatives because electors would be split among so many favorite son[3] candidates. This was always the major concern of the framers who always vehemently opposed Congress electing the president as was previously discussed.[53] The unofficial popular vote gave Vice President Adams a 53.4 percent to 46.6 percent victory over Jefferson.[54]

In 1796, each state legislature chose or elected their electors for whichever party and candidate they supported. Because the Constitution mandated each elector to choose two candidates without distinction for president or vice president caused each party to manipulate the results by having a majority of their electors cast one vote for the intended presidential candidate while a few of those same electors not choosing a second candidate, attempting to guarantee their choice for vice president. However, all electoral votes were cast the same day and communications between states electors was extremely slow causing difficulty in helping electors coordinate this effort.[55]

In this case, the election was won by the candidate who had a majority of the electoral votes needed to win. The total electoral votes were 138, meaning the majority winner needed seventy. Federalist Party candidate Vice President John Adams received one more than the required with seventy-one while Democratic-Republican Thomas Jefferson finished second,

---

[3] *Favorite son* candidates are ones who draw their support usually from their home state or from the broader surrounding region. Sometimes it also used to describe a candidate with little or no support outside of their home region. They are sometimes used as a bargaining tactic for political trade-offs for the vice presidency or other high cabinet or court appointments. One of the most popular of those favorite sons was Ronald Reagan in 1968.

receiving sixty-eight electoral votes, which automatically made him the vice president. History was made by this early electoral process of electors choosing two candidates, Adams and Jefferson, from separate political parties to become president and vice president.[56] It immediately raised major issues that would eventually lead to the Twelfth Amendment in 1804. Having a president and a vice president from different political parties with different views could not work effectively. A major concern was the Constitution also designated the vice president as the president of the Senate, allowing him to make the deciding vote if there was a tie vote in the Senate. That gave Vice President Jefferson and his newly formed Democratic-Republican Party significant additional powers over the president.[57]

These major flaws caused both the Federalists and Democratic-Republicans to agree that a constitutional remedy was needed to have the president and vice president elected either as a joint ticket on a single ballot or on two separate ballots, one for each office. This change could have parties predetermine whom their designated presidential and vice-presidential candidates should be. This solution would eliminate the likelihood of political opponents serving as president and vice president. However, it was introduced to the House of Representatives three times, and each time it was denied because partisan politics interfered over which party would get credit for such a proposed amendment.[58]

There were some potential "what if" scenarios that could have changed the results in 1796, making Jefferson the president. This election exposed the beginning of what is still known as faithless electors.[4] In this case, three electors (one each from three different states) voted for a different candidate than all the other electors in that state. Had these faithless electors maintained their loyalty it would have flipped the election to Jefferson 71-68. These single *faithless electors* were in Virginia, North Carolina, and Pennsylvania, and they broke with their party to vote for Adams.

Another potential scenario would have required some backroom politics. If Jefferson was able to strike a political *quid pro quo*[5] deal with Federalist John Jay by offering him the Secretary of State in exchange for Jay bowing out while securing his five electoral votes from Connecticut. Jefferson would have totaled seventy-three and won the presidency, but Adams would still get seventy-one and the same issue of two separate political parties serving as president and vice president.

---

[4] *A faithless elector* is an elector who as a member of a group on the electoral college in their state that does not vote for the candidate for whom they had been previously pledged to vote. Forty-eight of fifty states require electors to pledge their vote to whomever state.

[5] A *quid pro quo* is Latin for "something for something," describing an agreement between two or more parties in which there is a reciprocal exchange of goods or services.

Table 2.1: Presidential Election Results 1796

Presidential Candidate	Party	Popular vote		EC votes-+
		Count	%	
John Adams	Federalist	35,174	53.3%	71
Thomas Jefferson	Democratic-Republican	30,860	46.7%	68
Thomas Pinckney	Federalist			59
Aaron Burr	Democratic-Republican			30
Samuel Adams	Democratic-Republican			15
Oliver Ellsworth	Federalist			11
George Clinton	Democratic-Republican			7
John Jay	Federalist			5
James Iredell	Federalist			3
George Washington	Independent			2
John Henry	Federalist			2
Samuel Johnston	Federalist			2
Charles Pinckney	Federalist			1
	Total	66,034	100.0%	276-x
			Needed to win	70

x- Prior to 12th Amendment each elector had 2 votes each for president +
is EC Vote= Electoral College Votes

Reference: Wikipedia (https://en.wikipedia.org/wiki/1796_United_States_presidential_election)

1800: Thomas Jefferson vs. John Adams— "Yes… We Have a Tie?"

The 1800 election was a rematch between Federalist President John Adams and Democratic-Republican Vice

President Thomas Jefferson. The election of 1796 caused political parties to become political enemies, refusing to work together effectively in passing and enacting legislation. As defined by the Constitution, as President of the Senate, Vice President Jefferson had tremendous legislative power.[59] A president and vice president from different parties gave politicians concern that larger groups of candidates would try for the presidency sending several elections to Congress to decide by contingent election. This possibility infuriated the Framers who did not consider the consequences in our Constitution. The other major concern was if there were more elections of presidents and vice presidents from different parties it would cause more political bargaining, corruption, and power struggles in our Executive branch.[60]

The election of 1800 ushered in a new type of politics as both parties started the process of attempting to designate the chosen candidates for president and vice president unofficially running mates for the first time. The party leaders would strive for a team concept with party choices campaigning jointly. The accidental result of this development quickly became obvious in this presidential election, which has always been referred to as the Revolution of 1800 because several issues surrounded the methods of voting by the electors.[61]

Both parties used congressional nominating caucuses to formally nominate what their joint ticket designations for president first and vice president second would be. The Federalists easily nominated incumbent President John Adams for reelection and their intended vice-presidential candidate was Charles Pinckney from South Carolina, a state Jefferson got eight electoral votes last time. The Federalist Party felt Pinckney could help Adams wrestle that state away from Jefferson and maybe take the entire election itself.[62] The Democratic-Republicans continued to significantly broaden their presence within the anti-Federalists. Key leaders like James Madison and Alexander Hamilton changed their political stances by 1800. Previously being the main figures shaping the Constitution, they emerged as party organizers for the Democratic-Republican Party.[63] Their caucus gathered and again nominated Vice President Thomas Jefferson of Virginia for president and teamed him up with Senator Aaron Burr of New York for vice president hoping to help Jefferson gain the electorally important state that Adams had won in 1796. This Jefferson-Burr ticket had felt extremely confident that the total of thirty-three electoral votes from New York (12) and Virginia (21) would be significant in reaching the seventy electoral votes needed to win.[64]

These new congressional nominating caucuses were organized to stop the split of separate parties occupying the presidency and vice presidency that caused extreme partisan and outright nasty internal politics. Leaders of the Adams Federalists and the Jeffersonian Democratic-Republican parties knew that the key to the presidential election was controlling the manner of selecting how loyal electors would vote for both candidates in the designated fashion designed along party lines.[65]

Another factor was Virginia and Rhode Island were the only states to choose their designated presidential electors by a statewide popular vote that chose a designated slate for president and vice president. Democratic-Republican and Federalist Party members distributed their list of electors to help the legislative voters understand what was needed to win those states. The Virginia electors pledged their support to both Jefferson and Burr for the Democratic-Republican Party, while Rhode Islanders supported the Adams-Pinckney ticket. They were given instructions on who would be the first choice for president and their second choice for vice president.[66]

The popular vote was still unofficial which gave those opposed to a popular voting process more judgement that it was unreliable and caused detractors to this day to call it an unconstitutional way of electing presidents. Nevertheless, these unofficial results gave a landslide popular vote victory for Jefferson and his Democratic-Republicans with 61.4 percent to President Adams with only 38.6 percent. The electors would still be casting the official votes, and that is exactly where this controversy begins.[67]

Prior to the Twelfth Amendment, the Constitution allowed electors to cast two votes without specifying which party they were from and did not designate which one was for president and which was for vice president. Another significant issue was that each state chose its own election day, causing voting to last anywhere from four to nearly six months from April to October. There were still 138 electoral votes with seventy the magic number for a winning majority.[68] The ticket of Jefferson and Burr won the same electoral votes in each of the same states that Jefferson had won in 1796 and additionally won electoral majorities in New York and Maryland. Adams picked up electoral votes in Pennsylvania and North Carolina, but these votes were not enough to offset the Democratic-Republican gains elsewhere. However, the results were still a failure to provide a clear winner because the problems of electors voting for two candidates continued to interfere with who would be president or vice president. Party leaders had assumed the joint ticket they nominated for president would gain most of the electoral votes for president, while their preferred second choice would become vice president.[69]

Unlike today, the ballots themselves did not describe which electors the party preferred would cast their two votes for president or vice president. In addition, the party faithful probably cast two votes across the board for the same two candidates. This could result in two candidates getting the same amount and the same majority of electoral votes. In these early elections, the states used several different methods to choose electors with no standard. Some states had the state legislature pick the electors, while in others, the people chose the electors by popular vote. Many states eventually used a winner-take-all statewide at-large vote, a system where the voters are choosing the electors based on their choice for president and vice president.[70]

The two parties needed to devise some political strategy to have one candidate get at least one vote more than their other preferred candidate. To accomplish this, the Federalists arranged for one elector in Rhode Island to vote for John Jay rather than Charles Pinckney. This plan would produce a presidential plurality of one more vote for President Adams. The Democratic-Republicans had devised a similar plan; however, their congressional nominating caucus failed to execute this due to the lack of communication that existed in 1800. So rather than one lone elector voting for a different candidate, every Democratic-Republican elector cast all of their votes for both Jefferson and Burr, giving both the same exact electoral vote majority of seventy-three from the cast of faithful Democratic-Republicans.[71]

According to the Constitution in the case where two candidates obtained the exact majority vote and tied it would cause the same contingent election in the House of Representatives. Federalists tried to deny the Jefferson-Burr ticket of four electoral votes in Georgia on the basis that the electoral ballots were ruled defective and therefore rejected by the state level due to these technicalities. If they remained disqualified, Jefferson and Burr would have been left with 69 votes each, or one short of the required majority of 70, causing a contingent election between the top five in the House of Representatives. Constitutionally, Jefferson as the Vice President had the power of being President of the Senate and he immediately ruled the four electoral votes in Georgia would count without any objections on the floor of Congress. Many believed Alexander Hamilton used his powers with anti-Adams Federalists to forego any disputes on Georgia.[72]

Although the Democratic-Republicans gained dominant control of Congress in 1800, contingent presidential elections then would be cast by the outgoing House, which was still controlled by Federalists. The four Georgia electoral votes secured for Jefferson and Burr a seventy-three electoral vote majority tie, so they would be the only two considered. Publicly, Burr remained quiet between Election Day and the day the Electoral College counted their votes in February 1801. Behind the scenes, he faced mounting pressure from his party to step aside to allow Jefferson to win the election. He refused to withdraw, but it was no secret that the Democratic-Republican caucus supported Jefferson over Burr for President.[73]

There were two possible outcomes to a contingent election. First, the outgoing Federalist Party could attempt a coup to gain a victory for Burr as they controlled the House. However, they were tied with the Democratic-Republicans on states controlled at 8-8, as each state would have one vote in a contingent election. Second, the Federalists could refuse to break any stalemate by abstaining their electoral votes, allowing Federalist Secretary of State John Marshall to become the acting president. If the Adams Federalists succeeded in their attempt to keep the presidency from Jefferson, it would set the stage for what could have been the first major constitutional crisis of our new federal government.[74]

In February 1801, a contingent election was held by the members of the House to determine if Jefferson or Burr would become president. There were sixteen states, each congressional delegation with one vote, so a majority of nine was required for victory. Most Federalists voted for Burr to stop Jefferson at any cost. On the first ballot, six of the eight states controlled by the Federalists (Delaware, South Carolina, Connecticut, Massachusetts, New Hampshire, and Rhode Island) voted for Burr. Seven of the eight delegations controlled by Democratic-Republicans (Kentucky, New Jersey, New York, North Carolina, Pennsylvania, Tennessee, and Virginia) plus Georgia voted for Jefferson, giving him eight states. Two other Federalist states, Maryland and Vermont, remained divided and did not cast a ballot. Without a majority of nine, the Democratic-Republicans still wanted Jefferson and needed Burr to come onboard. They were concerned the Federalists might try to engineer a continuous deadlock that would cause the appointment of an acting president. Fortunately, Alexander Hamilton stopped that from happening by recommending to his disgruntled anti-Adams Federalists to support Jefferson as the not as dangerous man as Burr.[75]

Neither of those occurred and over the course of seven days, from February 11 to 17, the House cast a total of thirty-five ballots, with Jefferson and Burr continuously receiving the same eight to six state delegations with two abstaining. Hamilton finally got together with and convinced his former Federalist cohorts to go with Jefferson on the thirty-sixth ballot on February 17, electing Jefferson with his same eight states, while Federalist James Bayard of Delaware to finally get his allies in Maryland and Vermont to change their stalemate to vote for Jefferson, giving him ten states and the election.[76]

Prior to the Twelfth Amendment, the electors could choose among five candidates, meaning if the Maryland slate of electors were persuaded to cast all ten of its faithless electors to vote for Adams and Pinckney, Adams would have been reelected with exactly seventy electoral votes and Pinckney would have got the second most with sixty-nine. Jefferson and Burr would have lost Maryland and also the election with only sixty-eight ballots each.

Table 2.2: 1800 Presidential Election Results

Presidential Candidate	Party	Popular vote		EC Votes
		Count	%	
Thomas Jefferson	Democratic-Republican	45,511	60.6%	73
Aaron Burr	Democratic-Republican			73
John Adams	Federalist	29,621	39.4%	65
Charles Pinckney	Federalist			64
John Jay	Federalist			1
Other		10	<0.1%	0
Total		75,142	100.0%	276-x
Needed to win				70

x= Amount prior to 12th Amendment when Electors vote for 2 candidates EC Votes = Electoral College Votes

Table 2.3: 1801 Contingent Presidential Election Results

1801 Contingent United States Presidential Election		
February 11–17, 1801 – 1st through 35th ballots		
Candidate	**Votes**	**%**
Thomas Jefferson	8	50
Aaron Burr	6	37.5
Divided	2	12.5
Total votes	**16**	**100**
Votes necessary	**9**	**>50**
February 17, 1801 – 36th ballot		
Candidate	**Votes**	**%**
Thomas Jefferson	10	62.5
Aaron Burr	4	25
Blank	2	12.5
Total votes	**16**	**100**
Votes necessary	**9**	**>50**

The Twelfth Amendment - 1804

This Twelfth Amendment was an extremely important amendment with regards to future presidential elections. The major factor was it now required electors to vote separate ballots, one for president and one for vice president, reducing possibilities of ties and preventing candidates from different parties in the White House.[77] It further required a quorum of two-thirds of all the states to be represented in order to have future contingent elections; however, individual states could still determine their own quorum base regarding electors from their own states.[78]

Political party loyalties were cutting across state loyalties, thereby creating more problems in choosing the president. As the influence of politics in government grew and political parties formed, the systems problems became clear. By making seemingly small changes, the Twelfth Amendment fundamentally altered the design of the Electoral College by recognizing political parties as a fact of life in America. It is worth noting that electing a president by direct popular vote was not presented as an alternative due to the fact the demographics had not changed in twelve short years.[79]

The elections of 1796 and 1800 were the driving force for the passage of the Twelfth Amendment. It introduced electors voting separate ballots for president and vice president. After all, the 1796 election led us to a president and vice president from two different political parties. That was followed by the debacle of 1800 where we had a tie of seventy-three electoral votes, leading to a contingent election in our House of Representatives where each state would vote as a whole with just one vote each. This amendment reduced the possibilities of accidental ties and separated the voting in the back-up contingent election process preventing candidates for president and vice president being from two different parties. This prevented contingent elections to happen only one more time in our history in 1824.[80]

The amendment prevented any future situation of electing a president and vice president from different political parties. It changed voting method of the electors, requiring them to name on their ballots the person for whom they are selecting as the president and a second vote for whom they chose to be the vice president. Elections based on this Twelfth Amendment also required that a quorum of two-thirds of all the states must be represented in order to take a vote. However, each state can determine their own quorum base regarding electors.[81] At that time, the Twelfth Amendment would alter the original design of the Electoral College by recognizing political parties and therefore alleviate some future problems. However, electing a president by direct popular vote was not presented as an alternative because the population demographics had not changed.[82]

It clearly defines how if no person reaches a majority of votes for president, then the House of Representatives will still select the president from only the top three instead of the top five candidates. This would free any electors who voted for candidates that did not reach the top three to vote for whomever their choice would be for president and vice president.[83]

No longer would the person who finishes second automatically become vice president, but instead, that candidate would also require a majority. If not, the US Senate would choose the vice president. All of the rest of the Electoral College would remain the same, including the prevention of favorite son candidates because each elector had to choose at least one candidate that is not from his or her home state.[84]

The Twelfth Amendment did more than fix the broken Electoral College in 1800 because it drastically reduced the chances that elections would keep getting thrown to the House of Representatives. By recognizing organized parties and joint tickets, it made the presidency a national political office that would appeal to national coalitions. As political parties cut across state loyalties, their influence of politics in government grew moving forward. Also, by upholding Article 2, Section 1, Clause 3, this amendment gives all states, large or small, equal representation in selecting the president if there is a necessity for it to go to the House of Representatives as it would still be in the form of one vote for each state in a contingent election.[85]

In order to prevent deadlocks and denying a leader, the Twelfth Amendment provided that if the House is unable to choose a president by March 4 (this was inauguration day and the first day of the presidential term in 1800), the individual elected vice president, assuming they had a majority, would become the acting president. However, there was still no timetable on how long the vice president would act as president, which was one of the few drawbacks. By making these significant changes, the Twelfth Amendment altered the overall design of the Electoral College to accommodate political parties as a fact of life in American presidential elections going forward. All presidential elections since 1804 have been conducted according to the provisions of the Twelfth Amendment.[86]

Many of our framers who helped make the Twelfth Amendment possibly believed it would cure any future problems, such as those in these early contests, reducing the possibilities of future contingent elections, or until 1824 at least. This Twelfth Amendment to the Constitution regarding the election of president and vice president, passed Congress December 9, 1803, ratified June 15, 1804, just in time for the election of 1804. All this was believed to fix a broken piece of the Electoral

College, as it upheld Article 2, Section 1, Clause 3, giving equal representation to all states, no matter whether large or small, each state had only one vote each in a contingent election in the House of Representatives.[87] The final provision with regard to deadlocks denying a leader, and if House is unable to choose a president by inauguration day the individual elected vice president by majority would become the acting president. The one drawback was it still did not set a timetable on how long the vice president would be the acting president.

However, in no way did the Twelfth Amendment stop elections of potential wrong winners'[88] controversies as five elections since 1804 were granted to the candidate that lost nationwide popular vote to be the winner of the Electoral College. There were many other controversial issues, such as faithless electors who ignored their states choices, favorite son candidates holding up the Electoral College majority, and of course, the potential for quid pro quo of political maneuvering and corrupt deals and bargains.

The serious problems and questions about the Electoral College system will be taken up later in this book when we discuss whether abolishment, reform, or other remedies. Here is the text of the Twelfth Amendment.

Twelfth Amendment as written in the Constitution[89]

The electors shall meet in their respective states and vote by ballot for president and vice president, one of whom, at least, shall not be an inhabitant of the same state with themselves. They shall name in their ballots the person voted for as president and, in distinct ballots, the person voted for as vice president, and they shall make distinct lists of all persons voted for as president and all persons voted for as vice president and of the number of votes for each, which lists they shall sign and certify and transmit sealed to the seat of the government of the United States, directed to the president of the Senate. The president of the Senate shall, in the presence of the Senate and House of Representatives, open all the certificates, and the votes shall then be counted. The person having the greatest number of votes for president shall be the president. If such number be a majority of the whole number of electors appointed and if no person have such majority, then from the persons having the highest numbers not exceeding three on the list of those voted for as president, the House of Representatives shall choose immediately, by ballot, the president. But in choosing the president, the votes shall be taken by states, the representation from each state having one vote; a quorum for this purpose shall consist of a member or members from two-thirds of the states, and a majority of all the states shall be necessary to a choice. And if the House of Representatives shall not choose a president whenever the right of choice shall devolve upon them, before the fourth day of March next following, then the vice president shall act as president, as in the case of the death or other constitutional disability of the president. The person having the greatest number of votes as vice president shall be the vice president. If such number be a majority of the whole number of electors appointed and if no person have a majority, then from the two highest numbers on the list, the Senate shall choose the vice president; a quorum for the purpose shall consist of two-thirds of the whole number of Senators, and a majority of the whole number shall be necessary to a choice. But no person constitutionally ineligible to the office of president shall be eligible to that of vice president of the United States.

Source: The National Constitution Center: Interactive Constitution, Twelfth Amendment, Election of the President and Vice President: https://constitutioncenter.org/interactive-constitution/amendment/amendment-xii

CHAPTER 3
Electoral College Changes
1804–2022

As we previously discussed, Congress, in 1804, finally passed and ratified the Twelfth Amendment. It is the only constitutional amendment that directly affects the way in which the electors would be counted. Several other amendments and laws over the course of our history were made but only a few laws were enacted that either directly or indirectly affected the Electoral College system. Those few changes relate to one of the most antiquated election systems ever devised to elect the most important and powerful world leader.

Remember in 1789 only white property-owning tax-paying males twenty-one years or older were allowed to vote, which represented only 6 percent of our population. It also was intentionally left out of the Constitution by the early framers and founders who felt common people were not qualified to make decisions on who their leaders should be. That practice slowly changed during the early nineteenth century when states extended voting rights to wider segments of the population, and by 1832 only South Carolina had not transitioned. Because the United States is a compilation of fifty different distinct states, there are also fifty different voting laws that are still changing every day, even now in the twenty-first century. Here are some of the core achievements of better voting rights and their effect on the Electoral College.

Another factor with regards to the Electoral College shows the growth of our population growing from five million in 1800 to over 107 million in the 1920 census. During that time, the Electoral College rose from 138 votes to 538 based on the incoming of new states and the increases in state populations. However, the population in the last one hundred years rose to 331 million with zero changes to the Electoral College number, which is still 538. That brings up several discussions about the necessary changes that need to take place regarding our presidential elections.

Aside from the Twelfth Amendment in 1804, here are the only changes that indirectly effected the Electoral College system.

The Apportionment Act of 1792

The Apportionment Act of 1792 was first passed by Congress on April 10, 1792. This first act would set the number of members in the House of Representative (then at 105) and how they would be allotted to each state based on the population provided by that most recent census, in this case, the first decennial census in 1790. Subsequent apportionment legislation would be done every ten years after each US Census, changing the number of members in Congress each time based on increased populations.[90] The result of the changes to the number of members in the House added to the number of Senators directly relates to the total of electors who will vote in the Electoral College for the next decade.

However, this would all change after the Census of 1920. After Congress was dominated by the rural politicians who stood to lose their power to a forever growing urban population, they failed to reapportion it seats following the 1920 census. This was the beginning of setting in process the Reapportionment Act of 1929, which permanently set the House at 435 members, and now it stands at 438 with the addition of Alaska, Hawaii, and Washington, DC.

The Apportionment Act of 1842

This act set a ratio of one member of Congress for every 70,600 residents. This act decreased the size of Congress from 240 to 223 for the first and only time in our history. However, the key to this act required for the first time that states be split into actual congressional districts according to their apportionment and that a single representative be elected from each district.[91] The Electoral College effect was the only time we had decrease in the number of electors for a presidential election. The split in the congressional districts having one representative each would effectively change the choices of electors in that individual district and state. It stopped the at-large districts many states had that allowed that state to vote for an individual who represented the entire state.

The Presidential Day Act of 1845

Originally, Article 1, Section 4, Clause 1 of the Constitution granted state legislatures the right to choose the times, places, and manners for holding all federal elections for Congress and the presidential elections. So from 1787 to 1844, Congress was authorized—but not required—to determine the day and time for federal elections.[92] Article 2, Section 1, Clause 4 governs presidential elections but merely provided Congress a method to determine the timing for choosing the electors, and the deadline for which they will give their votes. During those early years, our federal government allowed the states to proceed to have elections at different times and dates if they were completed before the designated date for Congress to count the electors. This procedure became a problem during the 1840s.[93]

Obviously, the knowledge of voting results in the earlier voting states could affect voter turnout in other states holding their elections on different dates. Later voting states and decisions of last-minute voters had the power to sway the outcome of an entire state. This large window across the nation also enabled massive voter fraud. The votes cast increased from 1.5 million in 1836 to 2.4 million in 1840 as different states voted on different days from November 1 through December 4.

So-called floaters were able to cross state boundaries to vote in another state after voting in their own state, while the pipe-layers claimed they were in town to lay pipes, allowing them to vote several times, and repeaters were voters who changed their clothes and appearance to vote in different precincts. All these issues were because there was no voter registration.[94]

In order to prevent potential fraud, Massachusetts was the first state to require voter registration in 1800, followed by

Maine (1821), Pennsylvania (1836), and Connecticut (1839) as more and more states established the same prerequisite to register. But as voter registration continued during 1860–1916, it reduced turnout by as high as 19 percent in some states over concerns of discrimination. The first time white non-property owners twenty-one or older could vote was in 1828.

On January 28, 1845, the Presidential Election Day Act was adopted by the Twenty-Eighth Congress. The act provides that presidential elections will be held nationwide "on the first Tuesday after the first Monday in November every four years." This established a uniform time for holding elections for the Electoral College electors of the president and vice president in all the states. The winning electors in each state formed the Electoral College that would formally vote in their state capitals on the first Monday after December 12, and Congress was now required to meet to certify the election results in a joint session held on January 6.[95]

Many ask why is Tuesday Election Day? Back in 1845, a large percentage of voters were farmers who had to travel long distances to vote which would have caused for a shorter working week. Weekends were impractical because most voters spent their Sunday in church. Plus, farmers commonly sold their crops Wednesday to Friday. Therefore, Tuesday became the most logical day. November was also the best month since the harvesting season would be over, and it was logically prior to the arrival of the cold winter. The Tuesday after the first Monday would also prevent elections occurring on November 1, the Catholic All Saints Day.[96]

The Fourteenth Amendment - 1866

The Fourteenth Amendment in 1866 gave persons the right to vote with equal protection. All citizens born or naturalized in the United States and subject to the jurisdiction thereof, upon becoming a citizen of the United States, has the right to vote in the state wherein they reside. No state shall make or enforce any law, which shall abridge the privileges or immunities of citizens of the United States, nor shall any state deprive any person of life, liberty, or property without due process of law, nor deny to any person within its jurisdiction the equal protection of the laws.[97]

Section 2 of this amendment says that our representatives will be apportioned to the states in proportion to their respective populations. It also set the standard that all male inhabitants of twenty-one years of age and citizens of the United States will be eligible to vote.[98]

The Fourteenth Amendment's Equal Protection Clause requires the states to practice exactly that, equal protection. Equal protection forces a state to govern impartially and not draw distinctions between individuals based solely on the differences that are irrelevant to a legitimate government objective.

The Fifteenth Amendment - 1870

Although the Fourteenth Amendment originally protected three fundamental values: racial equality, individual rights, and economic liberty, it never addressed the real inequality.

Therefore, four years later in 1870, the Fifteenth Amendment continued where the Fourteenth left off by clearly stating the right to vote cannot be denied by any state or the United States on account of race, color, or previous conditions of servitude, which is a condition of completely submissive to and controlled by someone more powerful.[99] Servitude is included in the language because it differs from slavery because it has a form of debt bondage, such as unpaid labor generally replaced by housing, clothing, and being fed.

The Electoral Count Act - 1887

The Electoral Count Act (ECA) of 1887 is a federal law adding to the procedures set in the Constitution for counting the electoral votes following a presidential election. Enacted by Congress in 1887, ten years after the disputed the 1876 Tilden vs. Hayes presidential election when several states submitted different elector slates causing a divided Congress to filibuster and unable to resolve the deadlock for several weeks. The elections of 1880 and 1884 were extremely close elections that raised the possibility of no formally established counting procedure. This ultimately would lead to a partisan Congress to use the counting process to force a desired result, like that which was attempted on January 6, 2021.[100]

Prior to 2020, the ECA was merely a simple formality that was seldom covered by the news media live. However, following the 2020 presidential election this could not have been more important as it faced more controversy and challenges than ever before. The act is aimed at minimizing involvement by

Congress and placing the primary responsibility upon the states. The only thing Congress can do is (a) resolve a dispute of a governor certified slate of electors, or (b) if a state fails to certify results according to the ECA in a timely manner, or (c) an ineligible elector according to the Constitution.

The ECA sets guidelines that order the states to have the responsibility to resolve disputes, certify results, and send those results to Congress. If these "safe harbor" deadlines for states are met and done properly and the governor submits one set of electoral votes, it guarantees that Congress must accept those results.[101] Contrary to some beliefs, Congress does not have the authority to overturn the state certified electoral ballots.

The ECA sets the first Monday after the second Wednesday in December as the date for all Electoral College electors to meet in their individual state. Each state legislature designates where the meeting takes place. This leaves plenty of time after Election Day for elector balloting, resolving controversies, and counting Electoral Votes for the January 6 joint session of Congress after an election.[102]

The Republican-controlled Senate passed four versions of the act in 1878, 1882, 1884, and 1886, but all failed in the Democrat-controlled House of Representatives, which had a sensitivity toward state rights in presidential elections. There was significant debate over the powers of Congress to determine the validity of electoral votes and setting rules for the states. The drafting of the act involved significant debate over many of its provisions, primarily the "relative balance of power between federal and state authority concerning the counting of electoral votes" and the "distribution of congressional oversight across the two chambers and the federal judiciary."[103] Again this became very significant following the 2020 election that ultimately led to the insurrection of our capital on that awful day in the history of our democracy.

Two of the biggest challenges to the ECA came after the 2000 and 2020 elections. The Supreme Court in 2000 (*Bush v Gore*) concluded that when "the safe harbor deadline arrives (Florida) without a specific recount procedure in place that complies with the standards, the recount ordered by the state court would be terminated, effectively ending the election."[104] Then, of course, there was the December 7, 2020, deadline set by the Supreme Court. That case was filed by Texas in *Texas v Pennsylvania,* which was a request to throw out the Pennsylvania state's mail-in voting results by denying the application for a writ of injunction, which the Supreme Court denied.[105] As we know several other states, such as Georgia, Michigan, Wisconsin, Ohio, and Arizona, were included in the same suit with only a few reaching the Supreme Court, and all without success because they argued the ECA was not binding on Congress.[106]

The electors are listed on seven copies of the certificate of ascertainment by each state they are appointed. Also, since forty-eight of the fifty states (all except Maine and Nebraska) are winner-take-all based on those states popular vote, the names of the presidential and vice-presidential candidates do not need to appear on such certificate; they only need the names of the certified electors for those candidates.[107] This is submitted by the archivist, or the secretary of that state, which they must receive by the fourth Wednesday in December. Today, the Electoral College is handled by the Office of the Federal Register (OFR) who are the responsible party for delivery of the Certified Electoral Votes.[108] In many cases, the OFR responsibilities has included retrieving certificates from a variety of places, checking mailbags, calling state police to help find electors who forgot to sign the certificate, and correcting them before this very important date of January 6.

By imposing strict limits on the procedures, debates, and recesses, the ECA is designed to ultimately help Congress complete an election prior to the outgoing presidential term ending on January 20. The counting of the Electoral College votes has specific instructions, which were significantly expanded in the Twelfth Amendment that awards the "the president of the Senate (the vice president holding office at that time whether he/she won or lost in November), in the presence of the new incoming joint session of Congress, opens all the certificates from each state and reads them and announces their count."[109] And that is it, the vice president has *no* authority to question these certificates. The vice president hands those certified ballots to the four tellers as they are opened. The tellers read the votes to the joint session as they are counted and recorded.

For objections to be considered they must be entered by one senator and one congressman in writing, prior to 2022. Objections have happened in 1969 as an objection about a faithless elector in North Carolina. Then in 2005 when a formal challenge was made about an ineligible Ohio elector. Then on January 6, 2021, when several other objections came up, one was that the Arizona electoral votes were challenged, but it was denied by both the Senate (93-6) and the House (303-121). Another objection challenged the Pennsylvania electors as being fraudulent was denied by the Senate opposed (92-7) and the House opposed (282-138).[110]

When considering objections, the ECA requires that if only one set of returns has been received, no electoral votes that has been lawfully certified can be rejected. In the case of multiple returns, if one is compliant with the safe harbor rule, then that return must be counted as the true return. But if two or more returns from a state claim safe harbor, neither will be counted, which could be cause for concern in future elections considering the voter suppression laws placed in the last four years in over thirty states. When multiple sets of returns are not claimed to have safe harbor, some organizations believe the governor of that state has the authority to choose, which again is false.[111]

One of the major issues on January 6, 2021, centered around the "Role of the Vice President" and, more specifically, what powers he/she has. Because several times either (1) the sitting vice president was running for reelection or (2) he/she was a candidate for president could make them partisan to the outcome. The key purpose of the ECA procedural provisions limits the powers of the Senate president (the vice president holding office at that time) for this purpose.[112] Therefore, he/she is essentially powerless and acts only as a custodian opening and eventually reading the individual state certificates. The goal of the ECA was to reduce the Senate president's discretionary power as gatekeeper to the absolute minimum. On January 6, 2021, there were several attempts to present "alternative electors," who were not appointed nor certified by their state, therefore, cannot be recognized or counted. When the votes are certified by each state, the results are final, and no alternate electors can be recognized.[113]

If Congress rejects a state or several states electoral votes, it could create a situation where the leading candidate does not have the majority (270) needed for election. Historical precedent on this issue has been split, whether to reduce the total electors, thereby reducing what a majority is, or according to the Twelfth Amendment, "if no candidate achieves a majority, it is required the House to hold a contingent election where each state has one vote."[114]

To reduce this problem, the strict ECA guidelines on procedure or debate is designed to help Congress to achieve an election result before the outgoing president term ends. But in accordance with the Twelfth Amendment if no president or vice president achieves the required majority of electors, the Speaker of the House would be sworn in as acting president. It also states that an outgoing president and vice president cannot extend their term past noon on January 20. This is something we can debate forever because there is no precedent on how long, other than "a reasonable amount of time," the acting president would serve.[115] Future elections could undoubtedly see more disputes initiating the Supreme Court to make decisions on the constitutionality of these presidential elections.

The Seventeenth Amendment -1912

On March 13, 1912, and ratified on April 8, the Seventeenth Amendment modified Article 1, Section 2 of the Constitution by allowing voters in each state to cast their votes directly for their US Senators. Prior to this amendment, our senators were chosen by the individual state legislatures. During the nineteenth century, several legislatures had severe splits in political parties causing many deadlocked elections for their senators. This resulted in Senate seats remaining open for many months or sometimes even years. Therefore, the necessity for direct elections of senators became a constant in our politics.[116] This direct voting by the people of a state for their US Senators could go a long way toward the choice of electors that will be on the ballot for the presidential elections.

The Nineteenth Amendment: Women's Right to Vote - 1920

The Nineteenth Amendment to our Constitution prohibits the United States and all its states from denying any citizen the right to vote based on sex, which legally guaranteed women the right to vote. This amendment enfranchised twenty-six million women the right to vote in time for the 1920 US presidential election. Beginning in the mid-nineteenth century, several generations of woman suffrage supporters lectured, wrote, protested, and lobbied to achieve what was considered the most radical change to our Constitution at that time.[117] The pioneer of this movement was Susan B. Anthony who unfortunately died in 1906 and never saw the fruits of her work accomplished. She was the cofounder of National Woman Suffrage Association in 1869, alongside Elizabeth Cady Stanton. She was also the president of the association in 1892–1900. Nonetheless, the amendment became known as the Susan B. Anthony Amendment because of her tireless work toward its passage.[118] This amendment took place during the 1920 census. That census was ignored and overlooked, and therefore, we had twenty-six million women eligible to vote without receiving any further proper reapportionment for any additional electoral votes.

The Twenty-Third Amendment - 1961

The Constitution provides each state receives presidential electors equal to the combined number of seats it has in the Senate and the House of Representatives. The primary reason this was enacted was to give the District of Columbia three electoral votes even though it is not a state. Prior to this, Washington, DC, was not entitled to any electors. As early as 1888, journalists and members of Congress favored a constitutional amendment to grant the district electoral votes, but such an amendment did not win widespread support until the rise of the civil rights movement in the 1950s.

The Twenty-Third Amendment extends the right to vote in presidential elections to citizens residing in the District of

Columbia by granting the district the minimal three electors awarded in the Electoral College votes as if it were a state. The amendment was proposed by the Eighty-Sixth Congress on June 16, 1960, and ratified by the states on March 29, 1961, nine months and twelve days after it was proposed.[119] The amendment was ratified by forty states but was rejected by Arkansas, and nine other states took no action on the amendment (Florida, Kentucky, Mississippi, Georgia, South Carolina, Louisiana, Texas, North Carolina, and Virginia). The amendment was bipartisan with the ratification endorsed by President Eisenhower and both major party candidates in the 1960 election, Kennedy and Nixon. The ratification of the amendment made the district the only entity other than the states to have any representation in the Electoral College, but no representation in Congress.[120]

According to the terms of the amendment, the district is allocated as many electors as it would have if it were a state, but no more electors than the least populous state (Wyoming), which has three electors.[121] The amendment also gave Congress the power to determine how the District of Columbia's electors should be appointed. In October 1961, Congress enacted legislation providing the district's electors should be appointed based on the popular vote of the presidential ticket. Then in 1973, Congress enacted the District of Columbia Home Rule Act, delegating the Council of the District of Columbia legislative powers over the District (subject to Congressional override). Unaddressed in the Twenty-Third Amendment were the issues of no congressional representation. The DC Council was empowered to pass laws and enact administrative policies for the district, although Congress retained veto power if they chose to intervene. The DC Council subsequently passed legislation affecting the appointment of DC's presidential electors.[122]

While it was considered politically neutral and only somewhat liberal in 1961, the district has swung dramatically to the Democratic Party in the years after passage. African Americans started voting in greater numbers than in the 1940s and 1950s clearing away voting restrictions. Their share of the district electorate increased to 71 percent in the 1970 census. Black voters have historically strongly supported the Democrats, with the district sending its three electoral votes to the Democratic candidate in every single presidential election since 1964. President Nixon in 1970 signed the District of Columbia Delegate Act authorizing the district to elect one nonvoting delegate to represent them in the House of Representatives.[123]

In 1978, Congress submitted the District of Columbia Voting Rights Amendment, which would have granted them full congressional representation the same as a state. The amendment failed ratification by not reaching the required thirty-eight state votes but was vehemently rejected by many conservative members of Congress at that time.[124]

The Twenty-Sixth Amendment - 1971

Simply said it gives every citizen of the United States who are eighteen years of age or older the right to vote. This amendment must be abided by all fifty states and shall not be denied or abridged on account of age.[125] Although this amendment added several millions to the eligible voting list, this gained zero electoral votes and did not add any representation because of the failure to continue reapportionment in 1929.

At the time it took place, America was in the midst of a vicious war in Vietnam that literally was fought by our kids because a majority of the 500,000 troops there were between the ages of 18 and 21. This caused protesting by our youth that for good reason proclaimed that "if you can send me into a jungle with a license to kill the enemy, then I should be able to vote for or against the people who sent me there."

The Electoral Count Reform and Presidential Transition Improvement Act (ECRPTA) of 2022

On December 22, 2022, a bipartisan bill, the Electoral Reform and Presidential Transition Improvement Act (ECRPTA) of 2022, sponsored by Sen Susan Collins (R-Maine) and Sen Joe Manchin (D-West Virginia), passed by the Senate and the House and signed into law by President Biden on December 29, 2022, amending the Electoral Count Act of 1887.

The bill reaffirms that the role of the vice president in the counting of the electoral votes would be solely ministerial with no power to determine, accept, reject, or otherwise adjudicate or resolve disputes over the proper list of electors, the validity of those electors or the votes of those electors when the joint session of Congress meets to count the Electoral College votes on January 6 following the election.[126]

The bill also raises the threshold necessary for members of Congress to object to state certified electors.[127]/[128] Previously it only required one representative and one senator to object to a state's slate of electors. This new bill requires an objection to have a quorum of 20 percent of the House and 20 percent of the Senate to challenge electors. This act was a direct response to the January 6, 2021, insurrection. Much of this issue was because a large portion of the voters were misinformed that the vice president had the power to reject electoral votes already certified by the states.[129]

Any claims by candidates must go to US District Court of the Federal Judicial District in the state the claim is made. Appeals of negative decisions go directly to the Supreme Court where it must be expedited before the electors meet on "the first Monday after the second Wednesday in December" in their state.[130] Also, the bill limits the grounds for objection by Congress to either "(1) electors of a state were not lawfully certified or (2) an electors vote was not regularly given."[131]

The bill states that the revision and submission of certificates of ascertainment is the responsibility of the governor for submitting the certificates of ascertainment, unless otherwise specified in states laws or constitutions. Also, a revised certificate by state or federal court judgement must be received prior to the state electoral meeting to supersede all previous certificates.

Also, states selecting electors by popular vote can only modify them due to "extraordinary and catastrophic" events. And finally, the bill allows "apparent successful candidates" to receive federal presidential transition funds provided by the guidelines of the GSA (General Services Administration).[132]

Most of these bills were made due to some form of Electoral College glitches that was not an issue before its enactment. The only one that has not been challenged is the most recent reform of the Electoral Count Act. However effective these changes will be do not address the fact the Electoral College has been challenged more than 700 times without success. This is where partisanship has always stood in its way as whichever party in power has reached opposition from the other party simply due to the "who gains the most powerful" agenda. This is a separate act that stands today and is probably the single most challenge to enact either reform or abolishment of the Electoral College, which would be an amendment to our Constitution that in these political times of 2024 seem to be an impossible hurdle.

CHAPTER 4
Controversial Elections or Simply "Wrong Winners"
Was Electoral College Responsible for Controversial Outcomes?

We have had fifty-nine presidential elections between 1789 and 2020. Since the mid-nineteenth century when all the electors have been popularly chosen, the Electoral College has always elected the candidate who received the most popular votes nationwide, except the elections of 1824, 1876, 1888, 2000, and 2016. In two of those elections, Congress was called upon to decide the outcome in our House of Representatives. But in all of these elections, the candidate who won the popular vote was denied the presidency. These five electoral winners we will be refer to as possibly being the "wrong winners?"[133]

This chapter enlightens those controversial elections that will lay significant groundwork to the pros and cons of the Electoral College needing reform or abolishment. We also discuss some of the shortcomings of the Twelfth Amendment and how it affected these elections.

Chapter 4A
1824: Andrew Jackson vs. John Quincy Adams

This presidential election came on the heels of the collapse of the Federalist political party, leaving only one political party, the Democratic-Republicans. The consequences of this wide open single-party system caused a reduction in political party discipline as it became the first and only election in which the winner of both the popular vote and the electoral vote did not become president. The lack of two major political parties left no candidate with a majority of electoral votes, calling for a contingent election in the House of Representatives to choose the president. This was exactly what the framers of our Constitution did not want when they created the executive branch, but they had the sense to put the rules for handling this in the Constitution. This 1824 election was the first time popular votes were officially recorded in eighteen states who chose presidential electors by popular votes (six states still left the choice to state legislatures). Rather than creating unity, it caused factions to develop within the single party.[134]

In 1824, the presidential and vice-presidential nomination process was done by congressional group caucuses leaving the field of candidates wide open. With only one political party, the Democratic-Republicans, many believed John Quincy Adams (son of our second President, John Adams), who was the Secretary of State was the front-runner. However, the party caucus chose to nominate William Crawford, a candidate experiencing severely poor health and believed to be unelectable. This snub of Adams was a crucial issue that divided the party leaders. However, almost all the party leaders agreed that they wanted John Calhoun for vice president. The one certainty the caucus made was it vehemently opposed Tennessee Senator Andrew Jackson as a "radical rebel."

Jackson's platform was to cleanse the government of corruption and return it to its earlier values, and the national popular voters agreed with him.[135] Jackson supporters also chose John Calhoun for vice president, who eventually secured an electoral vote landslide majority.[136]

Andrew Jackson won the final popular vote by a comfortable 10.44 percent margin in the official eighteen voting states at 41.36 percent while percent, John Quincy Adams received only 30.92 percent, Henry Clay 12.99 percent, and William Crawford 11.21 percent. The six remaining states did not have a popular vote and appointed electors by their state legislatures. These states consisted of 25 percent of the total Electoral College votes. Another observation was the fact no candidate was on the ballot of all eighteen voting states which was cause for popular voter irregularities, giving those pro Electoral College groups an advantage in their quest to keep this system intact. On the Electoral College, Jackson got 99 electoral votes; Adams, 84; Crawford, 41; and Clay, 37. However, it left all of them short of the 131 needed to win.[137]

The candidates vying for electoral votes varied considerably and proportionately. First, Virginia, with its twenty-four electoral votes only had the same total popular votes as Indiana which only had five electoral votes. Second, three times as many people voted in Ohio than in Virginia, yet Ohio had only sixteen electoral votes. The cause was people did not understand their voting rights, causing turnouts to vary considerably. Some states were also won by extremely high percentages of the popular vote such as Jackson got 98 percent in Tennessee and 76 percent in Pennsylvania, while Adams took 94 percent in New Hampshire and 81 percent in Maine and Clay received 72 percent in Kentucky.[138]

The electoral map confirmed candidates had geographic support, with Adams winning in the New York and New England areas, while Clay dominated his home state of Kentucky, along with Ohio and Missouri, and Crawford won two Southern states, Virginia, and Georgia. Jackson, although a Southern Tennessee Senator, drew the widest voter appeal across the country, winning pluralities as far north as Pennsylvania and New Jersey, to the Midwest in Indiana and Illinois and most of the south in North Carolina, South Carolina, Tennessee, Alabama, Louisiana, and Mississippi.[139]

Without any specific way of choosing electors, the states used their own methods:

1) Twelve states had the voters choose the electors (Alabama, Connecticut, Indiana, Massachusetts, Mississippi, New Hampshire, New Jersey, North Carolina, Ohio, Pennsylvania, Rhode Island, and Virginia).

2) Six states had the state legislatures appoint the electors (Delaware, Georgia, Louisiana, New York, South Carolina, and Vermont).

3) Five states divided by congressional electoral districts had the voters of those districts each choose one elector (Illinois, Kentucky, Maryland, Missouri, and Tennessee).

4) And Maine was the one state (later on Nebraska joined this method) who had two electors chosen by the statewide popular vote and one elector to the winner of each congressional district by those voters, and this method in this state is still the same today.

This election was the first and only time in our post–Twelfth Amendment history of presidential elections where the House of Representatives had to conduct a contingent election in the post–Twelfth Amendment era to determine who would be president when no candidate could reach a majority of the Electoral College votes. This election was held by the rules of the Twelfth Amendment with each elector choosing two candidates, one designated specifically for president and the other specifically for vice president. John Calhoun won the vice presidency easily with overwhelming support from 182 of 261 electoral votes. This was the only election in history that the popular vote and Electoral College winner did not become the president, as Jackson fell short of a majority needed.[140]

According to the Twelfth Amendment, the House was restricted to considering only the top three electoral candidates: Jackson, Adams, and Crawford, who was in such poor health following his stroke made his electability impossible and maybe unqualified according to the Constitution.

Clay, who finished fourth, was the Speaker of the House held decisive power of who would win the necessary votes in a contingent election in the House and he had strong opposition to Jackson,[141] helping Adams win.[142] Clay used his influence with the Southern Kentucky House delegation to ignore its state legislature elector's choice and instead vote 8-4 for Adams. Clay also attempted to motivate state delegations where he won a plurality to vote for Adams. Rather than allowing Jackson to win, Clay forged an Ohio Valley-New England coalition that would secure the White House for Adams. Adams in return would guarantee that Clay would become his secretary of state, a position that had been a steppingstone to the presidency four previous times.[143]

Jackson expected the House to vote logically along the lines of the popular votes "of the people" and also the winner of the plurality of the electoral votes. Instead, with only one party, the Democratic-Republicans, this election should have sent politicians and constitutionalists over the edge to either abolish or reform the failing Electoral College system. On the first ballot in the contingent election, Adams had strong support in Congress.

According to the Constitution, each representative in the House would vote but each state as a group only had one vote for a candidate. Adams and Clay used this advantage to secure the thirteen states needed to win the presidency while Jackson received seven and Crawford four.[144]

Here is the breakdown of how the states voted in the House contingent election, which differed significantly from how the people voted:[145]

- Adams thirteen votes came from seven states where he won the popular vote (Connecticut, Illinois, Maine, Maryland, Massachusetts, New Hampshire, and Rhode Island), three states that had no popular vote recorded (Louisiana, New York, and Vermont), and three states that he lost the popular vote to Clay (Kentucky, Missouri, and Ohio).
- Jackson got seven votes were from six states that he won the popular vote (Alabama, Indiana, Mississippi, New Jersey, Pennsylvania, and Tennessee) plus one state that had no popular vote recorded (South Carolina).
- Crawford's four votes were one state he won the popular vote (Virginia), two states that had no popular votes (Delaware and Georgia), and one state that he lost the popular vote to Jackson (North Carolina).

The Adams-Clay coalition worked effectively in three states that Clay won and turned for Adams in an obvious political quid pro quo.[6] As expected, Clay was appointed Secretary of State by Adams.[146]

The fact that it was the only election in our history that the winner of both the national popular vote and the electoral vote

---

[6] Quid pro quo is a favor or advantage granted or expected in return for something of value.

lost the election because the lack of a multiparty system caused a contingent election by Congress, which was exactly what our Constitution framers feared the most. These factors lay groundwork for a future argument dealing with the smallest of states having the same power as the larger states. Remember in 1824, we had only twenty-four states, some with significantly more population than others, so the contingent election of one state, one vote was not true equality.[147] A good example today is California has over forty million people and fifty-four electoral votes, yet only one vote in a contingent election whereas, the two Dakotas combined have only 1.5 million people, with six electoral votes combined, yet they would have two votes in a contingent election.

Jacksonians claimed the Adams-Clay Alliance symbolized corrupt elite voter insiders pursuing their own interests instead of the will of the people. Congressional opponents of Adams rallied supporters for Jackson.[148] This would lead to a Jackson landslide victory in 1828 in both the popular and electoral votes.

The debacle of 1824 caused the Democratic-Republican Party to split into the creation of two separate parties, Jackson's Democrats and Adams National Republicans prior to the 1828 presidential election.[149] Jacksonian Democrats also gained control of the House and Senate in midterms, pretty much securing any possible contingent election in 1828. Vice President Calhoun, who supported expanding voter rights, joined the Jackson Democrats by becoming his running mate. In 1828, Jackson got 56 percent of the popular vote and 178 of the Electoral College while Adams only received 43 percent of the popular vote and only 83 electoral votes.[150]

Let's use our current two-party system to create a "what if" scenario of the 1824 election with the winner of the popular votes getting the Electoral College winner-take-all method of today, and use some demographics that could have changed these results:

- Adams won the popular vote in seven states (Connecticut (8), Illinois (3), Maine (9), Maryland (11), Massachusetts (15), New Hampshire (8), and Rhode Island (4) and most likely would have won three states that did not record any popular votes where he had territorial strength (Delaware (3), New York (36), and Vermont (7). If his political bargaining with Clay would have given him two more states, Missouri (3) and Ohio (16), that could have been a total of twelve states, totaling 123 electoral votes.

- Jackson also won the popular vote in seven states, Alabama (5), Indiana (5), Mississippi (3), New Jersey (8), Pennsylvania (28), Tennessee (11), and North Carolina (15); one state with no popular vote, Louisiana (5); and most likely would have won four strong southern territorial states, Georgia (9), South Carolina (11), Kentucky (14), and Virginia (24), total of twelve states, totaling 138 electoral votes. Therefore, the overall winner-take-all, two-party system would have given the election to Andrew Jackson with 138 electoral votes, exceeding the 131 needed for victory.

Here Are the States with the Closest Results

States where the margin of victory was under 1 percent:

- Maryland 0.32 percent (109 votes)–11 electoral votes won by Adams

States where the margin of victory was under 2 percent:

- Ohio 1.53 percent (766 votes) – 16 electoral votes- won by Clay

Reference: https://en.wikipedia.org/wiki/1824_United_States_presidential_election

Table 4.1: 1824 Presidential Election Results

Presidential Candidate	Party	Popular vote		EC Votes
		Count	%	
Andrew Jackson	Democratic-Republican	151,309	40.45%	99
John Quincy Adams	Democratic-Republican	122,440	32.74%	84
William H. Crawford	Democratic-Republican	41,222	11.02%	41
Henry Clay	Democratic-Republican	48,606	13.00%	37
Unpledged electors	None	10,449	2.79%	0
Total		374,026	100.00%	261
			Needed to win	131

https://en.wikipedia.org/wiki/1824_United_States_presidential_election

Table 4.2: 1824 Contingent Election in the House

1825 Contingent United States presidential election		
February 9, 1825		
Candidate	**Votes**	**%**
John Quincy Adams	13	54.17
Andrew Jackson	7	29.17
William H. Crawford	4	16.67
Total votes	**24**	**100.00**
Votes necessary	**13**	**54.17**

https://en.wikipedia.org/wiki/1824_United_States_presidential_election

Chapter 4B
1876: Samuel Tilden vs. Rutherford B. Hayes

At that time, the election of 1876 became the most corrupt presidential election tragedy in American history, between Democratic New York Governor Samuel Tilden and Ohio Republican Governor Rutherford B. Hayes.[151]

Nominations were now in the hands of the traditional delegate conventions, where wheeling and dealing takes place among party bosses. The Republican National Convention assembled in Ohio where it expected Senator James Blaine of Maine having a clear path to his second consecutive nomination. When he continuously fell short on several consecutive ballots Republican Party leaders concluded he could not win in November. When the anti-Blaine delegates could not agree on an alternate candidate, the Republican Party leadership conducted a backdoor meeting to consider alternatives. In that meeting, the party concluded the only candidate giving the Republicans a chance in November was Ohio's favorite son,[7] Governor Rutherford B. Hayes, who won the nomination 384 to Blaine's 351. The party nominated William A. Wheeler, a New York representative as his running mate for vice president.[152]

The Democrats gathered for the Democratic National Convention with the hope of gaining their first presidential victory in twenty years. Governor Samuel L. Tilden of New York faced large opposition from Governor Thomas Hendricks

---

[7] Favorite son is a famous person who is particularly popular and praised for his achievements in his native area or a person supported as a presidential candidate by delegates from the candidate's home state.

of Indiana. But on the third ballot, the convention nominated Tilden who received unanimous consent of 738 votes and agreed to have Hendricks as his running mate vice president.[153]

Tilden was a former federal prosecutor in New York who had strong opposition from the Tammany Hall Democrats because he convicted their legendary mob boss William Tweed. Also, Republicans raised the Civil War issue that "not every Democrat is a rebel, but every rebel is a Democrat."[154] Hayes was virtually unknown outside his home state of Ohio as presidential historians called Hayes "a nonentity whose only recommendations are that he is obnoxious to no one." But he was from the crucial swing state of Ohio, which to this day no Republican has won the White House without winning Ohio.[155] Many southern Democrats group during the late nineteenth century tried suppressing both blacks and Republican voter turnouts. They continuously disrupted meetings and rallies with intimidation during the post-Civil War era in the South.[156]

This election became the most controversial and contentious in all American history at that time. The results, until 2020, were the most disputed election returns ever. The nationwide popular vote total went to the Democrat Tilden with a 50.92 percent majority compared to Republican Governor Hayes 47.92 percent. The 3 percent victory of 254,000 votes made Tilden first presidential candidate in history who lost a presidential election while winning a majority of the popular vote.[157]

After the initial count of the electoral votes, Tilden won 184 electoral votes and Hayes 165, with twenty electoral votes unresolved and contested vehemently. Those electoral votes were four from Florida, eight from Louisiana, seven from South Carolina, and one from Oregon. The vote counts in those four states became the focus of sharp debate and manipulation.[158] The elector that would have given Tilden a victory at 185 was automatically disqualified by the state of Oregon because he was an elected official. However, Hayes needed all twenty of these contested electoral votes to win.[159]

In 1876, America had thirty-eight states. Governor Tilden's strength was New York, New Jersey, Maryland, Delaware, and most of the south, while Hayes's strength lay in New England, the Midwest, and the West, including the new state of Colorado that only had state appointed electors in this election. Early returns suggested Tilden had won as newspapers reported, but *New York Times* stated, "The results are still uncertain." Rumors spread by both parties made allegations of electoral fraud, ballot box stuffing, altered ballots, and voter intimidation at the polls. Each party attempted to decertify votes and actually paid bribes to correct voter's ballots, resulting in different voter counts in three southern states in dispute. Again, remember this was 1876 and we only had paper ballots, so fraud was easily widespread.[160]

The worst case of fraud appeared to be in South Carolina where 101 percent of all eligible voters participated in the popular vote. However, the Republican-dominated state electoral commission disallowed enough Democratic votes to award the popular vote by 0.5 percent and the seven South Carolina electoral votes to Hayes. This put the total for Hayes at 172.

Florida submitted two sets of presidential electors' votes, one from the Republicans giving Hayes a 922-vote victory, while the Democrats submitted ballots showing Tilden ahead by ninety-four votes. Both parties sent their disputes to the state Justice Department. The Florida governor was a Republican who finally certified the state for Hayes moving his Electoral College total to 176. In Louisiana, their Republican governor recognized and certified the results submitted by the Hayes electors. When Tilden's Democratic electors in Louisiana submitted that state for him; however, the Republican governor certified the votes for Hayes, and those three electoral votes put the two candidates in a tie at 184-184.[161]

Finally, in Oregon both parties agreed that Hayes had carried the popular vote, but the deciding elector was a former postmaster, disqualifying him as an elector according because Article 2, Section 1, of the Constitution does not "allow a person holding an office of trust or profit under the United States government unqualified to be an elector." The Democratic governor attempted to replace him with a Democratic elector, giving only two electors to Hayes and one to Tilden, which would have given Tilden a 185-184 Electoral College victory. However, the Republican state-controlled legislature dismissed the appointment as a faithless elector[162] and replaced him with a GOP elector, giving all three contested electoral votes to Hayes and the Republican secretary of state signed and certified all three electors for Hayes, giving him the electoral vote majority of 185 to 184. This issue brought the election to both parties screaming fraud, putting the nation in a state of utter confusion. Who was their president?[163]

According to the Constitution, it provides that the president of the Senate (the current vice president) shall, in presence of the Senate and House of Representatives, open all the electoral vote certificates, and the votes shall then be counted." However, there was no conclusive remedy of what to do when there were two sets of electoral results from several states. Congress argued the Constitution was unclear on what to do about multiple sets of popular votes.[164]

Republicans argued the president of the Senate (GOP Vice President Henry Wilson) should count the votes. Democrats wanted Congress to continue previous direction that clearly said, "No electoral vote objected to should be counted except by the concurrence of both houses." At that time, the Democrats held a majority in the House, which could have awarded the election to Tilden.[165] However, the election had no precedent in the Constitution or any laws for how to handle multiple states contested electoral votes. Historically, and as written in our Constitution as well as the election of 1824, it is still unknown why Congress did not hold a contingent election. This led Congress to pass the Electoral Commission Act on January 20, 1877 (at that time inauguration day was March 4), setting up a fifteen-member bipartisan Electoral Commission to study the contested votes and decide which contested electoral votes should be counted. The commission would have five House representatives, five senators, and five Supreme Court justices. Each majority party in each house would name three of their members along with two minority members and five Supreme Court members would be two chosen by each party and the fifth independent impartial justice chosen by the other four making the commission 7-7 with one independent.[166] Since there were no independents on the Supreme Court, the final seat went to a Republican appointed Justice Joseph Bradley, giving the Republicans an 8-7 advantage on every contested ballot. The commission's guidelines stated decisions could only be overturned by both houses of Congress. Because the Democrats were unable to overturn the decisions, they attempted to obstruct them, threatening a filibuster retaliation that could prevent the completion of the electoral vote count before Inauguration Day.[167]

As Inauguration Day came closer, the commission met on January 31. The cases of each electoral vote in Florida, Louisiana, Oregon, and South Carolina were submitted to the commission for hearing. Both parties submitted their version of the popular votes, giving the commission double sets of returns from each state. The commission did not question any returns. Consequently, a series of twenty votes were taken for each electoral vote individually with Republican Justice Bradley joining the other seven Republican committee members in a series of 8-7 votes, giving all twenty disputed electoral votes to Hayes. Finally, at 4:00 a.m. on March 2, 1877, two days before the inauguration, Hayes was declared the winner of the election by a 185-184 electoral vote margin.[168]

During intense meetings, the fifteen commission members did something that historians cannot explain. Rumor said a deal was struck where Democrats would withdraw federal troops from the last two occupied Southern states, South Carolina and Louisiana, and in exchange, Republicans would support some entitlements and the transcontinental railroad line through the south. There is no record of either promise ever being honored.[169] So this election continued Republican control of five consecutive presidents, from Lincoln in 1860 to Arthur in 1885. "The election discredited the Hayes presidency," according to Professor Alan Brinkley of Columbia University, and when his term ended, he did not run again.[170]

For obvious reasons, this election was clearly corrupt due to conflicting different elector results that created a major debate about Electoral College potential abolishment or reform. Also, Hayes is the last Republican elected president who did not carry Indiana.[171]

Here are some reasonable "what if" scenarios to this controversial second of five elections with another potential wrong winner[172] and how it impacts election results. These scenarios would change history and effect politics severely even today. It is also the only presidential election in history where the winner received a majority of the popular vote (50+ percent) but lost the election.

What if the Electoral College vote was a winner-take-all as it is in forty-eight of our fifty states today? Using our modern two-party system method, we set aside fifteen states dominated by one candidate or the other. Those states would have been nine states totaling ninety-three electoral votes for Tilden and six states for forty-two electoral votes for Hayes. These were states that were landslide popular vote winners getting 58 percent–72 percent. Next, the original electoral votes had Tilden at 184 and Hayes at 165. The Hayes campaign knew it would have to win all twenty of the contested electoral votes for him to get elected. All Tilden needed was one faithless elector or one congressional district in Maine and he would have been president.

Consider the South Carolina circumstance where Hayes won by his slimmest margin of 889 votes (or 0.49 percent). Remember Republicans cried fraud, and the commission disqualified 1,800 Democratic votes they claimed caused the 101 percent voter turnout. There was no proof the 101 percent was caused by only the Democrats. If those seven electoral votes were awarded to Tilden, he would have totaled 191 and won the presidency.

Hayes' only path to victory with 185 electoral votes was the commission awarding all twenty of the contested electoral votes in South Carolina, Florida, Louisiana, and the lone wolf dispute in Oregon. That is the only viable scenario that would and did give Hayes the victory. Consequently, an unbalanced fifteen-member partisan commission actually decided the outcome. This was the only that was an unqualified lone faithless elector in Oregon.

What if the election went to a contingent election in the House where the midterm 1874 election was dominated by the Democrats in the House of Representatives by a 182-103 margin over Republicans, and a 22-16 state congressional majority? Before the Twentieth Amendment in 1933, it would have been the outgoing Congress voting in a contingent presidential election with each state having one vote.[173] With no precedent for dealing with contested electoral votes, Congress could have used a contingent election method because no candidate got to 185. Assuming the states voted along party lines, Tilden would have won by the 22-16 state advantage.

Here Are the States with the Closest Results

Five of the thirty-eight states were considered close states representing fifty-four Electoral College votes.

States with a margin of victory less than 2 percent (fifty-four electoral votes):

1. South Carolina, 0.49 percent (tipping point state) - 7 electoral votes (889 votes) - Hayes
2. Ohio, 1.14 percent - 22 electoral votes (7,516 votes) - Hayes
3. Indiana, 1.26 percent - 15 electoral votes (5,515 votes) - Tilden
4. California, 1.80 percent - 6 electoral votes (2,798 votes) - Hayes
5. Florida, 1.97 percent - 4 electoral votes (922 votes) - Hayes

Table 4.3: 1876 Presidential Election Results

Presidential Candidate	Party	VP Candidate	Popular vote		EC Votes
			Count	%	
Rutherford B. Hayes	Republican	William A. Wheeler	4,034,142	47.92%	185
Samuel J. Tilden	Democratic	Thomas A. Hendricks	4,286,808	50.92%	184
Peter Cooper	Greenback	Samuel Fenton Cary	83,726	0.99%	0
Green Clay Smith	Prohibition	Gideon T. Stewart	6,945	0.08%	0
James Walker	American National	Donald Kirkpatrick	463	0.01%	0
Other			6,575	0.08%	
		Total	**8,418,659**	**100%**	**369**
				Needed to win	**185**

Chapter 4C
1888: Benjamin Harrison vs. Grover Cleveland

The election of 1888 was the third since 1824 and the second in twelve years that a candidate who won the popular vote lost the election to the Electoral College vote. The election was between Republican former Senator Benjamin Harrison and incumbent Democratic President Grover Cleveland, who was seeking a second term as the first Democratic president since the Civil War. Harrison was the grandson of former president William Harrison.

The Democratic National Convention was very harmonious and unified behind President Cleveland who was first Democratic president since the Civil War and the first incumbent Democrat renominated since Martin Van Buren in 1840.[174] President Cleveland stayed close to tradition and chose political leader Allen Thurman of Ohio for vice president. Cleveland's major asset was the economy was prosperous and the nation was at peace.[175]

The Republican National Convention placed thirteen candidates into nomination taking a total of eight ballots before nominating Benjamin Harrison from Indiana over James Blaine, the 1884 nominee who withdrew because he believed party unity and harmony would yield a Republican candidate that could defeat incumbent President Cleveland.[176] Republicans believed that Harrison, from Indiana, could wrestle that important swing state and its fifteen electoral votes away from Cleveland, and they also wanted to gain another larger state, New York, by nominating one of their Congressman Levi Morton for vice president.[177] Harrison ran an energetic campaign funded by major party activists and he refrained from the hostilities that marked the 1884 campaign.[178]

The candidates knew their focus would be the swing states of New York, New Jersey, Connecticut, and Indiana. On election day, Harrison swept most of the North and Midwest, with the exceptions of Connecticut and New Jersey, and narrowly carried the swing states of New York and Indiana (his home state) by a margin of 1 percent or less. However, it was rumored Harrison won New York and Indiana with the help of notoriously fraudulent balloting.[179] But this was still sufficient to gain a majority of the electoral votes needed. Contrary to his election in 1884, the powers of the Tammany Hall political machine in New York City denied incumbent Cleveland his home state and all its electoral votes. Had Cleveland won New York as he did in 1884, he would have been reelected by a 204-197 margin in the electoral votes. Instead, Harrison conquered New York and ultimately received the national popular vote total of 47.80 percent, with President Cleveland obtaining 48.63 percent, which was popular vote victory margin of 90,596 votes or 0.83 percent of 11,838,320 votes. However, despite his slim popular vote defeat, Harrison won the Electoral College majority 233 to 168, thirty-two more than the majority needed for victory.[180]

Four states had results that the winner won the popular vote by 1.09 percent or less. Three of those states—Connecticut, Virginia, and West Virginia—were won by Cleveland. Harrison won the other, Indiana, gaining all fifteen of their electoral votes in the process. As previously mentioned, the election came down to who would win New York? Harrison carried the state by a miniscule margin of 1.09 percent (14,3737 votes out of a total of 1,319,748), taking all thirty-six electoral votes. It was the tipping point state because had Harrison lost New York and all its electoral votes he would have fallen short of the 201 needed to be elected, allowing Cleveland to be reelected.

The consequences of this election caused America to have a third wrong winner[181] candidate and the second in twelve years who had a minority of the peoples votes for the presidency. It created several organized protests from anti-Electoral College protestors, whose actions fell on deaf ears and the nonaction continued. This disastrous Electoral College would cause this same tragedy in two more elections (2000 and 2016), with much more serious consequences that effectively changed the course of politics and political policies into the future.

In 1892 former president Cleveland won the Democratic presidential nomination and he easily defeated incumbent Republican President Benjamin Harrison by an electoral majority of 277 to 145 as he regained his home state of New York and took away states in the Midwest and California that he lost in 1888. He became the first and only presidential candidate in history to be elected to a second term in nonconsecutive order. It was also the first time an incumbent was defeated in two consecutive elections.

Here Are the States with Closest Results

Margin of victory of 1.09 percent or less

1. Connecticut, 0.22 percent - 6 electoral votes - Cleveland
2. West Virginia, 0.32 percent - 6 electoral votes - Cleveland
3. Indiana, 0.44 percent - 15 electoral votes - Harrison
4. Virginia, 0.53 percent - 12 electoral votes - Cleveland
5. New York, 1.09 percent (tipping point state) - 36 electoral votes - Harrison

Table 4.4: 1888 Presidential Election Results

Presidential Candidate	Party	VP Candidate	Popular vote		EC Votes
			Count	%	
Benjamin Harrison	Republican	Levi P. Morton	5,443,892	47.80%	233
Grover Cleveland	Democratic	Allen G. Thurman	5,534,488	48.63%	168
Clinton B. Fisk	Prohibition	John A. Brooks	249,819	2.20%	0
Alson Streeter	Union Labor	Charles E. Cunningham	146,602	1.31%	0
Other			8,519	0.07%	
Total			11,383,320	100%	401
Needed to win					201

Reference: https://en.wikipedia.org/wiki/1888_United_States_presidential_election

Chapter 4D 2000: Al Gore vs. George W. Bush—Florida, Florida, Florida? One for the Ages!

The candidates for the presidency in 2000 were Vice President Al Gore and Governor George W. Bush of Texas, the eldest son of the forty-first president, George H. W. Bush. The election became the only election to date that was decided by the United States Supreme Court on December 12, 2000 (thirty-five days after election day, November 5), in the infamous *Bush v Gore* case that ended in a controversial 5-4 vote that ended a battle over who won the State of Florida. Adding more controversy was the fact that the Governor of Florida was Jeb Bush, the younger brother of candidate Bush and the youngest son of former president George H. W. Bush. Historically it was the second father-son combinations to become president, the last being John Adams (1797–1801) father of John Quincy Adams (1825–1928).[182] It also became the fourth presidential election in which the Electoral College winner did not win the national popular vote.[183]

The 2000 election replaced President Bill Clinton, who completed his two-term limit according to the Twenty-Second Amendment of Feb. 27, 1951. This process always opens doors for widespread maneuvering by multiple candidates interested in their party nomination and 2000 was no different.

The primaries started with the usual New Hampshire shocker as Republican Senator John McCain destroyed Bush 49 percent to 30 percent, and went on to win Arizona, Michigan, Massachusetts, Rhode Island, Vermont, and

Maryland convincingly while Bush only won South Carolina. The Republicans were concerned with Democratic crossover votes in open primary states and also Senator McCain had strong senate bipartisan ties.[184] Then McCain hit a huge bump in the road with consecutive losses in Georgia, Missouri, and Ohio. Bush went on a steamroller as he continued winning state after state by wide margins, and when he won Florida (where brother Jeb was governor) and Texas primaries (where he was governor), McCain was finished. Bush won the Republican nomination easily, making the GOP Convention a Bush family and friends coronation and the passing of the torch from father to son and the reemergence of Bush 41s Defense Secretary, Dick Cheney, as the vice-presidential nominee.[185]

Meanwhile, Democratic Vice President Gore had only minor opposition from a significantly liberal alternative Senator Bill Bradley.[186] Gore won every primary and caucus easily, won the nomination, and chose the first Jewish-American candidate for vice president, Senator Joe Lieberman of Connecticut.[187] A memorable convention speech by a thirty-year-old Congressman Harold Ford Jr., only the second black congressman from Tennessee and first ever African American keynote speaker. The speech left Democrats in awe of if they were watching the potential first future black presidential candidate. The speech was only surpassed by a little-known senatorial candidate named Barack Obama in 2004 that obviously catapulted him to the White House.[188]

The Gore-Lieberman ticket ran on the Clinton coat tails of continued prosperity, progress, peace, the highest home ownership rate ever, the lowest minority unemployment, the lowest amount of people on welfare along with the lowest crime rate in twenty-five years.[189] Bush was a status quo GOP candidate with conservative principles both economically and socially, which followed in his father's footsteps.

The polls showed the race extremely close the entire campaign. In fact, the final closing poll on election eve showed a 50/50 dead heat[190] while predicting a Gore popular vote victory with a Bush Electoral College victory.[191]

On Election Day, it was easy to realize just what kind of days, nights, weeks, or even months before this would end. Especially in Florida, where Democratic officials and angry voters complained about Election Day irregularities, confusing ballots, computer glitches, misplaced ballot boxes, and accusations minority voters were turned away due to improper identifications, and voters unable to vote due to actual traffic roadblocks.[192] Democrats argued that Bush's younger brother, Jeb, the governor of Florida made things appear lopsided and favorable to the GOP.

A memorable moment on election night occurred when the late Tim Russert of MSNBC held up a small white board and a sharpie, and proclaimed, "Here is what it comes down to," and when he turned the board around appeared the words "Florida, Florida, Florida," causing host Chris Matthews to state that "just at the point of this night when you have to be the most accurate, you just made us a little punchy. I could not write this as a movie script."[193]

As polls started closing all the major news networks (CNN, ABC, CBS, NBC, MSNBC, and even Fox News) were projecting Al Gore the winner in Florida. But that close race left egg on the faces of most of the media who had to finally admit that Florida was now "too close to call."[194]

What political history fails to mention is the real shocker was in the very small northeastern state of New Hampshire and its tiny 4 electoral votes that went to Bush. Nader received 3.90 percent in a state considered to be a Democratic stronghold. But little New Hampshire has only four electoral votes, so it doesn't register as a "swing" or "battleground" state when it theoretically determined the presidential election in 2000. New Hampshire has been won by Democrats Clinton in 1992 and 1996, Kerry in 2004, Obama in 2008 and 2012, Hillary Clinton in 2016, and Biden in 2020, with Bush being the lone GOP candidate to win it in 2000. In fact, President Obama carried it by over 10 percent in 2008 and 6 percent in 2012. These four electoral votes could have flipped a Bush 271-266 win to a Gore 270-267 win, even with Bush winning Florida. Gore only lost the heavily Democratic New Hampshire by 1.27 percent, which was only 7,211 votes. It was attributed to the fact third party socialist candidate Ralph Nader took nearly 4 percent of the vote.

As the night rolled on past midnight, the major networks claimed Bush had a 50,000 vote lead and win in Florida and declared him the president-elect which led Gore to call Bush to concede.[195] However, Gore's aides convinced him to retract his concession as the results continued to change in Florida by the minute and the Bush lead was in jeopardy.[196] The next day, the Bush margin shrank to a mere 1,784 votes while voting machine irregularities were contested as voters complained the punch card ballots were confusing or not working, creating the infamous *hanging chads*. This also caused an automatic full state machine recount based on Florida's 0.5 percent margin of victory law.[197]

The recount showed Bush hanging onto a miniscule 327 (0.009 percent of the total six million votes cast) vote lead and the GOP Secretary of State Katherine Harris declared the official recount completed but was denied by a federal judge. Harris ignored the judge and attempted to stop the hand recounts, which was also denied by the Florida Supreme Court as the Bush lead shrank to 286 votes.[198] But the Florida Supreme Court again blocked Harris from certifying the vote and the US Court of Appeals denied the Bush request to stop the recount when he led by 930,[199] ruling the manual recount to continue and setting a deadline to certify the votes by Monday, November 27. Bush filed a petition to US Supreme Court to overrule the Florida Supreme Court decision that the *dimpled (hanging) chads* should be counted and not excluded.[200]

The Florida Republican-dominated state legislature tried to step in and resolve the contest by December 12,[201] while the US Supreme Court ruled in *Bush v Palm Beach Canvassing Board* clarify the recount deadline. The Eleventh US Circuit Court of Appeals heard both sides challenging the Florida ballot count but denied any appeal to throw out manual recounts in three counties and denied stopping the recount with a Bush 537 vote lead.[202] The Florida Supreme Court reversed a lower court rejection by Gore and ordered a statewide manual recount of the undervote.[8] At this same time, the US Supreme Court began hearing oral arguments regarding the recount in *Bush v Gore*.[203]

Finally on December 12, the US Supreme Court rendered a decision to overturn Florida Supreme Court rulings for manual recounts, stating "it is evident that any recount seeking to meet the December 12 date will be unconstitutional and we hereby reverse the Florida Supreme Court decision to order a recount to proceed. It is obvious that the recount cannot be conducted in compliance with requirements of equal protection and due process without substantial additional work." This vote was 7-2 referencing the Equal Protection Clause, and 5-4 regarding the use of an alternative method. This decision allowed the previous vote certification to stay as made by Florida Secretary of State Harris and signed by Governor Jeb Bush, declaring George W. Bush the winner of Florida's twenty-five electoral votes by 537 votes and giving him a 271-267 electoral vote victory, making him the forty-third president-elect.[204]

Florida has become a huge "swing" or "battleground" state. Since 1996 it has voted Democrat three times (1996, 2008, and 2012), and Republican four times (2000, 2004, 2016, and

---

[8] What is considered an undervote? An undervote occurs when the number of choices selected by a voter in a contest is less than the maximum number allowed for that contest or when no selection is made for a single choice contest. An undervote can be intentional for purposes, including protest votes, tactical voting, or abstention.

2020), with the largest margin of victory 4.4 percent in 2004 when Bush beat Kerry. Political experts attributed the Gore loss in Florida to Green Party socialist Ralph Nader, who received 97,488 votes (1.63 percent) in a state Gore lost by only 537.

Here is a statistical analysis of the 2000 election that leads into later discussions about the pros and cons of the Electoral College system. The 1876, 2000, and 2016 elections are three of the worst presidential election tragedies in our history. It has been 236 years since our framers of the Constitution created this Electoral College system, but it leaves the majority of America to believe it needs some reform or abolishment.

Many anti-Electoral College leaders blame Congress (both Democrats and Republicans) for freezing the House at 435 members even though the population went from 107 million to almost 331 million since 1929. That is over a 300 percent increase in our population with no change in our Electoral College. Also, Washington, DC, is still not a state, and even though it has three electoral votes, it has no representation in Congress. Therefore, 700,000 Americans are left without congressional representation. Finally, the Electoral College has been challenged in Congress over 700 times since 1929 by both parties with no results. These are just a few of the many inequities of a system that needs to at least be reformed if not abolished completely.

Here Are the States in 2000 with the Closest Results

States where the margin of victory was less than 1 percent totaling fifty-five electoral votes:

1. Florida, 0.0092 percent (tipping point state) (only 537 votes out of 5,963,110) - 25 electoral votes - Bush
2. New Mexico, 0.061 percent - 5 electoral votes (366 votes) - Gore
3. Wisconsin, 0.22 percent - 11 electoral votes (5,708 votes) - Gore
4. Iowa, 0.31 percent - 7 electoral votes (4,144 votes) - Gore
5. Oregon, 0.44 percent - 7 electoral votes (6,765 votes) – Gore

Reference: https://en.wikipedia.org/wiki/2000_United_States_presidential_election

Table 4.5: 2000 Presidential Election Results

Candidate	Party	VP candidate	Popular vote		EC Votes
			Count	%	
George W. Bush	Republican	Dick Cheney	50,456,002	47.86%	271
Al Gore	Democratic	Joe Lieberman	50,999,897	48.38%	266
Ralph Nader	Green	Winona LaDuke	2,882,955	2.74%	0
Pat Buchanan	Reform	Ezola Foster	448,895	0.43%	0
Harry Browne	Libertarian	Art Olivier	384,431	0.36%	0
Howard Phillips	Constitution	Curtis Frazier	98,020	0.36%	0
John Hagelin	Natural Law	Nat Goldhaber	83,714	0.08%	0
Other			51,186	0.05%	0
(abstention)					1
		Total	105,421,423	100%	538
		Needed to win			270

Chapter 4E 2016: Hillary Clinton vs. Donald Trump—Just When We Thought 2000 Was Enough

Every four years presidential elections manage to have some sort of new twist. However, 2016 was by far one of the most unconventional, divisive, and controversial in American history. This election followed three eight-year cycles of term limited outgoing presidents (Bill Clinton, George W. Bush, and Barack Obama, 1992–2016). In was an extremely ugly battle of a New York business and real estate tycoon Donald J. Trump versus a former first lady, senator, and secretary of state Hillary Rodham Clinton for the right to become the Forty-Fifth President of the United States in what was the most disastrous fifth potentially wrong winner[205] election of another Electoral College winner losing the popular vote. However, this time the popular vote margin was a decisive three million votes or 2.09 percent of the total votes cast. This election was completely unlike any in our history as the real issues took back seats to two candidates literally waging a mudslinging war of personalities. However, there were many significant firsts:

1. Hillary Clinton became the first woman to win the presidential nomination of a major party.
2. Hillary Clinton was the first spouse of a past president to run for the office herself.[206]
3. Sarah McBride became the first transgender to speak at a major party convention about discrimination against the LGBTQ+ community.[207]

4. Donald Trump became the first president in more than sixty years with no prior political experience whatsoever (the last was Eisenhower in 1952).[208]
5. Trump became the oldest president ever elected at that time, to his first term when he was sworn in at the age of seventy (Ronald Reagan was sixty-nine and later Biden was seventy-eight).
6. Trump, seventy, and Clinton, sixty-eight, were the two oldest candidates to face each other in a presidential election in history.[209]
7. It was the first time in history that two of the most unpopular and least trustworthy candidates, even within their own parties to represent them in a presidential election.[210]
8. The first time the process has ever been interfered and directly struck by external and foreign interference (Russia, WikiLeaks, and Julian Assange) and social media hacking and misinformation (Facebook and Twitter) with misinformation.[211]
9. The largest and most widespread voter intimidation and suppression ever in our election history.
10. Donald Trump would also become the only twice impeached president.

Although early polling showed Hillary Clinton in full control of the Democratic nomination at 64 percent, Senator Bernie Sanders proved he could beat her because of the damaging ghosts and demons of from the infamous personal email server and Benghazi.[212] This left primary polls in a dead heat.[213] Meanwhile the GOP compiled seventeen candidates, including Trump, Jeb Bush (son and brother of the two former Bush presidents), senators Cruz and Rubio, and governors Walker, Christie, and Kasich, along with several other candidates.[214]/[215]

The GOP center-right establishment invested $150 million on Jeb Bush becoming the nominee for a White House family trifecta as they braced for a Bush-Clinton rematch.[216] This same early polling showed Donald Trump at 1 percent as many felt the campaign was a political joke that would end quickly. What staunch GOP regulars failed to realize is he stood alone while a group of political insiders divided the party regulars.

A primary tidal wave escalated Trump to eliminate the competition one by one as they continued to plunge.[217] He crushed opponents with his insult-laden rhetoric, middle of the night tweets, and his MAGA (Make America Great Again) followers loved it. He promised to "clean the swamp" of both Republicans and Democrats. The field continued to shrink as he gained an insurmountable delegate margin making him the presumptive nominee by May 4.[218] Nothing he said or did hurt his campaign and could not touch the "Teflon Don." Trump crossed the 1,237-delegate count needed to secure the nomination by early May.[219]

At the GOP Convention disgruntled GOP "regulars," anti-Trumpsters, prominent Republicans such as McCain, Romney, Kasich, the Bush family, and many GOP governors, senators, and representatives refused to attend. Trump won easily on the first ballot as he accepted and declared "nobody knows the system better than me, and I alone can fix it."[220] Governor Mike Pence of Indiana became Trump's running mate while GOP platform moved hard right conservative, promising the elimination of the LGBTQ+ community in order to eliminate gay marriage and transgenders, promised to reverse *Roe v Wade,* claimed they would recall the ACA (aka Obamacare) and a "get tough" on law and order and immigration policies by deporting illegals.[221]

On the Democratic side, Hillary and Bernie continued splitting wins in the two Democratic primaries and caucuses and the Sanders campaign argued against superdelegates who were already pledged to Clinton by five to one margin rendering the nomination process meaningless. Superdelegates are elected officials, governors, senators, state representatives, local state party bosses, and DNC members that remain unpledged until the convention. Naturally, they favored Clinton, a longtime Democratic insider, over the independent senator Sanders who refused to give up his campaign all the way to the convention. His supporters stated that "it is unfortunate that the media is in a rush to judgement and the DNC is wrong to count superdelegates before the convention."[222] At the DNC Convention, Clinton won the nomination 2,775 delegates to Sanders 1,889 on the first ballot; however, Bernie and his delegates never conceded. Many felt Sanders supporters boycotted the election and did nothing to help their party. Hillary chose Senator Tim Kaine of Virginia as her vice-presidential running mate. The 2016 DNC controversies displayed the least party unity or loyalty since the 1968 and 1972 debacles.

The DNC Platform was their most progressive, pledging a $15 per hour minimum wage, a public option in the ACA, promoting pro-choice to sustain *Roe v Wade*, equal pay for women, expanding Social Security to Americans age 55+, middle class tax relief, criminal justice reform, abolishing the death penalty, boosting police accountability, gun control, banning assault weapons, and education programs for K-12 program and encouraging neighborhood public schooling. It also supported the LGBTQ+ community by supporting same-sex marriage and recognition of transgenders.[223]

Most of this hid in the shadows of the scandalous investigations by Congress regarding the Benghazi matter and an investigation by former FBI director James Comey calling Clinton's email server "extremely careless." Carelessness was enough to show the cause of a breach of national security, which exposes personal servers to hacking. It supposedly ended by the end of July, as FBI Director Comey concluded that there would be no charges because there was no intentional criminal action. Then suddenly he reversed course ten days before the election by reopening the investigation. Then again on November 6, he reported again to Congress that the additional emails did not change his original decision.[224] Obviously the fatal damage was done whether Hillary was exonerated or not and the report was too little too late, becoming the most decisive issue in this race.

Trump opposition was fueled by reports of sexual misconduct, continued insults attacking the news media, verbal attacks on peaceful protesters, African Americans, Muslims,

Mexicans, Chinese, and other immigrants with undignified racist comments. He also waged a continuous scandalous war against Clinton, with the help of influence from our largest foreign enemy Russia, and continuously spreading fake social media misinformation.[225]

As in every election, polling is a major factor. The polls continued to give Clinton an average lead of 4 percent–6 percent, which remained within the margin of error; however, the real issue was about the consistent 15 percent–20 percent undecided voters in all the polls.[226] Undecided voters are usually the people who make or break the outcome.[227] Who were these mysterious 15 percent undecided voters hovering over both campaigns? Were they disgruntled GOP members or Sanders supporters, or people who never planned on voting at all?

After the October 28 Comey ordeal, polls (NBC, CBS, and Fox) maintained that Hillary would win the popular vote by only 2 percent–3 percent on election eve while there still remained 13 percent–14 percent undecided. Also, third-party candidates Gary Johnson, Jill Stein, and Evan McMullen were polling at a total of 6 percent–7 percent. These small amounts from third-party candidates can still disrupt the outcomes (1968-Wallace and 2000-Nader) in disputable and controversial elections.[228]

RCP (Real Clear Politics) and FiveThirtyEight.com released polling on the Electoral College with the map showing Clinton ahead of Trump 203-164, but there was 171 toss-up electoral votes. These battleground states in question were Florida (29), Ohio (18), Michigan (16), Pennsylvania (20), North Carolina (15), and Wisconsin (10), setting up a potential repeat of 2000.[229]

Election Day, November 8, 2016, was supposed to end this long, brutal presidential campaign when instead it gave American politics a huge black eye.[230] The day meant so many different things to different people as supporters of Trump claimed this date was a deliverance to their faith in a billionaire businessman getting rewarded as he tweeted, "Today we Make America Great Again, but if we don't win, I will consider it a tremendous waste of time, energy, and money."[231]

On the other side, Hillary Clinton supporters entered the Javits Center in New York City fully expecting a night of partying and history being made. Every possible scenario leaned in favor of America electing the first female president. The over confidence led Hillary herself to state that "it's the most humbling feeling to be in this position in history, and I will do the very best I can if I am fortunate to win." Jennifer Palmieri, Hillary's Communications Director tweeted, "I am just bursting with pride today. I want to tell everyone I see that I work for Hillary Clinton." They were all left shattered by the outcome.[232]

Considered the grand wizard of predicting election results, Nate Silver of FiveThirtyEight.com made his final analysis on election day at 10:41 a.m., predicting Clinton with a 71.4 percent chance of winning with electoral vote margin of 302-236. Of course, that was incorrect. In the popular vote, he had Clinton with an 81 percent chance of beating Trump by a 3 percent margin (Clinton ended up with a 2.1 percent victory here). But what these numbers also showed was 12.5 percent undecided votes which was one of the highest percentages on election day in the history of polling. The highest amounts of these undecideds were in the swing states that would decide the election.[233]

In the end, a presidential campaign that tested the stamina of the candidates and the American people ended with nerves dangling. The polls closed and early results revealing no surprises. Clinton aides were "feeling really good about Florida," where a Miami-Dade lead of over 300,000; however, she was not doing very well in other normally Democratic counties. At 9:00 p.m., CNN gave the ever-Democratic states of Delaware, Washington, DC, Illinois, Maryland, Massachusetts, New Jersey, and Rhode Island to Clinton, while Trump took Oklahoma, Tennessee, and Mississippi, and showing strength in Florida, North Carolina, and the Midwest, including the Democratic strongholds of Pennsylvania, Wisconsin, and Michigan. These were all too close to call. The night concluded with a Republican winning Wisconsin for the first time since 1984 and Pennsylvania and Michigan for the first time since 1988.[234]

As more states rolled in, Trump took hold of the ever-Republican base in the Dakota, Wyoming, Nebraska, Kansas, Arkansas, West Virginia, and South Carolina, while Hillary added New York. The *New York Times* reported her chance of winning the presidency was now only 50/50. It now looked like the Trump campaign might have been correct when they claimed for months that he had a secret army of supporters not captured in the polls. The financial world and Wall Street was not handling this well as the Dow dropped 600 points on election day, the largest election day drop in history.

By 11:30 p.m., CNN called Ohio and Florida for Trump, putting Clinton in an impossible position. The electoral total had Trump 238 to Clinton 215, but problems were growing for Clinton in three of the most Democratic states of Michigan, Wisconsin, and Pennsylvania and their forty-six electoral votes were all "too close to call." Without those three states, Clinton's path to victory was impossible. Democrats from Maine to California could not understand how that could possibly happen. It turned out that is the exact nightmare that occurred and when Wisconsin was called for Trump, CNN projected him the forty-fifth president-elect. Word was Clinton had already called him and conceded.[235]

At the Javits Center, a huge, subdued crowd became teary eyed and completely silent. Russian President Putin called Trump to congratulate him. Trump took the stage at his headquarters to give a victory speech proclaiming "the forgotten men and women of our country will no longer be forgotten." The following morning, Hillary publicly conceded and apologized to her supporters while Trump had successfully become another one of those presumably and potentially wrong winners.[236] He was comfortably ahead in the Electoral College vote 304-227, but the final popular votes went to Clinton who received 65,853,516 (48.5 percent) to Trump's 62,984,825 (46.4 percent), a 2,868,691 (2.1 percent) margin, which is the largest popular vote victory ever in our history for a losing candidate[237] in a presidential election. This was also the fifth Democrat who won the popular vote but lost the election to the Electoral College. Republicans have never suffered that unfortunate circumstance. It was also the first election in which the winning candidate (Trump) lost his home state (New York) since Woodrow Wilson in 1916.[238]

Like déjà vu, just two weeks before the inauguration, the office of the director of National Intelligence (DNI) James Clapper released a report concluding that Russians interfered with the election to "undermine public faith in the US democratic process, to denigrate Secretary Clinton, and harm her electability and potential presidency." In 2017, former FBI director Robert Mueller became a special counsel investigating rumors of possible collusion between Russia and the Trump campaign. The investigation took two years to submit findings to the Justice Department only to state there was not sufficient evidence of collusion between the Trump campaign and President Putin or Russia. However, it did conclude that Russian interference absolutely occurred "in sweeping and systematic fashion" and was made intentionally to harm Clinton while giving significant help to Trump. Allegations accused Russia of possible involvement in ballot and voter registration tampering and various dark media suppression, distribution of misinformation, and significant hacking.

As we have done in all of the supposed "wrong winner elections," we present evidence of "what ifs" that could have tilted this election. Although it appeared to be a wide margin of victory for Trump with the electoral vote, 304-227, it was much closer than those numbers appear as he lost the popular vote by nearly three million votes.[239] He was victorious in the four most important battleground states, Michigan, Wisconsin, Pennsylvania, and Florida, so let us look at those states.

One of the "what if" scenarios for Clinton to win lay on the normally Democratic swing state strongholds that she lost by less than 1 percent? Wisconsin, ten electoral votes and lost by 0.76 percent; Pennsylvania, twenty electoral votes was lost by 0.72 percent; and Michigan with sixteen electoral votes, she lost by 0.23 percent. That would have given her a 278-260 electoral margin. To understand how close and significant that was we need to dig deeper into each state.

Michigan, a state that was not won by a Republican since 1988, she lost by only 11,000 votes or 0.23 percent. Wisconsin, which had not been won by a Republican since 1984, was lost by only twenty-three thousand votes, a 0.76 percent loss out of nearly three million total votes cast. Finally, in Pennsylvania where Republicans also had not won since 1988, Clinton lost by 45,000 or 0.72 percent of over six million total votes. These three states totaled 79,000 votes out of 125 million votes and would have given her not only a popular vote victory by three million but also the White House by a 278-260 margin. However, the loss by any of those four states would have left her short of 270.

Here Are the States with the Closest Results

States where the margin of victory was under 1 percent (50 electoral votes; 46 won by Trump, 4 by Clinton)

1. Michigan, 0.23 percent - 16 electoral votes (10,704 votes) - Trump
2. New Hampshire, 0.31 percent - 4 electoral votes (2,736 votes) - Clinton
3. Pennsylvania, 0.72 percent - 20 electoral votes (44,292 votes) - Trump
4. Wisconsin, 0.76 percent - 10 electoral votes (tipping point state) (22,748 votes) – Trump

States/districts where the margin of victory was between 1 percent and 1.5 percent

1. Florida, 1.20 percent - 29 electoral votes (112,911 votes) - Trump
2. Minnesota, 1.52 percent- 10 electoral votes (44,765 votes) – Clinton

Table 4.6: 2016 Presidential Election Results

Presidential Candidate	Party	VP Candidate	Popular vote		EC Votes
			Count	%	
Donald Trump	Republican	Mike Pence	62,984,828	46.09%	304
Hillary Clinton	Democratic	Tim Kaine	65,853,514	48.18%	227
Gary Johnson	Libertarian	William Weld	4,489,341	3.28%	0
Jill Stein	Green	Ajamu Baraka	1,457,218	1.07%	0
Evan McMullin	Independent	Mindy Finn	731,991	0.54%	0
Darrell Castle	Constitution	Scott Bradley	203,090	0.15%	0
Gloria La Riva	Socialist Libertarian	Eugene Puryear	74,401	0.05%	0
Tickets that received electoral votes from faithless electors					
Bernie Sanders	Independent	Elizabeth Warren	111,850	0.08%	1
John Kasich	Republican	Carly Fiorina	2,684	0.00%	1
Ron Paul	Libertarian	Mike Pence	124	0.00%	1
Colin Luther Powell	Republican	Elizabeth Warren Maria Cantwell Susan Collins	25	0.00%	3

Faith Spotted Eagle	Democratic	Winona LaDuke	0	0.00%	1
Other			760,210	0.56%	
		Total	**136,669,276**	**100.0%**	**538**
		Needed to Win			**270**

CHAPTER 5
Should Electoral College Be Abolished? Yes, or No?

There have been more proposals for constitutional amendments on changing the Electoral College than on any other subject brought before Congress. Because the Electoral College process is part of the original design of the US Constitution, it would be necessary to pass a constitutional amendment to abolish it completely. There have also been staunch defenders of the Electoral College who, although they may be less vocal in their criticism, they offer arguments in its favor.

When the framers of our Constitution established the Electoral College, it was thought to be a compromise between Congress electing the president or a popular vote of qualified citizens. They thought these would be a disaster. First, they vehemently rejected Congress choosing the president for fear they would become beholden to that state legislature that elected them, eroding any federal authority over the executive branch. The second, the direct election was rejected because the framers had serious doubts that the public had the knowledge or understanding of candidates outside their own state, leading to continuous favorite son presidential candidates. It would also cause large numbers of candidates attempting to be elected president with no candidate emerging with a majority of the popular vote, leading to one contingent election after another which leads right back to the first problem, where Congress would make the decision anyway.

As a compromise our founders settled on the idea of using electors. Article 2 of the Constitution and the Twelfth Amendment simply refers to "electors" but not an "electoral college." Nowhere in the Constitution does the term "electoral college" appear.[240]/[241]

Michael McConnell, Director of Constitutional Law at the Hoover Institution and a proponent of the status quo of keeping the Electoral College, says, "No one would adopt an Electoral College today if we were starting from scratch. But reforming it does not rank high among our national problems. There are more urgent and promising topics for reform of our presidential election system.[242] Professors Jack Rakove, the William Robertson Professor of History and American Studies, and a professor of political science disagree with that theory and argue in favor of abolishment when they said, "Having the states play an autonomous role in presidential elections, it is said, reinforces the division of governing authority between the nation and the states."[243]

Before reviewing the significant attempts to abolish the Electoral College, we first discuss the pros and cons of the system. For some, the Electoral College is a legacy of the founders' vision. For others, it is an antique relic that enables tyranny of the minority.

The following opinions are strictly related to extensive research done of those who argue for the present Electoral College and those who wish to abolish it. They do not represent my own opinions on this subject and should not be confused with any future chapters regarding my personal remedies for this problem. What I am attempting to characterize is bipartisan views so you, as the reader, can come to your own conclusions. However, I will give you a brief opinion on each of the factors mentioned in this chapter. In later chapters, I will reveal my solutions on what would be best, whether it mean abolish, reform or continue to keep the Electoral College.

No: Arguments for Keeping the Electoral College

Advocates believed our founding fathers thought it was the best way because electors will safeguard against uninformed uneducated voters instead of Congress choosing the president. Therefore, the US Constitution should only be rarely amended. As it clearly states in Article 2, Section 1, that "each state shall appoint, in such manner as the legislature of the state thereof, a number of electors."[244] Reference is made of the NAEP (National Assessment of Education Process) that shows a decline in grade 12 reading performances, thus the theory of the less educated voters.[245] Of course, this is simply theory as more and more voters are very aware of the political landscape more than anytime in American history. Using the "uneducated" syndrome is not only incorrect it is downright discriminatory and potentially racist.

Trent England, founder and director of Save Our States and the David and Ann Brown Distinguished Fellow at the Oklahoma Council of Public Affairs, believes the Electoral College preserves the needed checks and balances, keeping states in charge of our elections, and ensures that our national politics stays national.[246] The issue here is the fact we have fifty different states with fifty different voting laws which absolutely does not keep our election of presidents on a national level. What it does is divide our presidential elections into fifty small state elections. Again, this is a theory, but it carries no weight.

The pro-Electoral College version is that we badly misunderstand it and elections such as 2000 and 2016 fuel that fire. Hence, many Americans contend that it is archaic, outdated, and irrelevant. But those theories dispel history and our founding fathers' knowledge of imperfections of human nature and the fact that simple democracies are unreliable. However, the framers could not predict all the changes in our society. But they still were able to design an electoral system that would change with the times.[247] The key here is the words "change with the times" because that is not true either. If we are to believe this system is still working, then why do we still have only 435 members in the House?

Tara Ross explains in her book *Why We Need the Electoral College* and believes it was created to protect the voices of the smaller populated rural state minority from being overwhelmed by the will of the urban states with larger population's majority. This balance would work against the risk of "tyranny of the majority" where the voices of masses of large populated urban states drown out minority smaller populated interests.[248] She believes this historical American system was is a unique presidential system that has served for centuries creating a decentralized process that ultimately makes it harder to steal elections.[249] The theory stops the larger populated states of undue influence between electing the president by popular vote because it would alleviate Congress from assisting in choosing the president. Ross, also the author of *The Indispensable Electoral College*, believes the Electoral College creates a balancing power between the small and large states creates coalition-building across many regions. Our framers were vehemently opposed to letting Congress have anything to do with the election of the president, and that is rightly correct because political leadership in our Congress should not have anything to do with the national election of the office of president.

The Electoral College ensures that all candidate campaigns will try to include all parts of the country to be involved in the selecting of the president. Depending solely on the popular vote would limit candidates campaigning to only the heavily populated areas or regions. Groups of people, such as farmers in states such as Iowa, would be ignored in favor of pandering to the metropolitan densely populated areas. This would leave rural areas and small towns marginalized. Tina Mullally of South Dakota reasons, "The Electoral College creates a needed balance between rural and urban interests."[250] Once again, I disagree with this because if we had a one person, one vote philosophy of a national direct popular vote, then each and every vote, no matter where it is from, would count equally.

Believers say it preserves Federalism because our country is made up of so many different regions and cultures. By allocating the electoral vote to over fifty states, it allows more states to have an impact on the choice of our president.[251] Yes, allocation to states is absolutely a definite plus for keeping the Electoral College. However, we again do not respect the wishes of our founding fathers and framers of our Constitution who consistently believed the number of representatives a state should have should be apportioned equally according to population. That allocation has not happened in ninety-five years.

Tara Ross, as a lawyer and writer, is one of the most nationally recognized for her expertise on the Electoral College. According to her several books in favor of the Electoral College states, "The Electoral College is part of the system of checks and balances, intended to check tyranny. We can no more outgrow it than we can create a world full of perfect human beings."[252] She argues that the Electoral College is grossly misunderstood because too many Americans believe it is outdated and archaic and is irrelevant by improved communication and technology.[253]

Another argument says it lessens the likelihood of calls for recounts or demands for runoff elections, giving uncertainty to presidential elections. Because popular vote elections seldom reveal a clear majority of the votes, we are continuously creating many minority presidents, such as Nixon in 1968 and Clinton in 1992 who both only received a plurality of 43 percent.[254] It is also a fact that fifteen presidents were elected by less than 50 percent of the voters.[255] If you believe in the Constitution that clearly begins with "We the people of the United States," it stands to reason that anyone who meets the qualifications of obtaining the office of president of the United States should do so. The believers say that the end result of this Electoral

College is clear because the winner must get "a majority of the electoral votes whereas you might have somebody winning by a mere 30 percent of the voters due to many candidates running for president creating a potentially extremist candidate," according to Chris DeRosa, chair of the Department of History and Anthropology.[256] Of course, elections will end with the winner only receiving 40 percent or maybe less, and if run-offs are needed to reach that level of 50 percent then maybe that is a concept we may have to look at.

According to another proponent, Allen Guelzo, elections that are won by small pluralities reveal the lack of support for one candidate. A president who is elected with only 25 to 35 percent does not create a mandate to govern and questions the legitimacy of the election outcome itself.[257] True, but what if the NFL said that if a team does not score on at least 50 percent of their possessions they cannot be declared the winner even if they scored more points than the other team.

America's unique presidential system has worked for centuries because it contributes to the cohesiveness of the country by requiring a distribution of popular support to be elected president. This state-by-state election process isolates voting problems and decentralizes the process making it harder to steal elections.[258] The first part is absolutely true that it distributes popular support across the board. However, the second part is one of the largest problems of presidential elections because if we are truly one country under God then every state must have the same set of rules for voting for the president of the entire United States, not fifty presidents.

There should be separate federal laws just for the presidential elections and they must be the same in all states.

Tara Ross believes the system rewards the candidate who does the best job of coalition building. These founders wanted a system that does not allow candidates to ignore issues that ignore geographical checks and balances,[259] making this state-by-state system harder to steal elections.[260] Yes, it does build coalitions, and yes, it does not ignore geographic policies, but neither of those have anything to do with stealing elections.

Ross continues by saying it creates a safeguard against voter fraud because it minimizes corruption. Her argument is if somebody votes in one state it only affects the outcome of the electoral votes in that one state whereas a national popular vote opens up a free-for-all for fraudulent voting in many states. Simply put her beliefs of this Electoral College was a crucial part of our founding fathers (from 200 years age?) avoiding the creation of an unconstitutional popular vote.[261] This I am sorry to say is just wrong. Yes, the vote affects only the outcome of the electoral votes in one state, but that makes every state have selfish beliefs in what the outcome of the election should be and takes away the national one person, one vote theory.

Yes: Arguments for Abolishing the Electoral College

We need to begin with Jesse Wegman, author of many books, including the infamous *Let the People Pick the President,* concurs, "It's hard to imagine a political institution less suited to the twenty-first century democracy than the Electoral

College."[262] And following are the many reasons why he shows that he is correct.

The first problem of the Electoral College is the fact that "it gives more weight to the voters in small states than in the most populated states," according to Chris DeRosa.[263] Smaller populated states have significant electoral power over the larger states.[264] A state such as Wyoming has one elector per 192 thousand people, while California has only one elector per 760 thousand people. Gautam Mukanda, a political scientist at Harvard, stated, "The fact that presidential elections of the people in Wyoming have four times the power of people in California is antithetical at the most basic level to what we say we stand for as a democracy."[265]

Another Electoral College example is North and South Dakota, who combined have six electoral votes with each having one member in the House plus two US Senators each. That is one US Senator for every 425 thousand people, while California has the same two US Senators representing forty million people, which is one for every twenty million people. That ratio gives Dakota a 47 to 1 advantage. We could go on and on, but the importance is the fact that there are many small or less populated states overwhelming misrepresentation in comparison to larger more populated states. When you take the overall average among the fifty states, small state representation has four times the voting power in Congress. These factors are all true and the responsibility of this problem goes back nearly one hundred years with the Reapportionment

Act of 1929, or should we call it what it is, the Permanent Apportionment Act.

The Electoral College also presents a problem of electoral inequality because every state starts with the same number of electoral votes of two US Senators no matter what the population of that state. Then the remaining are for the number of members in the House. This format gives an overwhelming representation to the small to medium sized populated states at the expense of the larger more populated states. Christopher Pearson, a Vermont state legislator, is on the Board of the National Popular Vote Inc. that promotes the belief the Electoral College should be eliminated because it does not follow the "popular vote of all the people." He claims, "it does not truly represent one person, one vote."[266]

This theory completely ignores the fact that 15 percent of American counties represent 64 percent of the nation's GDP (gross domestic product) which is directly related to the country's economic activity. This converts into the fifteen most prosperous states, having only thirty senators, while the less prosperous thirty-five states have seventy senators. These thirty-five states have greater political power to choose presidents and dictate public policy. That creates a mismatch between economic vitality and political power that will continue to cause discrepancies between the popular votes and Electoral College votes, causing the winners of the popular vote losing elections becoming the norm.[267]

Another reason for abolishment is the fact that people continue to move to the coasts, yet the Electoral College stays the same. States such as Wyoming, the Dakotas, and Delaware are worth more than the electoral votes in the four most populous state of California, Texas, Florida, and New York, leaving these four very large states underrepresented in the Electoral College. This imbalance has primarily been a late twentieth or twenty-first century phenomenon because of an act called the Reapportionment Act of 1929, which we thoroughly discussed in the last chapter. Over the last eleven decennial US Census, this act has frozen the Electoral College at its present day 538 while states that continue to grow, such as California and even New York, are losing electoral votes because of the redistribution of the same 538. Faith in our elections, trust in our government, and the legitimacy of elected officials gives the people the perception of antidemocratic, anti-majoritarian concept will be challenged by the will of the voters.[268] This unbalance electoral vote theory goes back to our Constitution that gave every state two senators, meaning states with only three electoral votes have significantly more power than the larger states, where every ten years we continue to poach and redistribute the same amount of electoral college votes takes place.

The theory that both proponents and opponents believe is that it takes a constitutional amendment to abolish the Electoral College. However, there are methods that could change the rules of the Electoral College system without using a constitutional amendment. Since its final ratification in 1788, the Constitution has been changed several times by means other than the traditional amendment process.[269]

The current system gives too much power and attention to the top eight states, allowing the presidential elections to be determined by only a handful of states without worrying about the nationwide popular vote totals. In 2024, if a candidate can win all eight of these states, it would total 223 electoral votes, leaving them only forty-seven electoral votes in forty-two states to be elected president, giving excessive power to the swing states. It also debunks the pro-Electoral College theory that candidate's campaign in more states. This false narrative of a coalition-building theory that the proponents believe does not make campaigns have a more national approach.

The Electoral College ignores the will of the people, when democracy should function as the will of the people, allowing one vote, one person. This leads to a failure of the theory that the national population of the American people are supported. Instead, the system puts presidential elections in the hands of only 538 people of the national population of 332 million in the United States decide who will be president. That is 0.00000162 percent (one elector for every 625,000) of the total population. In no way does that represent the one person, one vote theory. Even former president Trump who benefited from the Electoral College stated as recently as early 2016 that he believe the presidents should be chosen by a popular vote, "I would rather see it where if somebody gets 100 million votes and the other gets only 95 million votes, the person with the 100 million should win."[270] Jesse Wegman, author of *Let the People Pick the President*, stated, "If anything, representative democracy in the twenty-first century is about political equality. It's about one person, one vote—everybody's vote counting equally. You're not going to convince the majority of Americans that that is not how you should do it."[271] John Koza, Chairman of the National Popular Vote, warns us that "at this point I think changing the system to something better is going to determine whether there will be a dictator in this country."[272]

Opponents are disturbed by the possibilities of electing minority presidents, those five so-called wrong winners in 1824, 1876, 1888, 2000, and 2016 and other possibilities in 1960 and 1968, who won the Electoral College while they lost (or nearly lost) the national popular vote causing us to elect minority presidents. This possibility grows stronger each presidential election year.[273] In a perfect democracy, not everything needs a majority vote, which the Electoral College requires. Many Americans still do not understand why they do not actually directly vote for the president, when the reality is we choose electors who have the full authority and power to elect the president.[274] This cannot continue, so having a person who loses the popular vote win the presidency seriously undermines the legitimacy of the elections.

Wegman in *Let the People Pick the President* goes beyond those five and makes examples of the problems of the elections of 1796 and 1800 where in one case, the president and vice president were from different parties in the former while giving us an electoral tie in the latter. These only led to the passing of the Twelfth Amendment to ensure our president and vice president would be from different parties. He shows us his views on one-person, one-vote revolution of the 1960s was an attempt to drive a constitutional amendment for a national popular vote in 1969 and again in 1970.[275]

The Electoral College is deeply rooted in slavery and racism. James Madison stated, "There was difficulty of serious nature based on the right of suffrage being more diffusive in the northern states than the southern states, giving the latter no influence for the scores of Negroes." The Three-Fifths Compromise made the enslaved population only count as 3/5 rather than a whole person. Also, in 1788 all blacks, women, and white men who did not own property could not vote. Racism is at the root of the Electoral College by suppressing the votes of people of color in favor of voters from largely homogenic white states.[276]

The biggest problem with this part of the Electoral College is that it encourages voter suppression. Southern states have always had an advantage in the population count because they get electoral vote allotments based on the former slave population counting as a whole person instead of only the three-fifths. But black voter suppression is still running rampant as it did during the Jim Crow laws. "This further inflates the electoral count because this voter suppression on the black population causes an unfair electoral count for the white votes in many southern states. So, the Electoral College became a pillar of white supremacy," according to Chris DeRosa.[277]

Because electors are based on total population, the Three-Fifths Clause gave Slave Power states undue electors based on the population count of these nonvoters. Even after the Fourteenth and Fifteenth Amendments which gave the

African American population the power to vote, the violent disfranchisement throughout the south gave those former slave owner states additional electors as voter suppression of the former slaves was controlling voter turnout, thus benefiting the white male power holders.[278] So these southern states consume electoral votes that are not consistent with their voter turnout due to the voter suppression of the minorities.

Love it or hate it, eliminating the Electoral College is here to stay for now because changing it would require *constitutional surgery.* A constitutional amendment must be proposed by a two-thirds vote in both chambers (290 in the House plus sixty-seven in the Senate). Then the amendment must be ratified by three-fourths (38) of the state ratifying conventions, but clearly there are too many states suppressing the vote for the benefit of the Electoral College. Different states have several different methods; some simply have their state legislatures vote while others require a statewide referendum popular vote, which then would still need the ratification by the state legislature and the signing of its governor. Although the Constitution has been amended twenty-seven times, beginning with the Bill of Rights in 1791 up to the Twenty-Seventh Amendment in 1992, reaching the thirty-eight states needed is clearly impossible right now due to voter suppression laws in more than twenty states. The overall downside is "if you never have to appeal to the electorate because you're successfully suppressing some large part of it, then you have a broken system."[279] However, we do have five ways the Constitution can be changed or overridden by other methods to be discussed.

Another risk of the Electoral College is the so-called faithless electors, who, for whatever reason, choose to vote against their state's chosen candidate. There have been nearly 165 faithless electors over the years who pledged their votes to their party's candidate then voted for a different candidate. Today many states require electors to take a formal pledge that they will uphold their state's popular choice; however, twenty-one states still have no such requirement.[280] Let's say the electors in those twenty-one states form a *coup d'état* or a *quid pro quo* with a specific candidate to vote contrary to their state's popular vote; we could elect a president who is deeply entrenched in political corruption against the will of the people that could cause the deterioration of our democracy.

Winner-take-all (in forty-eight of fifty states as Maine and Nebraska does not apply) is creating problems for states and the country as 70 percent of American voters feel ignored, leading to lower voter turnouts. All a candidate needs to do is win a state by one vote and they get all the state Electoral votes, thus making it responsible for five presidents elected while losing the Electoral College. The possible role of the Electoral College causes a different form of voter suppression in the form of low voter turnouts. The argument is the electoral votes takeaway the incentives of many voters to go to the polls or sometimes not registering at all to vote because they are disenfranchised that their votes are rendered meaningless.[281]

There is also a simple fact that the Electoral College is no longer relevant in its present form because it is an antique relic from the eighteenth century. Remember it has been attempted more than 700 times to either abolish or at least reform it that cannot even pass Congress once over more than 200 years. Jesse Wegman mentions in his famous book *Let the People Pick the President: the Case for Abolishing the Electoral College* that it is hard to imagine a political institution less suited to the twenty-first-century democracy than the Electoral College. It was a convoluted compromise of the Constitutional Conventions of 1787 and 1788 that undermined voting in the very early nineteenth century. [282]

In recent years, state lawmakers have debated the continued use of the Electoral College and whether it should be left intact, reformed, or abolished. In September 2020, a Gallup poll found 61 percent of all Americans (Democrats, Republicans, and Independents combined) prefer amending the Constitution to use the popular vote to elect the president. Only 23 percent of those identify as Republicans, while 89 percent identify as Democrats, the highest preference for popular vote in two decades and 68 percent are Independents. This is up from 55 percent in 2019.[283] This poll makes things abundantly clear, the Electoral College as we have it now must go, whether it be a reformed version or an amendment to completely abolish this system. This is not just a 2020 issue as Gallup took polls from 1967 and 1980 that found majorities of 58 percent to 80 percent favored abolishing the Electoral College in favor of the popular vote.[284]

Aside from all this, the one thing that is abundantly clear to those who are in favor of abolishment is the Electoral College as we have it now must go.

All these arguments for or against leave plenty of unaddressed possibilities. Such as how do we count the popular votes in Maine and Nebraska if those states adopted the same plans of the other forty-eight states? What happens if some states lower the voting age to sixteen while others do not? What if there is a dispute as to who won the nationwide popular vote because the national popular vote gave a winner a less than 0.50 percent victory, which is the exact difference in most states usually causes an automatic recount. How would we conduct a recount?[285]

CHAPTER 6
Attempts to Abolish or Reform the Electoral College
Will Any of These Plans Fit What Americans Needs?

Over 235 years ago, our founding fathers and framers of our Constitution created our Electoral College system. Since 1800, there have been more than 700 attempts to either reform or abolish it according to the Congressional Research Service, which is more than any other issue regarding constitutional reform. The fact is the fight to reform or abolish this old antiquated Electoral College started as early as 1802 by Alexander Hamilton, one of the original founding fathers, who was so upset with how it was being executed that he drafted a constitutional amendment to fix it.[286] As discussed previously, the biggest problem is a constitutional amendment is the only means of abolishing this old system. That was the part of the Constitution the framers failed to consider when creating the executive branch in 1788. Only in 1969, was one of those attempts almost successful to being proposed to the states.[287]

The actual phrase "Electoral College" cannot be found anywhere in the Constitution. Instead, it has always been referred to the voters as presidential electors per Article 2, Section 1, Clauses 2 and 3 and ratified 1789.[288] It simply called for electors equal to the number of senators and House members in each state based on population. It chose to allocate one House member per a minimum of 30,000 people plus two senators per state without regard to population. The framers also gave states plenty of latitude on how to choose their congressional House members and senators. Some states used direct popular vote while others had state legislators choose. The Seventeenth Amendment in 1914 gave voters the right to choose senators for the first time.[289]

Changing or abolishing this Electoral College needs a constitutional amendment requiring ratification by three-quarters (38) of the states and needs the governor's certification signature of the governor. These are the largest hurdles to overcome. Although the Constitution has been amended twenty-seven times, reaching the thirty-eight states on the abolishment of this Electoral College is nearly impossible due to partisan politics.

The father of the Constitution, James Madison, never favored the system of electing president electors. Historian Garry Willis wrote, "As a framer and defender of the Constitution, he (Madison)had no peers." Madison proposed his preference was a national popular vote as early as 1787.[290] Also he would support choosing electors by district instead of at large stating that, "Most of our Framers assumed that the choice of electors by district was a given part of the system." The original Electoral College lasted seventeen years until the Twelfth Amendment in 1804 due to messy elections in 1796 and 1800. But that amendment still did not cure the problem that electors were chosen on a winner-take-all basis.[291]

In 1823, James Madison began to argue for a district plan that "was mostly, if not exclusively, in view when the Constitution was framed and adopted." His plan would subdivide "the electors to be chosen by congressional districts, naming the candidate with the most popular votes in a given district of that elector." He issued his strong opposition to states voting as winner-take-all blocs because he believed it disenfranchised districts that voted against the statewide preference. Madison felt that the use of a winner-take-all rule did not help smaller states while favoring the largest most populated states.[292] Madison is proof that 200 years ago needed reform of the original system.[293]

A major problem is the Constitution used the wording that House districts would have "a minimum size of 30,000" but never established a *maximum size,* resulting in the failure to continually increase the size of the House based on the US Census. The failure of using the words "no more than" that should have read "no less than."[294]

Today, forty-eight of fifty states allocate electors based on popular vote with the winner-take-all process in all those states. Only two states, Nebraska and Maine, award electors based on the district plan for the winning candidate of each congressional district gets one elector while the statewide popular vote winner gets two electors.[295] There are also several groups working on a state-by-state basis before they are presented to Congress as a replacement or reform of the present system.[296]

Following are the many alternative methods that have been seriously considered since the landmark 1929 Reapportionment Act that froze the House at 435, consequently freezing the

Electoral College at 538. That act simply allows for a redistribution of those numbers even if a new state is admitted later on.[297]

The Automatic Fractional Proportion Plan: The Lodge-Gossett Amendment – 1950

In 1950, a bipartisan amendment was proposed by bipartisan sponsors, Senator Henry Cabot Lodge (Republican-Massachusetts) and Congressman Ed Gossett (Democrat-Texas). Also known as the automatic fractional plan that would give the number of electoral votes each candidate awarded *automatically* on a fractional proportional basis carried out to three decimal points. It would allow a president to be elected by a simple plurality and not a majority. This plan would remove the possibilities of *faithless electors*[9] by eliminating the presidential electors that also eliminates the contingent election because the amendment would only require a candidate only need a plurality of the electoral votes. This amendment eliminating the electors, and the contingent election would require a federal constitutional amendment.[298]

Before it went to Congress, an adjustment was made requiring a candidate would need a minimum of 40 percent of the national popular vote. The joint resolution went to the US Senate in February 1950 and received a favorable vote of 64-27. However, the proposed amendment died in the House of Representatives.[299]/[300]

---

[9] Faithless electors are those who vote for a candidate other than the one to whom they are pledged.

Supporters argue it would maintain the Electoral College concept while eliminating the electors, also eliminating faithless electors while balancing federal and state power over elections. The elimination of faithless electors stops electors who vote opposite to the popular vote choice. Faithless electors have never changed the outcome of any presidential election it has happened only 165 times.[301] Proponents say it also preserves the two-party system with the state-by-state fractional proportional allocation of the electoral votes, and also rewards parties with a broad range of viewpoints by embracing larger areas of the nation.[302] It also does not violate Article 2, Section 1 of our Constitution, and automatically awarding electoral votes to the third decimal point increases the one person, one vote accuracy.[303]

Fractional Proportional Allocation Plan: Senator Howard Cannon – 1969

Shortly after assuming office in 1969 President Nixon threw his support and challenged Congress to create an amendment to abolish the Electoral College. He said, "I have supported a proportional plan in the past and I will support any plan that moves forward abolishing the individual electors in order to allocate presidential candidates the electoral votes of each state and the District of Columbia in a manner that may more closely approximates the use of popular votes that the present system does not have."[304] This message ignited a flurry of activity by the Ninety-First Congress as members stepped forward and introduced potential amendments to change or completely abolish the Electoral College.[305]

Immediately, Senator Cannon (Democrat-Nevada) proposed to Congress a constitutional amendment very similar to the Lodge-Gossett Amendment, calling for electoral votes distributed on a fractional proportion method to the third decimal place based on the percentage of votes each candidate received in each state. It also would require a 5 percent popular vote cut-off in a state for a candidate to have to receive any electoral votes. This would require a constitutional amendment because it needs to repeal Article 2 and the Twelfth Amendment and essentially dismantles and abolishes the entire Electoral College, including elimination of the presidential electors.[306]

Examples using the two-party system shows this fractional plan accurately reflects the nationwide vote in the closest electoral elections. In the close election of 2000, Gore who won the nationwide popular vote by 543,895 but would have still lost the Electoral College to Bush by 0.480, 269.240 to 268.760. Although it meets the necessary plurality, it would have still denied the winner of the popular vote a victory.[307] Looking at the second minority presidential election in this century in 2016, the popular vote winner would have proven the use of the fractional method would give us astounding results. Clinton, who defeated Trump by 2.9 million popular votes would have also won the Electoral College 272.368 to 265.632, also reaching the 270-majority of the electoral votes.[308] This brings up the inequity of at what point does the popular vote victor also win the Electoral votes? Obviously, a 500 thousand popular vote victory was not enough to win the Electoral vote, but a 2.9 million victory seems to put the popular winner over the top on the Electoral side. There is no formula for this because it could depend on several factors from (a) unequal turnouts in states with the same electoral votes, (b) how many electoral votes are from states with differences in electoral votes, and (c) how does third party candidates affect a state's electoral votes in states that they do not reach the 5 percent cut-off? There are no simple hardcore answers to these potential circumstances.

The fractional plan reveals how much the 2,000 bonus electoral votes given to each state automatically regardless of that state's population because the Constitution gives every state two Senate seats. An example of this is one electoral vote in Wyoming represents 192,573 people whereas an electoral vote in California represents 732,903 people, a 3.805-to-1 advantage to Wyoming. There is also an unequal apportionment of membership in the House in several states. Wyoming has the constitutional minimum one House member for a population of 577,719, while Delaware also has only one House member while representing a population of 989,948, giving Wyoming a 1.714-to-1 advantage over a state that has the same number of electoral votes that creates inequalities among the smaller states with only three electoral votes.[309]

Another negative is the fact that states with lower turnouts have a greater weight than votes cast in states with larger turnouts. In the last election four states, Nebraska (40.3 percent turnout), New Mexico (32.7 percent turnout), Utah (33.7 percent turnout), and West Virginia (35.5 percent turnout), all have five electoral votes; however, their turnouts do not relate equally to one person, one vote. This negative directly falls on the voters themselves who do not exercise their voting rights for various reasons.

To summarize, the fractional proportion approach is a more equal distribution of the electoral votes than they are today even with the deficiencies to the actual populations in each state. This method is dependent on the degree of civic participation in each state that also may vary in states having the same electoral votes. Unfortunately, Senator Cannon's proposal never got the needed support in Congress.[310]

Again, the largest hurdle is eliminating the requirements of a constitutional amendment which many of these new plans must pass. An amendment needs to (a) eliminate the actual electors while also eliminating the faithless electors, (b) the fractional proportions will minimize minority presidents that will eliminate the contingent election in Congress that our framers did not want, and (c) candidates needing only a plurality instead of the 270 electoral vote majority.[311]

Congressional District Plan: Senator Karl Mundt - 1969—used by Maine and Nebraska

Senator Karl Mundt (Republican-South Dakota) was the leader in the proposed federal constitutional amendment to implement a district plan in 1969. The District Electoral Plan is another proposal aimed at reducing the effects of winner-take-all voting while eliminating the need for a constitutional amendment by keeping the Electoral College and only changing the way electoral votes are distributed. The plan would still have electors, with two statewide at-large electors representing the candidate with the most popular votes in that state, which equals the two senators each state has. The remaining electoral votes would be distributed as one to each candidate that wins each congressional district. Today the only states of Maine and Nebraska have adopted this plan and have used it since 2008. Of course, those state with only three electors would remain status quo with all three going to the popular vote winner because those states.[312]

Nationally it makes the Electoral College more reflective of the partisan divisions The candidate will still be required to get a 270 majority of electoral votes to be elected president. This proposal goes one step further, stating if no candidate reaches that Electoral College majority, the president would be determined by a joint session of all 538 members in Congress instead of only the House making the final contingent election decision.[313]

This method would have affected several elections, including 1960, which would have yielded Nixon a 278-245 victory over Kennedy, and 1976, which would have been a 269-269 tie between Carter and Ford. The 2000 election would have been won by Bush over Gore 288-250, but the 2016 election would have been much closer with Trump winning by a slimmer 290-248 margin over Clinton.[314]

If we further analyze the 2000 election with this Congressional District approach of the Electoral College, George Bush won 228 congressional districts to 207 for Al Gore. To that we add sixty to the Bush total because he won the popular vote in thirty states while Gore would get only forty electoral votes for the twenty states he carried. Gore would also get all three of Washington, DC, electoral votes. And that is how the 288 to 250 Bush victory would be.[315] However, 2020 would have been much closer than the actual Electoral College, as Biden would have defeated Trump 275-263. They each won twenty-five states—Biden won 221 districts, twenty-five states, plus three electoral votes for Washington, DC; and Trump won 214 districts and twenty-five states.[316] In 2016, Trump carried 230 districts to Clinton with just 205. And Trump won thirty states to Clinton with twenty, giving Trump an overall win of 290 - 248.[317]

This Mundt proposal's advantages would be the fact it retained the presidential electors but eliminated the possibility of faithless electors. They would be eliminated by this amendment because each elector would take an oath to vote for the winning presidential ticket won in each Congressional district or their electoral vote would not count, avoiding those 165 faithless electors who voted for whoever they wanted, ignoring the popular vote in those states.[318]

As with other proposals, this idea had its shortcomings and never be presented for a vote in Congress because felt

1. it would not accurately reflect the "nationwide" popular vote.
2. it would not improve on the current situation where two-thirds of the states ignoring two-thirds of the people

    in presidential campaigns, creating less battleground districts and/or states; and

3. it would not make every vote equal because so many congressional districts have gerrymandered so many districts an unfair number of voters than others in the same state.[319]

The favorable parts of this plan say it (a) more accurately reflects the popular votes by considering each congressional district separately, making small states winners, and (b) that states dominated by one party give incentive for greater voter involvement resulting in larger turnouts. This would give the minority party an opportunity to take some electoral votes such as upstate New York versus New York City or Northern California vs. the Los Angeles and San Francisco areas and follow that up with additional congressional victories.[320]

Opponents feel this plan still promotes an indirect election, causing more minority presidents. Also, it makes the large competitive states losers. Also, it weakens the two-party system because it promotes narrow geographical or ideological areas. It also gives states that are dominated by one party encouragement for more gerrymandering.[321]

Direct Nationwide Popular Vote Election Plan: The Bayh-Celler Amendment - 1969

Of course, a nationwide direct popular vote plan draws the most attention from the public. It is simply designed to reward the candidate who receives the most direct popular votes the winner. In 1969, Gallup polls showed bipartisan support for the direct vote of the president was as high as 80 percent. The reason for this overwhelming swell of support was due to the messy 1968 presidential election which Nixon (43.4 percent popular vote) defeated Vice President Humphrey (42.7 percent) by a 301-191 margin in the Electoral College votes. The problem was third-party candidate, segregationist Governor George Wallace of Alabama managed to wrestle forty-six electoral votes from southern segregation dominated states with 13.5 percent, the most by a third-party candidate in modern history up until that time.[322/323] Wallace's wanted to throw the election into chaos, hopefully depriving any candidate of the 270 electoral votes needed to win, forcing the first contingent election in the House since 1824.

These factors are what led to Senator Birch Bayh (Democrat-Indiana) and Congressman Emanuel Celler (Democrat-New York), to cosponsor this historically proposed constitutional amendment that would replace the Electoral College with a simple direct nationwide popular vote that only needed a plurality vote of 40 percent to be elected president and vice president as a joint ticket. However, if the leading candidate did not reach the 40 percent bottom line earmark, there would be a runoff election held between the top two candidates.[324/325] It took place during the Ninety-First Congress in 1969–1971.[326] The runoff election could be a huge drawback today and even in 1969 because it could lead to lower turnouts. Those type of elections should remain on only local or statewide elections if any at all.

This amendment was the closest Congress ever came to abolishing the Electoral College. On September 30, 1969, the House of Representatives overwhelmingly passed a bipartisan vote of 338-70 for a federal constitutional amendment to abolish the Electoral College and replace it with a direct nationwide popular vote amendment and sent it to the Senate.

Jesse Wegman, a member of the *New York Times* editorial board and author of *Let the People Pick the President: the Case for Abolishing the Electoral College,* stated, "The Electoral College is long past its sell-by-date, and the people who run national campaigns know it. So, it's simple, what if we just count up all the votes for president and the one with the most votes wins." If it succeeded, it would have completely dismantled the Electoral College.[327/328]

This plan would obviously generate the highest voter turnout, which obviously receives the most attention. It is also a plan that has been supported by most contemporary presidents. Today, polls suggest that an overwhelming majority of more than 70 percent agree with this nationwide popular vote by giving everyone one person, one vote power. Those promoting this amendment felt it made the process simpler because it was a more accurate and democratic choice that puts the election in the hands of the people. Elections such as 2000 and 2016 that created minority presidents, a.k.a. wrong winners, would be eliminated because the winner would have been based on the direct vote of the people without an additional second level of electors voting.[329/330]

Opposition to this plan believe the use of a plurality president eliminates the filtering portion of the Electoral College. They also believe that close elections such as 1960, 1968, and 2000 could result in disastrous national recounts and lead to more US Supreme Court involvement which violates the values our constitutional framers emphasized.[331] They see more voter fraud could be more of a national problem causing continuous challenges by losing candidates. Another issue would be if no candidate reaches 40 percent there would be a runoff which would easily lead to lower turnouts in a runoff.[332] The fact is the runoff election is probably the major drawback because if people must go to the polls two times turnouts will drop lower dramatically than any level in our history.

Supporters of the Bayh-Celler Direct Nationwide Popular Vote believe it would have been a major improvement over the Electoral College because it not only needed plurality of the nationwide popular vote to be elected president and vice president. This amendment would have rendered electors useless, stopping the future possibilities of faithless electors.[333] Either way, it remedies the major problem of electing minority presidents while equalizing voting power amongst all fifty states. Although the larger most competitive states may lose some electoral superiority because it eliminates the winner-take-all electoral system of today, the increased turnouts would create extensive party competition.[334] But the biggest hurdle that so many plans have is the fact it needed an amendment to the Constitution.[335]

This direct popular vote still receives the most attention today because every vote would count equally with no state receiving an advantage or disadvantage because it would be a nationwide single system tied directly to only the popular election results.[336] American history has shown that the expansion of the direct vote is supported broadly amongst all the public sectors, and as recently as September 2023, nearly 70 percent of all Americans want a Nationwide Direct Popular Vote. Breaking this down by party shows 82 percent of those identified as Democrat, 47 percent of those identified as Republicans, and 65 percent of all independents support this way to elect their president.

One of the few arguments is the elected president may not be representative of the entire country by diluting the powers of the rural states. Other groups think geographically, concentration in large states could have their votes diluted. For example, the Jewish vote only represents 3 percent of all voters nationally, yet they have 14 percent representation in one of the largest states, New York. They argue that it may dilute the present electoral system in states with high Hispanic voter representation, such as in Florida, Texas, and California. However, every one of these theories is debunked because it simply does not violate the "one vote, one person" theory.[337]

Political parties, such as the Republicans, have become reluctant to the direct election because the current Electoral College system provides them more safe states than their rival Democratic Party. The five minority popular vote presidents elected in 1824, 1876, 1888, 2000, and 2016 were all Republicans who won by way of the electoral vote.[338]

The public majority who oppose the winner-take-all system, 65 percent to 33 percent because one person's vote in one state matters more than in other states. Bayh argued in his speech before Congress, "We are at long last arriving at the place and time in our history where meaning has been brought to the preamble of our Constitution—'We, the people of the United States.'"[339]

However, the Senate filibustered the idea until it finally died. Opposition was bipartisan as two prominent senators, Southern Republican Senator Strom Thurmond of South Carolina, and Democratic Senator Sam Ervin from North Carolina, led the filibuster on the amendment and argued that although the present system may have loopholes, it often worked well over the course of almost 200 years. A 54-36 vote resulted which came up six votes short of stopping the filibuster.[340] Consequently, Senate Majority Leader, Democrat Mike Mansfield of Montana moved to put the proposal aside so the Senate could take care of other "more important business." The proposal was never considered again and died when Congress ended its session on January 3, 1971.[341]

Throughout the 1970s, Bayh repeatedly introduced this amendment, yet it continued to face strong push back from members of both houses of Congress and both political parties. Then in 1977, President Jimmy Carter made a proposal to Congress to revisit the Bayh-Celler Amendment following a very close election in 1976 between himself and

President Ford, where Carter won both the popular vote and electoral vote winner. He wrote a letter to Congress, asking that consideration for an amendment be made to abolish the Electoral College in favor of a direct nationwide popular vote. It read: "My recommendation is that the Congress adopt a constitutional amendment to provide for direct popular election of the President. Such an amendment, which would abolish the Electoral College, will ensure that the candidate chosen by the voters becomes president that could have eliminated minority presidential elections of 1824, 1876, and 1888. I think the amendment process must be reserved for an issue of overriding governmental significance, which the election of our president is such an issue."[342] He believed the winner-take-all provision disenfranchised voters.[343/344]

A major bipartisan supporter was Senator Bob Dole, a Republican from Kansas who was the vice-presidential nominee in 1976 and the presidential nominee in 1996 stated, "The candidate for two most powerful positions in America should be elected by a direct vote of the people is one that I have supported for a long time. Candidates will soon realize that all voters are important from small and large states, therefore, to me it represents each vote carrying equal importance." Several other bipartisan politicians agree.[345]

This problem persisted as independent candidates continued to disrupt elections continuing with third-party influence on the Electoral College when Ross Perot's attracted 18.9 percent of the nationwide vote in 1992, rekindling the interest in reform. Perot grabbed anywhere from 10 percent to as much as

30 percent in every state except two. Many other attempts supporting the Nationwide Popular Vote amendment continued in 2005, when Every Vote Counts Amendment was presented that would allow presidential elections to be determined by a simple plurality. This never received a vote by Congress.[346]

The Direct Election is still the most highly supported method of public opinion. Every poll in the last four decades consistently found the public favoring the direct election as the only one that is truly one person, one vote. Many congressional members continue to push for the popular vote method over the present Electoral College. Recent polling also shows that the direct election would increase voter turnout.[347] Despite these facts, the deterrents who continue to worship the Electoral College as the most functional method for more than 200 years, and simply say that "if it isn't broke, it doesn't need fixing."[348] The United States is still the only democracy in the world where a presidential candidate can get the most votes and still lose the election.

The most recent September 25, 2023, Pew Research Center poll revealed that nearly two-thirds, 65 percent to 33 percent, favor changing how we vote to the popular vote over keeping the Electoral College. When broken down by Democrats favor the popular vote 82 percent to only 47 percent of those Republicans that were surveyed.[349]

Whole Number Proportional Approach – 2004

The whole number proportional approach was considered by Colorado voters in 2004, and it was defeated in a referendum.

The whole number proportional approach substantially differs from the fractional proportional method of Senator Cannon because instead of going to the third decimal point, it simply rounds off to the *nearest whole number, higher or lower.*[350]

Using this whole number method, the 2000 election would have ended in a 269 to 269 Electoral College tie between Gore and Bush, sending the election to the House for a contingent election. It also reveals the battleground states of Florida (25), Pennsylvania (23), Michigan (18), Ohio (21), and little New Hampshire (4) totaled eighty-seven electoral votes to end up Bush 271 to Gore 267. The whole number method would have split these states, as they were so close it would have caused a shift of two Electoral Votes for each candidate, causing a tie at 269-269 and would have caused a contingent election in the House.[351]/[352]

If you move forward to the 2016, minority winner numbers are astounding. Doing the numbers using the whole number system gives Clinton a 272 to 266 win over Trump. The reason is rounding off some of the battleground states would have affected four states, Florida (29), Michigan (16), Pennsylvania (20), and Wisconsin (10) who account for seventy-five electoral votes. Trump won all of these states to get to the 304 with the winner-take-all method. However, because these states were so close, the whole number would have split Clinton (38) to Trump (37) resulting in the 272-268.[353]/[354]

The whole number method has many unexpected and undesirable methods. First it turns the "one-person, one-vote" theory to a "one-state, one-vote" with only twenty-six of the 538 electoral votes in play. Winning one electoral vote in twenty-six "battleground" states could have thrown the presidential elections in 1976, 1992, 2000, and 2016 to the House for a contingent election, which our framers of the Constitution vehemently denied elections decided by Congress.[355]

Although this method would be executed by the states because electors are needed to create the whole number Electoral College vote, leading to more minority presidents and more faithless electors time after time. The problem stands to reason because one electoral vote in play in all the states that ended with a close popular vote. There lies the "one-state, one-vote" theory because the states that have odd number electoral votes means it takes only one electoral vote in almost any of these states could be won. Overall, the whole number proportional approach (a) does not accurately reflect the nationwide vote, (b) would not improve the current system as it puts less states in play because twenty-six of them become a 1 vote victory, and (c) it fails to make every vote count equally.[356]

CHAPTER 7

Why 435? The Reapportionment Act of 1929

(or The Permanent Apportionment Act of 1929)

"It is the sense of the people of America, that the number of Representatives ought to be increased, but particularly that it should not be left to the discretion of the Government to diminish them, below that proportion which certainly is in the power of the Legislature as the constitution now stands … I confess I always thought this part of the constitution defective."

-James Madison[357]

When our founding fathers designed and ratified the legislative branch of the Constitution the population was around four million people, concentrated in eleven ratified states consisting of only fifty-nine House members and twenty-two senators. Also, only white male landowners over twenty-one years of age were eligible to vote. By the time we reached a point where all citizens of any race or gender were allowed to vote without discrimination, our population had grown to 122 million according to the US Census in 1920.

The first United States Census was done in 1790 and the Apportionment Act that provided for the decennial apportionment was signed into law by President Washington on April 14, 1792, increasing the ratio of House members from one every 30,000 to one every 33,000 people. This act increased the number of seats in the House to 105. This is based on the Constitution, Article 1, Section 2, which requires all states to have a minimum of three electors, counting their two senators. The apportionment is a process by which we fairly divide the seats in the House among the states based on population counts from the decennial US Census numbers. This decennial apportionment became the most important function for measuring the population of each member in the US House of Representatives.[358]

In all future decennial census, the population count for all following decennial census included all residents living in the United States, regardless of age, race, both citizens and noncitizens, regardless of their immigration status at the time of the decennial apportionment.[359] A new legislative apportionment has followed every decennial Census from 1790–1920. However, the Constitution does not set the size of the House of Representatives or specify any specific method for apportionment, which is the power of each state legislature. The changes in the decennial apportionment of the population also automatically increased the total number of electors each state has based on that same continuous increase of their populations.[360]

After the first census was completed in 1790, political thinkers, such as Alexander Hamilton and Thomas Jefferson, began suggesting different methods. The plans generally differed according to whether they favored the large or small states in future post-census allocation of representatives.

The apportionment in 1792 gave every 33,000 people a representative and would change every ten years thereafter. Subsequent Apportionment changes continued in 1800 to increasing the number of House members to 142, followed by the 1810 Census setting the House at 181 based on one for every 35,000. In 1820 as America grew to over nine million people, the apportionment of the House was 213 members, which would represent an average of 40,000 people per member district. Then in 1830, the House increased to 240 seats representing 47,700 for each member based on the population increase to 12.9 million people.[361] All of these apportionments of course increased the number of presidential electors, or the Electoral College, to 288 by the election of 1832.[362]

The Apportionment Act following the 1840 Census authorized the establishment of a centralized census office during each decennial enumeration. This act set the ratio to one House member for every 70,680 residents and also decreased the number of House members from 240 to 223 for seventeen million people. This act also required states to split their House members into congressional districts for the first time. This caused several disagreements of how the members should be apportioned because it caused the elimination of a significant amount of at-large congressional districts. But we must remember that even though this act took place states still had the controlling interest in how the seats would be divided. In 1850, the House grew again to 234 House members representing twenty-three million people, and 241 in 1860 representing 303 electoral votes and an ever-growing population of thirty-one million, or one representative per 130,470.[363]

Following the Fourteenth Amendment in 1868, the population apportionment increased dramatically because the black population in the South was changed by that amendment. Now African Americans counted as one whole person rather than only 3/5 of a person, which became a large part of the population increase to over thirty-eight million people, adding forty-two members, increasing the House to 283 after the 1870 census.[364] In 1881, a provision for equally populated single member districts was added to the reapportionment laws increasing the House to 325 seats and the Electoral College to 401, and this was echoed in future decennial reapportionments acts until 1900. From 1890 through 1910, the increasing membership of the House was calculated in such a way as to ensure that no state lost a seat due to shifts in apportionment population. In 1890 the House went to 356 members, and 1900 increased to 386 seats that now represented an ever-exploding population of over seventy-six million. Remember that each increase in House members would also affect the total of the Electoral College by the same amounts.[365]

Following the Census of 1910, Congress passed the *Act Fixing the Size of the House of Representatives* on August 11, 1911. It was also otherwise known as *the Apportionment Act of 1911,* which set the size of the House of Representatives at 433 seats, which now increased the Electoral College to 531. This apportionment was based on a 1910 census of just over ninety-two million people which represented a huge 21 percent shift in population from 1900. It also included a provision to add an additional seat each for the anticipated statehood of the new states of Arizona and New Mexico, which would take us to the 435 House seats.[366]

The 1920 census represented an America that was making a large shift from a rural-to-urban nation, and more than ever, a nation of immigrants as the population grew to over 106-million people, an increase of almost 15 percent over the 1910 census report. Less than half of the population lived on farms in rural areas or in towns smaller than 2,500 people. Prior to the 1920 census, Congress and the White House had a Republican majority that historically supported rural controlled right wing conservative states. This political majority strategy in Congress failed to pass an apportionment act because it would have caused a shift of population away from the rural states, moving them to the more urban states. So, Congress left allocations after the act of 1911 in place until the 1930 Census. However, this problem has continued for the last one hundred years.[367]

The fact that Congress did nothing about apportionment set off a firestorm between the rural and urban politicians. The Republican-dominated Congress believed that any reapportionments would put the rural state members in jeopardy of losing seats due to population shifts in their respective states, as the power was moving in the direction of a quickly urbanizing nation. This significant shift in population to urbanization took place as the urban population grew from only 28 percent in 1880 to 55 percent in 1920, whereas the rural population did the opposite, shrinking from 72 percent in 1880 to 45 percent following the 1920 census. These dramatic shifts in population consequently led to the reasoning for freezing the number of House members.[368]

Beyond urbanization shift, rural politicians feared any subsequent redrawing of their districts would force individual members of Congress to have to compete against each other for the same seats. In some cases, the shift would have caused elected members of Congress of the same party to compete for those redrawn district seats creating a game of musical chairs. This created a significant increase in districts of different sizes compounding the rural dominated states in Congress to stand by and do nothing about reapportionment.[369] This would trickle down to the rural controlled state legislatures who then began redrawing district boundary lines that made absolutely no sense geographically or evenly populated districts. This allowed the creation of districts so they would remain more favorable to rural populations. This method of unfair districting is known as gerrymandering[10], which continues today as frequently as it did one hundred years ago. This gerrymandering is directly related to whichever political party controls the state legislatures who have the power to change the shape, size, and population of every House district in our federal government.[370]

The next thing that occurred is probably the most significant time in the history of our House of Representatives. A year prior to the 1930 Census on June 18, 1929, Congress passed

---

[10] Gerrymandering—the political manipulation of electoral district boundaries with the expressed intent to create undue advantages for a political party, group, or social economic class within the constituency.

what was called the Reapportionment Act of 1929 and the Act Providing for the Fifteenth Census and the Apportionment of Representatives in Congress (actually was the Permanent Apportionment Act of 1929 or the Permanent Redistribution of House Members Act of 1929). Because the act permanently froze the House at 435 members, reapportionment became a redistribution of the same number of House seats for the next one hundred years. This 1929 Act set up a permanent mathematical process that would automatically redistribute the same House members according to each subsequent Census and fixing that number at 435.[371]

The US Census in 1930 was over 122 million people, resulting in another fifteen million people increase from 1920. The reality is this is the Reapportionment Act of 1929 became a redistribution of the same fixed 435 seats which continues today and all future population expansion growth as the nation continues its move toward more urbanization. However, without an amendment to the Constitution or repeal of the *Reapportionment Act of 1929*, Congress does not have the power to intervene and determine if additional house seats and electoral votes can be added in the future.[372]

Unlike any earlier apportionment acts, 1929 neither repealed nor restarted the requirements of previous acts that would make congressional districts contiguous, compact, and equally populated proportionately. It was not clear whether these requirements were still in effect in 1932 when the Supreme Court ruled in the case of *Wood v. Broom* that the provisions of each apportionment act affected only the apportionment for which they were written. Thus, the size of the population requirements expired with the enactment of the 1929 Act.[373]

This is completely the reverse of proposals made by James Madison, as one of our Founders, who stated 250 years ago in Federalist 58 that "one of the unequivocal objects of the population census is to augment (increase) the number of representatives under the sole limitation that the whole number of representatives shall not exceed one for every thirty thousand inhabitants." The use of gerrymandering became part of the means that makes it possible for powerful partisan politicians to draw district lines in such a manner to maintain the rural population power.[374]

The Reapportionment (or let's call it what it really is, the Permanent Apportionment) Act of 1929 allowed states to operate at their own discretion of redrawing districts without intervention by the federal government. This also became the act which allowed states to redraw districts of varying sizes and shapes and allowed them to abandon districts altogether to elect at least one representative at-large, which is what several states did. From 1920 to 2020, congressional district sizes tripled from an average of 210,238 people to 760,919 people according to our current 2020 Census, due to the unchanging size of the House.[375] There is a large disparity of the redistribution of House seats, not only geographic but in population sizes.

Urban states such as Delaware have only one House district representing 989,948 people, while the rural state of Montana has two House seats, as one was added after the 2020 Census, with an average of only 542,113 people per district for the 2024 elections. This gain of one seat in Montana was based on an increase of only 95,992 in population from 989,415 in 1910 to 1,085,407 people in 2020. Delaware increased by 92,014, going from 897,934 in 2010 to 989,948 in 2020 with no additional representation. This disparity of congressional districts has been exposed every ten years by state legislatures controlling urban vs. rural states.[376]/[377]

The urbanization of America continued from 1960 to 2020 as it went from 70 percent to 80 percent urban, while the rural population shrunk continuously from 30 percent to 20 percent. In the 2020 US Census, there were approximately 57.47 million people living in rural areas compared to 274.03 million people living in urban areas. The fact of the matter is by 2040 if there are not any changes made by our state legislatures on how we reapportion the House each member of Congress could represent an average of one million people or more.[378]

The 1929 act took away the power of Congress and delegated the power to reapportion to state legislatures to redistrict, redraw or reapportion their individual states and did away with any mention of districts at all. This would cause partisanship and political self-interests to affect any possibilities for further reapportionment. The lack of these recommendations concerning districts had several significant effects.[379] Because the act also did away with any mention of districts, it allowed political party leaders in control of their individual state legislature the ability to draw district boundaries at will and allowed them to elect some or all representatives at large.[380]/[381]

The actual law that made redistricting members into a single member per district did not happen until the Uniform

Congressional District Act of 1967. And that law still allowed states to elect their representatives at-large if they wanted to do so. All the state legislature in a state needs to do is group all the candidates as at-large candidates, competing in a general election regardless of party, and electing their members as at-large House members. According to Grant Tudor, a coauthor of *Protect Democracy*, "The House's electoral system began evolving immediately after the founding—just as the framers intended. In that tradition, this is about imagining what the next iteration of a more representative House might be."[382]

This Permanent Apportionment Act of 1929 was the result of the continuous battle between rural and urban areas of America after the 1920 Census because the formula used for distributing seats in the House was based on a population favoring urbanized districts, which left the rural states politicians from smaller populated states screaming they were being unjustly penalized. Therefore, their congressmen would disagree with any future reapportionment plans. So, what did Congress do? It passed this act in 1929 that sealed the number of House members at the level established after the 1910 census of 435 House members permanently. US Rep. William B. Bankhead of Alabama, an opponent of this legislation, called the "Permanent Apportionment Act of 1929 an abdication and surrender of vital fundamental powers. The number of seats in Congress should reflect the number of people living in the United States". And of course, any limitations of the number of House members will always affect the total number of electoral votes a state has. And they call that democracy?[383]

This set up a one-hundred-year period of decennial census from 1920 to 2020 with a frozen 435 House members even though our population more than tripled from 106 million to 331 million according to the 2020 US Census Bureau Report. Freezing the size of the House when our population tripled creates a situation that awards less populated states more power.

Following the US Census of 1940, the 1941 Apportionment Act became the only change to the 1929 Reapportionment Act, when it made the apportionment process self-executing automatically after each decennial census based on a redistribution of the same maximum number of 435 House members. The exact formula adopted by Congress in 1941 for the purpose of apportionment was created by mathematicians and politicians and adopted by Congress, called the Method of Equal Proportions. What this method fails to recognize are the shifts in population density. Instead, this method increases the population size in each House District to adhere to the mandated 435 House seats. This formula is part of Title 2, Section 2a of the US Code, which gives each state one seat while the remaining seats are distributed using a formula that computes "priority values" based on each state's apportionment population.[384] This took away any responsibility of Congress to pass any future apportionment acts following each census, ensuring a continuous repeat of the events surrounding the 1920 census.[385]

Expanding the House of Representatives and creating additional Electoral College votes is completely in line with what our founders envisioned would happen regularly. Repealing the Reapportionment Act with a simple vote of Congress is all that is needed to bring voters closer to their representatives without the requirement of any constitutional amendment. We would then have the House that our founders envisioned of having an ever-expanding House that would make it more democratic (with a small *d*) and more responsive to the voters in the individual states.[386]

In 2017 a memo was sent from the Commerce Department attorney to the Commerce Secretary, who oversees the Census Bureau, pointing to a key section of the Constitution's instructions for dividing up congressional seats states that "the Apportionment Clauses do not address the exclusion of noncitizens or illegal aliens from the population when apportioning the United States Representatives. Using this population count and more detailed demographic results from the census, defines each states geographic boundaries of its congressional districts through the process of redistricting."[387] What they were saying is redistribution is redistricting?

Our census includes children under the age of eighteen, citizens and noncitizens, US Armed Forces personnel and federal civilian employees that are stationed outside the United States and any dependents living with them for apportionment purposes. However, it excludes the population of 700,000 in Washington, DC, 4.5 million in Puerto Rico and other US. Island Areas because they are not considered states because they do not have any voting seats in Congress.[388]

Advocates for the increase in the number of seats in the House strongly believe that it would increase the quality of representation by reducing the number of constituents each member of Congress represents which is now more than

761,000 people per district, whereas in 1790 there were sixty-five members in Congress, or one for every 35,000 constituents. Not only are such massive districts contrary to the founders' vision that according to the American Academy of Arts and Sciences to explain that "the chambers lack of growth over the past 100 years has had serious and harmful consequences for both representatives and the voting public, leading to worse representation and bolstering the feeling among voters that their voice does not matter. The principle of proportionally equitable representation has been abandoned," the group argues.[389/390]

The very first amendment proposed in our Bill of Rights had an *Article the First* which intended to ensure that "the total number of representatives would forever increase along with the total population." Unfortunately, this proposal was never ratified. This continuous increase in representation was obviously not a new idea because our nation's founders intended that the number of Representatives would forever increase in direct proportion to the total population when they wrote the Constitution. James Madison wrote in part of Federalist Paper 55, "First, a small number of representatives will be an unsafe depositary of the public interests; secondly, they will not possess a proper knowledge of the local circumstances of their numerous constituents; thirdly, that they will be taken from that class of citizens which will sympathize least with the feelings of the mass of the people; and finally it will most likely aim at a permanent elevation of the few on the depression of the many." He went on to say in Federalist Paper 58, "First, adjust from time to time the apportionment of representatives to the number of inhabitants in each state, with the single exception that each state shall have a minimum of one representative while the number of members of representatives will be augmented (to be made larger in size) from time to time (every ten years with the US Census) as the progress of population demands considered in the manner provided by the Constitution; therefore, the number of representatives should be left to the people, not the discretion of the government. Second, a gradual increase must at least keep pace with that of its constituents. Third, one branch will be larger to represent the citizens (the House of Representatives) while the other will represent the states (the Senate)."[391] Clearly, Madison's visions were always far ahead of his time. He predicted that America with its democracy would become an ever-increasing source of freedom for people from all over the world and would eventually want this safe democracy that led us to be the nation of all nations that it should be forever.[392]/[393]

Another argument advocating that the size of the House should be increased is the belief that it would diminish the influence of lobbyists, while increasing the relationship of lawmakers to their constituents, making it less likely to cater to the wishes of special interests. Many Americans feel extremely disconnected from their representatives with studies showing voters in smaller populated districts felt more connected with their representatives.[394]

Those in favor of continuing to freeze the size of the House of Representatives argue that the quality of legislating improves because House members get to know each other on a more personal level, and the same number of members reduces the cost of paying for salaries, benefits, and travel for House members and their staffs.[395]

As an advocate for a larger House, these arguments look like what the problems really are in Congress today. Do we really want our federal lawmakers to have more personal relationships with their constituents or the outside lobbying interests causing more quid pro quo legislation? The other reasoning has no merit because the fact is as members leave the House with tenure, they increase the taxpayers' burdens and indebtedness because we pay their pensions, free healthcare for life and other benefits with our federal taxes. Besides that, is it really good value to judge the way we govern by how much it costs to get things done for this country with unequal representation? The cost factors are probably the most ridiculous reasons for not expanding the House.

Another part of our long history has been advocated for more members since 1789. One of our Framers, James Madison, in Federalist 55 believed that the success of the new republic would be predicated upon "the number of representatives in the House that should forever increase in proportion to the nation's total population." In fact, which is exactly what the founders promised when another, James Wilson, stated in 1787, "the House of Representatives will, within a single century in 1887, will consist of more than six hundred members."[396]

Another argument was made by James Madison in the Federalist 55 papers in February of 1788 that "it will not be thought an extravagant conjuncture that at the expiration of twenty-five years the number of representatives will amount to 200, and in fifty years to 400. This is a number which, I presume, will put an end to all fears arising from the smallness of the body. I take for granted here what I shall, that the number of representatives will be augmented (to be made larger in size) from time to time in the manner provided by the Constitution; therefore, the number of representatives should be left to the people, not the discretion of the government."[397] Yet here we are 200 years later, and we have 435 House members while we reshuffle and redistribute the same representatives from state to state, adding to the problem at hand of ignoring the one person, one vote concept. Our very first amendment proposed in our Bill of Rights could have solved many of the issues of the last 235 years.[398]

Herein lies the angle for which the Permanent Reapportionment Act was passed and has never changed. Freezing the House of Representatives by allowing only the redistribution of Representatives never considers the quality of representation given to the people in every district. It is abundantly clear that the same number of members for the last 200 years cannot faithfully represent over 330 million Americans. Thomas Jefferson argued 240 years ago that "when the people fear their government, there is tyranny; however, when the government fears the people, there is liberty."[399]

This permanent apportionment causes the ratio of how many people are represented by one house member to continuously climb in one state while doing the reverse in others. The 1929 Act gave the states exclusive powers to draw congressional district boundaries leading to substantially unequal political party populations because they cater to whatever party has the power in that state. Maps show the crazy looking redrawn districts by state legislatures maintains a certain parties' political powers at home as well as Washington, DC.

Another fact is enlarging the House and Electoral College will not give any significant advantage to one party or the other as suggested by its opponents. The authors of *The Case for Enlarging the House of Representatives* ran over 10,000 simulations of all presidential elections since 2000 that did not give either party any more than a 3 percent advantage of controlling the House chamber.[400]

Apportionment has always been a concern in the allocation of congressional seats because it is based on the political power in the various states. The history of apportionment provides a remarkable view of the larger political demographics in our society. Urbanization has always been an issue with the rural population, but the numbers do not lie. The most logical way to correct this issue is to (a) repeal the *Reapportionment Act of 1929,* (b) find an equitable apportionment replacement method to restore the government back to the people with more House members and electoral votes, or (c) attempt to pass an amendment to the Constitution to elect the president who is the winner of the people's popular vote. Unfortunately, with the current political landscape it is extremely unlikely because electing the president simply by who wins the nationwide popular vote requires an impossible bipartisan passage of an amendment to the Constitution.

Table 7.1: Average House District Size 1790-2040

**Average House District Sizes
per Reapportionment Act of 1929**

Census Year	Average Constituents per House District
1790	34,436
1800	34,609
1810	36,377
1820	42,124
1830	49,712
1840	71,338
1850	93,020
1860	122,614
1870	130,533
1880	151,912
1890	173,901
1900	193,167
1910	210,583
1820	243,728
1930	280,675
1940	301,164
1950	334,587
1960	410,481
1970	469,088
1980	510,818
1990	571,477
2000	646,946
2010	709,760
2020	761,169

2030x	810,000
2040x	874,000
x = Estimated Future Numbers	

Source: Part II: The Case for Enlarging the House of Representatives https://www.amacad.org/ourcommonpurpose/enlarging-the-house/section/3[401]

If you need more convincing how outdated the *Reapportionment Act of 1929* is, all you must do is take a look at the progression of the size of each House seats in Table 7.1 above, from 34,000 constituents in 1790 to 211,000 in 1910. Then from 1920 to 2020, after the House of Representatives was frozen at 435, the district size has never grown proportionately. It begins with each district's size at a respectable 280,000 in 1920 but continues to rise rapidly to 470,000 in 1970, to the present day 762,000 in 2020. Then it makes projections using the US Census calculations for the future to 874,000 by 2040, while the smallest district size being 520,000 and the largest individual district exceeding one million people. That gives credence to the fact that the smallest of states will enjoy more than a two-to-one individual voter power over the larger urbanized states.

In the upcoming chapters, we will analyze the effects of our present Winner-Take-All Electoral College, the future of the NPVIC, enlarging the House of Representatives, and the Wyoming and Cubic Root Rules. We will reach some important conclusions of achieving every vote is equal in accordance with the one person, one vote principles.

CHAPTER 8

Today's Effects of the Winner-Take-All Electoral College

Our Current System and Its Problems

Today's winner-take-all Electoral College system awards all the presidential electors of a particular state to the winner of the popular vote is the system used in forty-eight of our fifty states, with Maine and Nebraska being the exception. Voters do not actually vote directly for electors of the Electoral College, but instead vote for the president and vice-presidential joint ticket on the ballot. Then the chosen electors for each candidate pledge to vote for the popular vote winning candidate in their state when they meet. Of course, 165 times we have had faithless electors[11] who voted contrary to their pledge to a certain presidential ticket. It is no secret that the winner-take-all electoral system was done because of partisan powers.[402]

The most interesting thing about our current winner-take-all Electoral College is the fact that it is not mentioned anywhere in the US Constitution. Instead, it is left up to the individual states to determine how they select their electors according to Article 2, Section 1, Clauses 2, 3, and 4 of the Constitution. The complete text can be found in its entirety in Chapter 1, "How the Electoral College Was Created," and was amended

---

[11] A faithless elector is an elector who does not vote for the candidate that his/her slate is committed to by choosing to vote at their own discretion for another person that may or may not be on the ballot.

by the Twelfth Amendment where its entire text can be found in Chapter 2, the "Early Electoral College Failures, and the Twelfth Amendment." In 2020, in forty-eight of the fifty states their electoral votes using the winner-take-all method, with the only exceptions being the states of Maine and Nebraska.[403]

When the presidential election of 1824 gave us the only contingent election in our history to date, several states began using the statewide winner-take-all voting method. The states that split their electoral votes lead to the first and only hostile contingent election in the House of Representatives. By 1832, every state was awarding its electors on a winner-take-all basis of the popular vote except South Carolina. It is now a natural system that has become a fundamental part of the American democracy. Presidential candidates compete to win individual states to get to the magic number of 270 electoral votes needed to win the election.[404]

In the first thirteen presidential elections, many states experimented with different electoral systems that Article 2, Section 1, Clause 2 of the US Constitution empowered each state legislature to determine how that state chooses its electors. The only restriction is the Constitution prohibits any federal office holders from being electors.[405]

According to Jesse Wegman, a member of the *New York Times* editorial board, explains, "The Constitution grants states total authority as to how to decide to award their electoral votes. All but two states, Maine and Nebraska, have chosen to award their electors by winner-take-all rules. While winner-take-all rules are not in the Constitution, the Constitution grants the states exclusive power to independently choose the manner in which they award electors. Winner-Take-All rules are distorting because they erase all of the people in a state who didn't vote for the person that won the popular voter of that state. But all of those votes are treated as invisible because the candidate does not get any of those electoral votes in the winner-take-all. When you look at a map that has no correction for populations and illustrates the winner-take-all you have blocks of red and blue states that give you inaccurate and distorted images of American politics. The binary map might suggest that most people live in the heartland, which is not the case. These maps are a clear illustrator of the harms caused by the Electoral College."[406]

Today forty-eight of the fifty states have mandated that the candidate that wins the plurality of the statewide popular vote in that state receives all that state's electoral votes. In thirty-three of these forty-eight states, it is required that the electors make a pledged commitment to cast their vote for whichever presidential ticket they represent. However, in the other fifteen states and sometimes even the ones who made a commitment, 165 have been faithless electors who voted contrary to what the people's choice of the popular vote of that state.[407] That is where the use of the winner-take-all electors is based solely on state laws and is not mandated in the US Constitution. However, following the 2016 presidential election the Supreme Court refused to "free faithless electors" from their pledged commitment to vote for the popular vote winner. The court sided with the states of Washington and Colorado who were imposing penalties on several faithless electors. This led many state officials to say that faithless electors threaten the integrity of American democracy.[408]

The other two states, Maine and Nebraska, have used a different method similar to the District Plan. Those two states split the electoral votes by awarding one electoral vote to the candidate who wins each congressional district, then awards the candidate who won the statewide popular vote two electoral votes, which is equal to the number of senators each state has. These two states show that creating an Electoral College system like this would create a better reflection of each state. Another example is the electors can decide—as many states have already planned the National Popular Vote Interstate Compact—to award the state's electoral votes to the winner of the national popular vote. Of course, there are strong incentives now to move away from the winner-take-all allocation for the same reasons they went to the system originally as it dilutes their power in the election of the president.[409]

There are very strong political incentives to keep the winner-take-all allocation for the same reasons they moved to the system originally. It would dilute their partisan powers to elect the president. Since it came about due to partisan political power, once some states came to this conclusion the others had no choice but to follow to avoid hurting their side.[410]

Contrary to many believe, the winner-take-all is not biased toward the larger battleground states. It has become biased toward the smaller states that have a distinct advantage over the much larger populated states when you use a population-to-electoral vote comparison. Every state has two bonus electoral votes given to each state automatically regardless of that state's population because the Constitution gives every state two Senate seats. When we compare the average population of the group of seven least populated states that have three electoral votes, including Washington, DC, it is 698,003 versus the average population of the seven most populated states with the most electoral votes is 19,664,063. So, each bonus constitutional senate electoral vote in the seven smaller populated states averages 349,001 per bonus electoral vote, whereas each bonus constitutional electoral vote in the seven most populated states averages 9,832,031 per bonus electoral vote. Obviously, this is not anything close to equal representation or one person, one vote because the guaranteed two senatorial electoral votes in the smaller states have a fourteen-to-one political power advantage over the larger states. This totally disagrees with any of the pro-Electoral College groups.[411]

Using another smallest state to largest state advantage in overall representation, we have already discussed how every electoral vote in Wyoming represents 192,573 people whereas an electoral vote in California represents 732,903 people, giving Wyoming a 3.8-to-1 advantage. There is also the unequal apportionment of membership in the House where the largest congressional district, the state of Delaware has only one House member representing a population of 989,948, while Montana now has two House members with an average of 542,703 people per House member giving them almost a two-to-one advantage in 2024 presidential election. It should be noted that Delaware has had the same one House member for nearly 200 years. And they also have only 13,000 less people than the State of Rhode Island, which also has two House members.[412]/[413]

One of the most vocal proponents of the winner-take-all is Tara Ross, a distinguished writer about the Electoral College, says in her book about the *Indispensable Electoral College,* "The Electoral College, in combination with the winner-take-all allocation of electoral votes, reinforces the two-party system."[414] Her argument of this reinforcement of the two-party system is one of her best arguments regarding the Electoral College but only to a certain extent because although it may reinforce the two-party system while it disenfranchises potentially strong third-party candidates.

An opponent of the system, Thomas Hart Benton wrote in 1824 about the unfairness of this the winner-take-all method when he said, "the winner-take-all rules segregate states by drawing them against each other. It also fills them with hostile feelings amongst them as the president elected only represents the states that elect him, casting coldness and resentment on those who oppose him." This is because winner-takes-all misrepresents and erases those people who voted for the person who did not win the popular vote in their state by literally tossing their vote aside and awarding all of the electoral votes to the state popular vote winner. It creates a division between the blue and red states because plenty of voters that took their time to go vote are ignored at the end of the day.[415]

On the matter of its constitutionality matter, Jason Harrow wrote an editorial in *USA Today* calling "the winner-take-all presidential system is unconstitutional way to pick the electors who cast votes for president. There is no legal justification for states to use the winner-take-all." If a candidate wins by a single vote, it can lead to a huge haul of electoral votes; however, the opposite of losing a state by a single vote leaves candidates empty-handed. This leads to votes literally being tossed aside that leads to the question: Is the winner-take-all allocation of the Electoral College votes even legal? Many say of course it is legal because America has done it this way for centuries and voters believe it is required by the Constitution, which it is not. Even former President Donald Trump claimed on election night 2012, when he thought Romney might win the popular vote but lose the electoral, factually stating that "the Electoral College is a disaster for democracy as more votes equal a loss … time for a revolution." Trump continued by stating emphatically, "it should be a very simple process, one candidate gets seventy million votes when the other gets only sixty-five million votes, of course the candidate with the seventy million is the winner, period." We are talking the president of the United States, probably the most powerful leader in the free world justifies the use of this winner-take-all simply because since it supposedly worked most of the time since 1788 it should work now.[416] Naturally, Trump completely changed his mind the day after the election of 2016 and stated, "The Electoral College is actually genius in that it brings all states, including the small ones, into play. Campaigning to win the Electoral College is much more difficult and sophisticated than the popular vote."[417]

To summarize this is simpler terms, let's challenge the winner-take-all defenders. If we take away the "we've always done it that way" argument that does not matter legally, or "it's in the Constitution" argument, which winner-take-all is not, and the "states can choose presidential electors however they want" because they cannot because they need to comply with one person, one vote, the foundation of the current system becomes unstable or crumbles. Fact is, there is no argument that can legally justify states using winner-take-all to allocate their electors. Although those conclusions may seem dramatic, it's a straightforward application of the principle of fairness and equality of citizenship that really has been in our Constitution since the Equal Protection Clause that came following the Civil War.[418]

First, there are many other shortcomings of the winner-take-all method. First, it disenfranchises voters in 80 percent (forty out of fifty states) because candidates with huge leads or deficits in certain states do not even bother campaigning in those states. Between 1988 and 2020, over two-thirds of the states were completely ignored by presidential campaigns. It also has shown that the thirteen least populated states are basically spectators.[419]

Secondly, the current system does not reliably reflect the nationwide popular vote as shown in five elections that have been won by the candidate who lost the popular vote. Third, not every vote is equal. As described in Chapter 4, "Controversial

Elections or Simply Wrong Winners," states with exceptionally close popular votes are not truly reflected in the winner-take-all process. For example, in 2000, five states were won by margins of only 0.0092 percent (537 votes out of almost six million in Florida) to 0.44 percent. In that election, those states totaled fifty-five electoral votes in which case any one of those states would have swung the election to Gore who won the popular vote. Then in 2016, three states that were won by less than 1 percent, 0.23 percent in Michigan with sixteen electoral votes, 0.72 percent in Pennsylvania with twenty electoral votes and 0.76 percent in Wisconsin with ten electoral votes all went to the loser of the popular vote, Donald Trump. If these states had gone to the popular vote candidate, it would have given forty-six more electoral votes to Hillary Clinton, which would have given her 278 electoral votes, enough to win the election. And let's not forget she won the popular vote by over three million votes equaling more than 2 percent.[420]

Compounding the problems of the current winner-take-all are the facts showing that fewer than 26 percent of the voters elect the president. According to calculations performed by MIT Professor Alexander Belinsky, using actual voter data reveals an Electoral College majority with the winner-take-all current system, could have won 16 percent to 22 percent of the national popular vote in nineteen elections between 1948 and 2012. He also found that twelve of the biggest states were won by only a slightly over 50+ percent majority in every election from 2000 to 2016, essentially ignoring the 49+ percent of the voters which in many cases were in large battleground states. This winner-take-all gives candidates very little appeal to campaign the cross-section of Americans because this small path to victory runs through only a few states or regions.[421] The election should be about voters everywhere rather than appealing to a small base of voters in key battleground states, creating more space for policies that will be better addressed by the whole nation.[422]

Moderation is necessary in our presidential elections. One Democratic consultant, Joel Benenson, said, "If every vote counted equally at the end of the day you would have candidates who could not write off any group of states or groups of people completely." Right now, Matthew Dowd who is a Republican strategist believes, "One party has the demographic advantage while the other has a geographic advantage and the best forcing mechanism to solve that would be a national popular vote. This would force Democrats to campaign in rural states and for Republicans to campaign for the blacks, the Latino, and LGBTQ voters, and the urban states."[423]

Why are all these statistics so important? Because they go back to the fact that a candidate who wins the popular vote in only twelve states by only one single vote in each state can accumulate 283 electoral votes that surpasses that 270-magic number of the majority of the electoral votes. In fact, it only takes eleven of those twelve states to get exactly 270. They can accomplish this with the current winner-take-all system without their name ever appearing on the ballot in the other thirty-eight or thirty-nine states. This is a complete violation of democracy and the one person, one vote theory. To eloquently quote

Jesse Wegman again, "the winner-take-all rules are distorting because they erase all of the people in a state who didn't vote for the person that won the popular voter of that state. But all of those votes are treated as invisible because the candidate does not get any of those electoral votes in the winner-take-all."[424]

Table 8.1 shows the population density based on the 2020 US Census. Each box represents one electoral vote of the 538 and demonstrates the actual proportionate size of each state based on population and electoral votes. This map eliminates square mileage and replaces it with the actual density of those states if all electoral districts were equal in size.

Table 8.1: Map that Illustrates Population Density by States

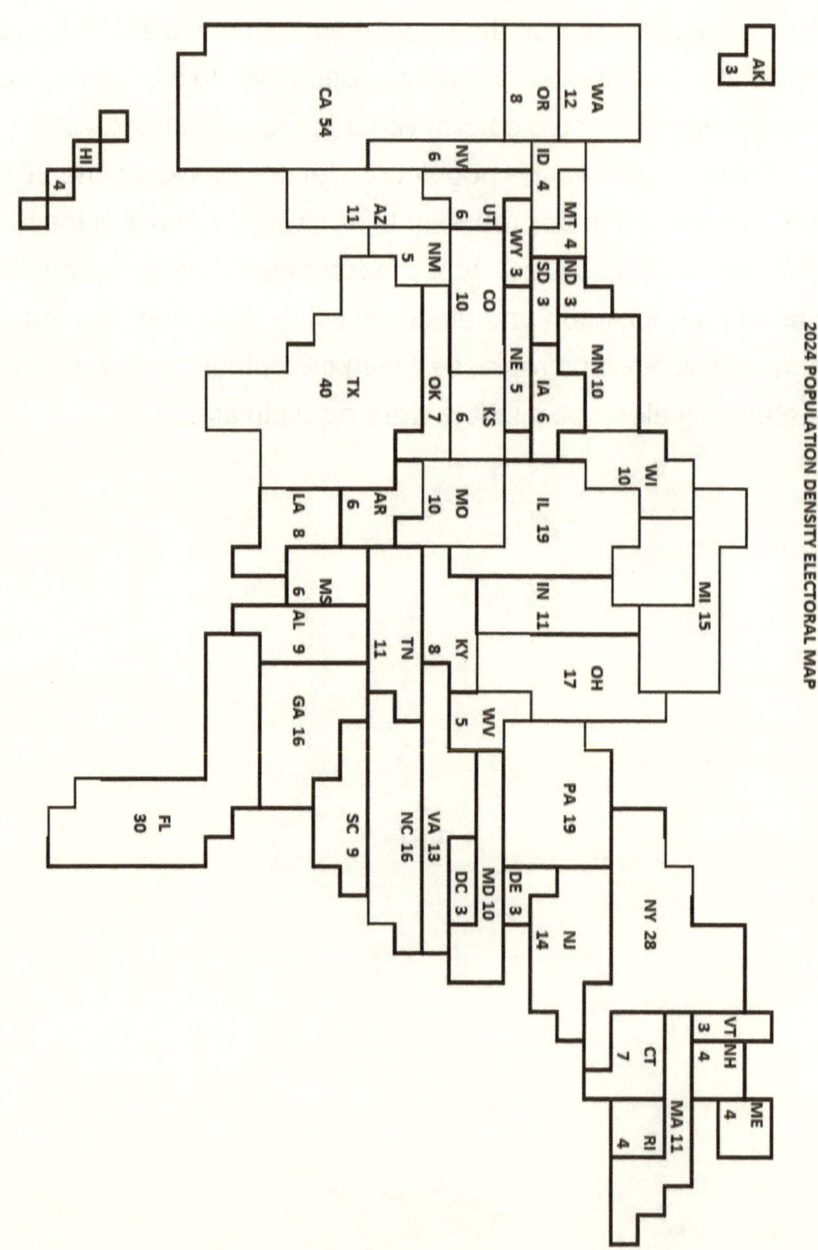

The 8.1 Map Illustrates what the actual Population Density (not square mileage areas) of States compared to the Electoral College Votes of each state.

Ex.: The 7 states or areas with only 3 Electoral Votes because of their population (i.e. North Dakota, South Dakota, Wyoming, Delaware, Vermont, Alaska, and Washington D.C.) have significantly smaller populations than the 7 states with significantly more Electoral Votes because these states have larger populations (i.e. California 54, Texas 40, Florida 30, New York 28, Pennsylvania 19, Illinois 19, Ohio 17), therefore the size of those states boxes are compared

To compare how the winner-take-all system effects the Electoral College, we have (1) Table 8.2 that represent those near certain Democratic and Republican states and their current electoral votes, and (2) Table 8.3 that represents the states that are considered battleground states or swing states in all the elections from 2000 to 2020. These are the states which usually determine the presidential election winners and finally (c) states that are what we will refer to as floaters, which are the states that have close to 50/50 from 2000 to 2020 election cycles.

Table 8.2: Republican and Democratic Stronghold States

Republican Strong Red States	Win Streak	EC	Democratic Strong Blue States	Win Streak	EC
Oklahoma (1968-2020)	14	7	District of Columbia (1964-2020)	15	3

TODAY'S EFFECTS OF THE WINNER-TAKE-ALL ELECTORAL COLLEGE

Kansas (1968-2020)	14	6	Minnesota (1976-2020)	12	10
Utah (1968-2020)	14	6	New York (1988-2020)	12	28
Nebraska (1968-2020)	14	5	Washington (1988-2020)	9	12
Idaho (1968-2020)	14	4	Massachusetts (1988-2020)	9	11
Wyoming (1968-2020)	14	3	Oregon (1988-2020)	9	8
North Dakota (1968-2020)	14	3	California (1992-2020)	8	54
South Dakota (1968-2020)	14	3	New Jersey (1992-2020)	8	14
Alaska (1968-2020)	14	3	Maryland (1992-2020)	8	10
Texas (1980-2020)	11	40	Illinois (1992-2020)	8	19
Alabama (1980-2020)	11	9	Connecticut (1992-2020)	8	7
South Carolina (1980-2020)	11	9	Maine (1992-2020)	8	4
Mississippi (1980-2020)	11	6	Hawaii (1988-2020)	9	4
Montana (1996-2020)	7	4	Rhode Island (1988-2020)	9	4
Tennessee (2000-2020)	6	11	Delaware (1992-2020)	8	3
Missouri (2000-2020)	6	10	Vermont (1992-2020)	8	3
Kentucky (2000-2020)	6	8			

Louisiana (2000-2020)	6	8		
Arkansas (2000-2020)	6	6		
West Virginia (2000-2020)	6	4		
Red Strongholds (20 total)	**155**	**Blue Strongholds (16 total)**		**194**

Sources: https://en.wikipedia.org/wiki/List_of_United_States_presidential_election_results_by_state and https://www.270towin.com/state-electoral-vote-history/

If you take a closer look at the numbers, they show that the top ten ranked Republican states will give them eighty electoral votes, while the top ten ranked Democratic electoral votes is 173. Nine of the top ten Republican states are an absolute certainty as these states have fourteen presidential election winning streaks dating back to 1968. The number ten state of Texas has had an eleven-cycle winning streak back for the GOP nominee since 1980.

On the Democratic side, Washington, DC, with three electoral votes, has a winning streak back to 1964. The remaining nine of the top ten have winning streaks starting anywhere between 1968 and 1976, with Minnesota having the longest winning streak of ten election cycles dating back to 1976, with others having eight election winning streaks that date back to 1992. These top ten represent 169 electoral votes that have been a certainty.

Overall, all the major pollsters show the Democrats have a stronghold on at least sixteen states that total 194 Electoral

Votes and the Republicans have twenty states that would easily accumulate 155. This leaves the Democratic nominee only seventy-six electoral votes short of winning whereas the Republican nominee most likely would need 115. This would give us a total of thirty-five states that are pretty much locked up by one party or the other. That will leave us with the remaining fifteen states deciding the 2024 election.

These tables show where there is a major flaw and problem with awarding Electoral College votes by a winner-take-all system. These are not only the "strong" red or blue states across the nation, but they have been such a sure win for decades by either party that it sometimes causes candidates to see no reason to campaign in the opposing parties' stronghold states. This is where the winner-take-all basically ignores and the voter of the people who did not vote for the person that failed to win the popular voter in their state, which sometimes causes smaller voter turnouts by whichever party does not have this "stranglehold" of power over these states for as long as four decades in some cases.

Maine and Nebraska are the only exceptions to the winner-take-all system. Those states use an alternative method similar to the district plan, as it encourages voters to "get out the vote" because each of their congressional districts counts as one electoral college vote while the overall state popular vote winner only gets two electoral votes. The reasoning is the two represent how many US Senators are in each state. This method has been in use in Maine since 1972 and Nebraska since 1996.

The following Table 8.3 below shows the "battleground states" (a.k.a. swing, toss-up, or purple states) that can make or break a presidential election. 2020 and 2016 are reflected in the first three, Wisconsin, Pennsylvania, and Michigan, which did decide the last two presidential elections. Those three states won the 2016 election for former president Trump, as he secured the total forty-six electoral votes that put him thirty-four votes over the 270-magic number. Then in 2020, those same three states flipped to President Biden giving him a total of 306 Electoral vote or thirty-six more than needed to win.

Even going back to 2012, former president Obama took those three states plus twenty-nine Florida electoral votes that put him at his 332, which made any three of the four enough to make it over the top. In 2004, former president Bush had to win either Michigan or Pennsylvania or Florida to get over the 270, and of course, we know that Florida gave him that slim victory of 271 in 2000. So, except for 2008, these four states have decided every presidential election in the twenty-first century.

The following Table 8.3 represents the remaining 15 states and are in order by significance of a battleground or swing state based on past trends and the comparison to what is expected to be the most significant in 2024.

Table 8.3: The Battleground and Swing States 2000–2020

Battleground/ Swing States	DEM	REP	2024	2020	2016	2012	2008	2004	2000
Wisconsin	*5*	*1*	*10*	*D*	*R*	*D*	*D*	*D*	*D*
Pennsylvania	*5*	*1*	*19*	*D*	*R*	*D*	*D*	*D*	*D*
Michigan	*5*	*1*	*15*	*D*	*R*	*D*	*D*	*D*	*D*
Georgia	*1*	*5*	*16*	*D*	*R*	*R*	*R*	*R*	*R*
Arizona	*1*	*5*	*11*	*D*	*R*	*R*	*R*	*R*	*R*
Nevada	*4*	*2*	*6*	*D*	*D*	*D*	*D*	*R*	*R*
North Carolina	1	5	16	R	R	R	D	R	R
Florida	2	4	30	R	R	D	D	R	R
New Mexico	5	1	5	D	D	D	D	R	D
Colorado	5	1	10	D	D	D	D	R	D
Iowa	3	3	6	R	R	D	D	R	D
Virginia	4	2	13	D	D	D	D	R	R
New Hampshire	5	1	4	D	D	D	D	D	R
Ohio	2	4	17	R	R	D	D	R	R
Indiana	1	5	11	R	R	R	D	R	R
Total Swing/ Battleground EC			189	189	189	190	189	189	186
Total Swing Dem EC				110	37	137	164	52	64
Total Swing Rep EC				79	152	53	25	137	122
Winner Total EC				306	304	332	365	286	271
% of 270 EC Won by Winner				56.9%	56.5%	61.7%	67.8%	53.2%	50.4%
Winner				Biden	Trump	Obama	Obama	Bush	Bush

Sources: https://en.wikipedia.org/wiki/List_of_United_States_presidential
_election_results_by_state and https://www.270towin.com/state-electoral-
vote-history/

Using the winner-take-all system and adding to that what
most pollsters are considering the most probable winners in the

2024 election, here is how the 2024 election will be determined. Table 8.3 gives us all the battleground states since 1988. The first level of those battleground state includes Wisconsin (10), Pennsylvania (19), Michigan (15), Georgia (16), Arizona (11) and Nevada (6) for a total of seventy-seven electoral votes. The second level of potential battlegrounds is Florida (30), and North Carolina (16), which is another forty-six electoral votes that could come into play. If the Democratic state winning streaks continue, they get the certain 194 Electoral Votes and the same with the Republicans winning streaks that give them their 155; there are all kinds of combinations for a candidate to get to the magical 270 needed to win the White House through the many possible combinations of battleground states.

Looking back to 2016, former President Trump swept all of these states except Nevada. Adding these battleground states 117 electoral votes to the 155 of the Republican certainties, he would have secured a total of 272, which is two more than he needs to win. In 2020, President Biden secured all of these same battlegrounds plus the next level of battleground states, New Mexico (5) and Colorado (9), minus Florida and North Carolina, giving him a total of 279 electoral votes. Colorado (9) and New Mexico (5), totaling fourteen more electoral votes which the Democrats won those in every election since 2008.

These are a lot of assumptions but that is what polling is all about. This year is an election for the ages, with the possibilities for the closest numbers ever, like 2000 or even closer. These Electoral College numbers feed the abolitionists view that the only way to go is a Nationwide Popular Vote that is the truly makes every vote equal, the one person, one vote theory.

There are historical facts not listed in the tables. The first is the fact no Republican has ever won a presidential election without winning Ohio. On the Democrats side, only one has been elected president without carrying Maryland, Truman in 1948. An interesting state is Florida where only three Democrats won without that state, Kennedy in 1960, Clinton in 1992, and Biden in 2020. In total, the Florida winner has won the presidency in twenty-six of the thirty-eight elections since 1860. Here is a list of the states who voted for the winner in the last thirty-eight elections since 1860:[425]

1. Ohio – 34 (89.5 percent)
2. Illinois – 33 (86.8 percent)
3. California – 31 (81.6 percent)
4. Nevada – 31 (81.6 percent)
5. New Hampshire – 31 (81.6 percent)
6. New York - 30 (78.9 percent)
7. Wisconsin – 30 (78.9 percent)

So, on election night, if you want to crunch the numbers, the tables in this chapter give you a good place to start. There will always be that unusual landslide, such as Roosevelt (four in a row, 1932–1944), Eisenhower (1952 and 1956), Johnson (1964), Nixon (1972), Reagan (1980 and 1984), and Bush, 41 (1988), but these were the exceptions not the norm. Every election in this century has been extremely competitive as Republicans have won the Electoral College in 2000, 2004, and

2016, while Democrats have won the Electoral College in 2008, 2012, and 2020. But Democrats have won the Nationwide Popular Vote every time except 2004, which is the only election that the Republicans won the popular vote. All this statistical information shows how certain trends happen in our history changes.[426]

Table 8.4: Swing and Tipping States 2000-2020

Year	Electoral College Winner	Decisive State	Decisive State D/R Margin	National Popular Vote Margin
2000	Bush (R)	Florida	+0.01%(R)	+0.52%(D)
2004	Bush (R)	Ohio	+2.11%(R)	+2.46%(R)
2008	Obama (D)	Colorado	+8.95%(D)	+7.27%(D)
2012	Obama (D)	Colorado	+5.36%(D)	+3.86%(D)
2016	Trump (R)	Pennsylvania	+0.72%(R)	+2.10%(D)
2020	Biden (D)	Wisconsin	+0.63%(D)	+4.50%(D)

CHAPTER 9
Analyzing False Myths

There are plenty of myths surrounding the Electoral College system. We have chosen some of the more important and challenging misinformation. They have all been reviewed for their validity, and this chapter exposes those fictitious assumptions that many voters are led to believe act the facts when they are only a myth. This misinformation significantly plays out in all our elections of the presidents of these United States of America.

Myth #1: A Federal Constitutional Amendment is necessary to change the current Winner-Take-All method of electing a president.

Answer: False

Winner-take-all is presently used in forty-eight of the fifty states. The other two, Maine and Nebraska, award two electoral votes to the state popular vote winner then one electoral vote for the winner of each congressional district.[427] This winner-take-all method is not anywhere in our Constitution; therefore, an amendment is *not* necessary to do away with it. In those forty-eight states, rules were adopted instructing their presidential electors to vote on a winner-take-all method, automatically awarding all the electoral votes to the candidate that won the popular vote in that state. In theory, this is true. However, practically the electors may vote their conscience for whomever they please, and on rare occasions, they are those faithless electors.

In a tight election, such behavior might deny either candidate a majority of the electoral vote and throw the election into the House of Representatives. While the founders wisely and intentionally made it difficult to amend the Constitution, they made sure the document contained the necessary instruments for modest changes the future might demand. The Constitution grants the states the full authority to award their electoral votes as they see fit. In fact, the words or phrase "winner-take-all" method of awarding electoral votes is not written or seen anywhere in the Constitution.[428]

The use of the winner-take-all may be repealed and/or replaced by any process used by individual state legislature for enacting or repealing state laws.

Myth #2: The Electoral College would be abolished by the National Popular Vote (NPVIC)

Answer: False

The NPVIC would preserve the Electoral College and would not affect the structure of the Electoral College as contained in our Constitution. Rather, it is based on the state's power of how they award their electoral votes, which is retained by the NPVIC. What it does replace is the current winner-take-all system, which takes away every vote is equal theory because it ignores those who voted for a candidate that loses a state.

The myth can also be debunked by the laws of Maine and Nebraska.[429]

The NPVIC would only change how we award electoral votes as described in Article 2, Section 1 of the United States Constitutions, which states, "Each state shall appoint, in such manner as the (state) legislature thereof may direct, a number of electors equal to the number of senators and representatives to which that state is entitled and that those electors shall meet and vote for president."[430]

Myth #3: The Electoral College Saves America from "Mob Rule"

Answer: False

Over 240 years ago our founding fathers believed, and for good reason at that time, that the public did not possess sufficient information about candidates to make an accurate decision. They argued Americans could have posed a threat to order and stability of the government. Therefore, this misleading "mob rule" is attributed to those who believed we needed an intermediary (Electoral College presidential electors) to elect the president of the United States.[431]

Many politicians declare that mob rule refers to large turnouts of voters expressing their choice through a national popular vote. There was a time when many Americans were unable to cast votes in every state; therefore, those who could vote were referred to as mob rule. The belief was debunked since 1880 when all Americans in all states were able to cast votes for President.[432] Naturally, Electoral College advocates attribute the so-called mob rule to the winner of the popular vote because it represents the victor of all the people.

The Oxford Languages meaning *mob rule* is "the control of a political situation by those outside the conventional or lawful actions that typically involves violence and intimidation."[12] And the Collins Online English Dictionary defines *mob rule* as "the fact or state of large groups of people acting without the consent of the government authorities."[13] Neither of these definitions are true of a popular vote election.

Neither of those represent the privileges afforded us as Americans to express ourselves by voting. However, if we want to find an example of true mob rule that was directly caused by the Electoral College, we only need to look back at the unlawful insurrection of January 6, 2021, when large groups of unlawful people violated our sacred United States Capital while they plotted a coup to overthrow the 2020 election and our government. This is conclusive evidence that the Electoral College can be related to causing mob rule and damaging our democracy.

---

[12] *Mob rule* meaning can be found in the Oxford University Press–Oxford Languages, https://languages.oup.com/google-dictionary-en/.

[13] Collins English Dictionary, https://www.collinsdictionary.com/us/dictionary/english/mob-rule.

Myth #4: Wrong Winner Electoral College Elections are Rare.

Answer: False

This is the furthest from the truth, especially since 2000. There have been five wrong winner (see Chapter 4) elections out of fifty-nine total presidential elections between 1789 and 2020, which is a failure rate of one out of twelve (8.3 percent), with the popular vote winner losing the election to the Electoral College. Another statistic is in this century since 2000, two out of the last six (33 percent) elections, 2000 and 2016, the national popular vote winner has lost the Electoral College to a wrong winner. Because half of the presidential elections have been landslides (those with a popular vote margin of victory of more than 10 percent), the non-landslide failure rate of the Electoral College is 1 out of 6 (16.7 percent).[433]

Every election from 1988 to 2020 have all been non-landslide victories. If the current trend continues, we can expect many additional wrong winner elections in the future. For instance, take a look at 2004, where a shift of 59,393 votes in Ohio would have made Senator John Kerry a wrong winner.[434] That year 5,627,908 voters went to the polls in Ohio, which means a 2.11 percent shift would have changed the election.

There are others that with a small shift in popular votes in certain states would have changed outcomes in at least three more elections in the twentieth century, 1960, 1968, and 1976. So, it may have been rare in our first fifty-three elections,

33 percent of the last six elections yielding a wrong winner, obviously debunks the theory that it is a rarity in the future.

Myth #5: A National Popular Vote favors the Democrats over the Republicans

Answer: False

Naturally, on paper this is an obvious talking point because Republicans have had five Electoral College wrong winner victories but lost the popular vote to a Democrat. Below is a statistical elections breakdown since the last apportionment in 1910 to 2020:[435]/[436]

Political Party	Total Votes 1910-2020	Pct of Votes	Popular Vote Wins	Electoral Wins
Republicans	996,939,966	48.56%	13	11
Democrats	991,854,943	48.31%	15	15
Independents	64,151,381	3.12%	0	0

These numbers obviously debunk the Republicans myth that the popular vote for presidential elections favor Democrats. The two parties are in a virtual tie with 0.0025 percent votes out of over two billion voters since the last apportionment that was done in 1910.

More recently during the 1970s and 1980s, it was believed the Republicans had a "lock" on the Electoral College since they won every election from 1968 to 1988 except 1976 when Carter just barely squeaked out a victory. Then in the 1990s, it was believed the Democrats built a solid "blue wall" for Bill

Clinton and again for Obama in 2008 and 2012. But all that changed in 2016 with the Hillary Clinton loss due to the "blue wall" came crashing down in Pennsylvania, Wisconsin and Michigan, leading to her defeat even though she won the popular vote by 2.9 million votes (2 percent).[437]

Another situation to remember since 1910 is the fact that there were eleven landslides where the winners won by more than a 10 percent popular vote victory, four Democrats to seven Republicans. That is eleven out of twenty-eight elections, or 39.28 percent. There have also been two Electoral College wrong winners, both Republicans, Bush 43 in 2000 and Trump in 2016. Another statistic is the Republicans have had an over 50 percent majority of the popular vote ten times to the Democrats 8 in that same 1912 to 2020 elections. [438]/[439]

Numbers like those above throughout most of the twentieth and twenty-first centuries showed Republicans supporting a national popular vote for only slightly less than the Democrats until the 2000 election. Conservatives believed the Democrats attacks on the Electoral College damaged the legitimacy of President Bush 43. But by 2011, most Republicans supported the national popular vote, well at least until 2016.[440] Looking at Table 12.5 (Chapter 12), the Pew Research Center Polling that in 2012, 54 percent of Republicans supported a national popular vote to 69 percent Democrats. After the 2016 election, those figures dropped to 27 percent of Republicans compared to 74 percent Democrats backing the national popular vote.[441]

Statistics are mathematical facts which cannot be disputed. Therefore, the Republican myth that they are at a disadvantage with the national popular vote is false. Their reasoning is solely based on the fact Democrats have won seven out of the last eight national popular vote since 1992, with 2004 being the only exception.

Myth #6: A National Popular Vote would Destroy our Two-party System

Answer: False

Our Constitution only has three qualifications for the presidency: (1) the president must be at least thirty-five years of age, (2) must be a natural born citizen, and (3) must have lived in the United States for at least fourteen years.[442] Therefore, the myth that a national popular vote will cause the end of the two-party system is easily contested by factual evidence.

First, those who think eliminating the Electoral College would cause a multitude of candidates running for the presidency, thus destroying the two-party system is false. The reason is there is no cap on how many candidates can run for president of the United States, assuming the person meets the qualifications in our Constitution, and obtaining the required voter signatures (if necessary) to be on each individual state ballot can be a candidate. We call it a two-party system, but we always have third-party candidates in every election.

Tara Ross, a popular conservative who is an opponent to a national popular vote and writer of the book *The Indispensable Electoral College: How the Founders' Plan Saves Our Country from Mob Rule,* predicts that "a national popular vote would lead to a multitude of candidates that would fracture the electorate, leaving us with presidents elected with only 15 percent of the votes nationwide." She also writes, "The most likely consequence of a change to a direct popular vote is the breakdown of the two-party system."[443] If the Electoral College system avoids this theory, there must be evidence of this outcome in elections that did not employ the winner-take-all system.

When elections are based on the most popular votes, candidates do not win with only 15 percent. The best example of this process is the election of 1,000 governors elected since 1948. In 100 percent of those elections, the winner received at least 35 percent, with 99 percent of those getting 40 percent, 98 percent received 45 percent, and 90 percent received a majority of 50 percent or more. United State Senate elections and other statewide type elections confirm the same pattern. There is no proof of any situations where multitudes of too many candidates cause fracture the electorate, debunking the myth that a national popular vote will destroy our two-party system.[444]

Jesse Wegman of the *New York Times* Editorial Board writes in his book *Let the People Pick the President: the Case for Abolishing the Electoral College* that "in particular, the state winner-take-all rule discourages candidates who don't have a good shot at winning a state's popular vote, and even those with the nerve and the money to dive in often come up empty." The reality is fifteen out of our forty-six presidents did not win a majority of the popular votes due to our winner-take-all

Electoral College system that has also given us five presidents who lost the national popular vote. Americans are okay with a non-majority candidates on the state level, so why should a state require a presidential candidate to earn a majority of the vote in order to get the electors.[445]

This theory is supported by Duverger's law, named after a mid-twentieth century sociologist, named Maurice Duverger. His law supports the theory that plurality. He writes that two-party systems are supported by plurality elections. First, parties with similar interests tend to form alliances to improve their chances to win; and second, voters ultimately realize that they are harming their own interests by wasting votes on third-party candidates that do not have a chance of winning. The 2000 Ralph Nader debacle that cost Al Gore the election supports this theory. So, it is fair to say America's two-party system is protected and preserved by the plurality elections we hold in all fifty states, not by the Electoral College.[446]

The current winner-take-all Electoral College system of electing the president has affected the outcome of 38 percent. This is due to minority-party candidates have shifting enough states from one candidate to the other to cause one party or the other to lose a presidential election.

Teddy Roosevelt became so dissatisfied with fellow GOP President Taft; he chose to run in 1912 as the Bull Moose Party nominee. He did not win, but finished second, received 27.4 percent and eighty-eight electoral votes, denying his fellow Republican a second term.[447] Another candidate, Strom Thurmond, a former Democrat who ran as a Dixiecrat that opposed civil rights, voting rights, and racial segregation, hoped to deny Truman the presidency. Instead, he probably cost Republican Thomas Dewey the election by winning four southern states, South Carolina, Alabama, Mississippi, and Louisiana that accounted for thirty-nine electoral votes with only 2.4 percent of the national popular vote. This is a classic example of how the winner-take-all Electoral College system is not consistent with a one person, one vote theory.[448]

Another anti-civil rights, anti-voting rights anti-racial and segregationist platform candidate was George Wallace a Democrat, that in 1968 ran as an American Independent. His motive was to destroy and splinter the Democratic Party, which he was successful at doing by winning forty-six electoral votes from five segregationist states of in the south: Georgia, Alabama, Mississippi, Louisiana, and Arkansas. His ten million votes and 13.5 percent single handedly stole the election from Vice President Humphrey.[449]

Of course, we probably all remember Ross Perot in 1992, a Texas billionaire who received 19 percent of the popular vote. However, his twenty million votes were spread so thin across our fifty states that he did not receive a single electoral vote.[450] He was a former conservative Republican whose ideals have been the blame for costing Bush 41 reelection because nearly all his votes were drawn from conservative Independents and anti-Bush Republicans.[451]

Then you have Ralph Nader in 2000, a self-proclaimed Liberal Independent who ran under the Green Party label, got only 2.74 percent of the vote but was literally responsible for Al

Gore's defeat. Almost everyone credits the Bush victory by 537 votes in Florida for his winner-take-all win of 271 to 267. However, the state that has been overlooked was New Hampshire and its four electoral votes that were solidly Democratic in seven of the last eight presidential elections since 1992. Nader received 22,198 votes, 3.90 percent, in a state that Gore lost by only 7,211 votes. If Gore had won New Hampshire, he would have had the 271 to 267 while losing Florida those.[452]

Finally, Gary Johnson in 2016 received 4,489,221 votes, 3.28 percent, and no electoral votes as a third-party Libertarian candidate. Even though Clinton won the popular vote by 2.09 percent, or 2.9 million votes, she was the loser to Trump, who crashed the so-called blue wall by defeating Clinton in Pennsylvania, Wisconsin, and Michigan. Those states accounted for forty-six electoral votes in three states Democrats won in seven of the last eight elections. Flipping those states to the Democrat Clinton would have won her the electoral vote 273 to 258.[453]

Theoretically, voters tend to abandon candidates that have little or no chance of winning, thus supporting the theory that two-party systems with plurality voting discourages the formation of viable third parties. Therefore, the two-party system remains safe with a national popular vote as evidenced by independent third-party candidates who drew national attention could only achieve a few if any electoral votes or for that matter even less than 15 percent of the popular vote in nearly 90 percent of all presidential elections.

Myth #7: States with Small Populations would Lose Political Clout under a National Popular Vote

Answer: False

The opposite is true. Under a national popular vote, the nature of presidential campaigns would fundamentally change to encompass all fifty states, regardless of size, population, or voting histories. As things now stand, twelve so-called "battleground" states with a propensity to "swing" from one party to another consume virtually all of the candidates' time, money and attention. The remaining thirty-eight states and the District of Columbia are virtually ignored because candidates see no reason to campaign in places where they are so far behind, they can't possibly win or so far ahead they can't possibly lose. By having a National Popular Vote, candidates would make use of every vote they can get no matter what the size of the state.[454]

Myth #8: A Constitutional Amendment is the only Legitimate way to Reform our Presidential Election System

Answer: False

While the founders wisely and intentionally made it difficult to amend the Constitution, they made sure the document contained the necessary instruments for more modest change as future times would demand. The founders explicitly gave states authority under the Constitution to form compacts like the National Popular Vote interstate compact. The Constitution also grants the states authority to award their electoral votes as they see fit.

CHAPTER 10

Enlarging the House and Expanding the Electoral College

Saving Our "One Person, One Vote" Democracy

Thomas Jefferson observed that "when the people fear their government there is tyranny; when the government fears the people there is liberty." This tyranny is dominated by political powers of incumbents dominating reelections, increases lobbyist influence, and gives a partisan political party control of our government by reducing the size of each district compared to the nation's population. Jefferson believed that the solution to these problems is to continuously increase the number of seats in the house to restore political power to the people.[455]

When the executive branch of the Constitution was ratified, the population was only 3.9 million people, representing eleven states, consisting of fifty-nine House members and twenty-two senators for a total of eighty-one presidential electors (Electoral College). Also, only white male landowners over twenty-one years of age were eligible to vote. Not until 1920 did we reach a point where all citizens of any race or gender were allowed to vote without discrimination when the population was 105 million according to the US Census. The continuous growth in our representation was obviously not a new idea because our nation's founders intended that the number of representatives would forever increase in direct proportion to the total population when they wrote the Constitution.[456]

What many people do not know is the original Bill of Rights had twelve amendments. This first of those amendments was famously known as Article the First of the Bill of Rights ensuring "the total number of representatives would forever increase along with the total population." As an arithmetically complex amendment, this proposal was affirmed by the many states before a subtle, but fatal, defect in its formulation eventually became evident. The purpose was intended to fix the Electoral College defects by requiring a *minimum* number of representatives proportionate to the total population. Strangely, this proposal was never sent to the states for ratification. Instead, a seemingly identical defective version was substituted which effectively sabotaged the implementation of this solution. The defective part of the Constitution implies the "number of representatives shall not exceed one for every thirty thousand," but it failed to establish a corresponding maximum size.[457]

Unfortunately, this Article of the Bill of Rights was a proposed but never ratified.[458]

One of the founders, James Madison, had envisions way ahead of his time when he wrote in Federalist Paper 55, "A small number of representatives will be an unsafe depositary of the public interests because it will take away the feelings of the mass of the people," and continued in Federalist Paper 58 that "we must adjust the apportionment of representatives to the number of inhabitants in each state ... so the number of representatives should be left to the people, not the discretion of the government."[459] These increases with every apportionment would have also increased the number of presidential electors.

This equally proportionate increase of these electors would support the democracy theory of our presidential elections because democracy itself is not only about words, laws, and policies. Democracy is also about math, which is one of its most interesting features. And with math comes the word *census*, that means the counting of people. Over time, the census became a basis for social statistics. Democracy is also about the fact math is used for decision making, usually by a majority of 50 percent plus 1. And finally, democracy is about the principles of one person, one vote.[460]

Over the years of 1790 to 1920 our nation's population continuously grew along with our House members, changing the Electoral College with every decennial apportionment. Our congressional districts grew from 34,400 average to more than 243,700 by 1920, while continuously growing the Electoral College from 105 members in 1790 to 531 in 1913/. These numbers remained consistent and directly related to the population of each congressional district.[461]

The last increase came after the 1910 Census when the House reached 433 and the Electoral College was 531 when the total population was 92 million. The only additions to this number came when Arizona and New Mexico were admitted to the states bringing the total to 535. The 1920 U.S. Census represented an America that was shifting from a rural-to-urban nation, and more than ever, a nation of immigrants as the population grew to over 106-million people. This was an increase of almost 15 percent over the 1910 census report.[462]

Dalton Conley, a professor of sociology, medicine and public policy at New York University, and Jacqueline Stevens, a professor of political science at Northwestern University wrote, "After the 1910 census, when the House grew from 391 members to 433 the growth of the House of Representatives stopped. That's because the upcoming 1920 census indicated that most Americans were concentrating in the urban cities, and rural nativists and conservative politicians worried about the power of 'foreigners' (a.k.a. city people) would block efforts to give them more power over representation."[463]

If there was a proper decennial apportionment following the 1920 Census, the size of the House would have increased 433 to 483, an increase of fifty seats which would have awarded the Electoral College to also increase from 531 to 583. However, as it had never previously done before in our history, Congress decided it would choose to ignore the results of the 1920 US Census and do nothing about the reapportionment of the House of Representatives. Subsequently the House and the Electoral College was frozen following the Reapportionment Act of 1929 and are the same numbers today. This 1929 act would be a total contradiction to Article 1, Section 2 of the US Constitution, which mandates that an apportionment of representatives among the states be carried out each ten-year period.[464] Because the act permanently froze the House at 435 members, reapportionment became a redistribution of the same number of House seats for the next one hundred years, which has kept the Electoral College stymied at 538. This 1929 Act set up a permanent mathematical process that would automatically redistribute the same 435 House members according to each subsequent census and fixing the number at 435.[465]

This shift in the population has not stopped as the urban population grew from only 28 percent in 1880 and continued to grow to 80 percent per the 2020 US Census. During this same period, the rural population did the opposite, shrinking from 72 percent in 1880 to only 20 percent following the 2020 census. The correct redrawing of districts where the most population expansion took place would clearly create more urban metro areas, giving so the called city people the opportunity to vote for one of their own.[466] A century later and we are stuck at the same 538 Electoral College votes while the population has tripled to 331 million people on the 2020 US Census.

The cause for no apportionment was the Reapportionment Act of 1929 (or the Permanent Apportionment Act of 1929), which was the major setback passed by Congress that has become one of the major discussions surrounding the abolishment of the Electoral College. It produced an irrevocable effect on the Electoral College, which is still 538 because the House was frozen at 435 members. This has affected representation of each House district and every presidential election from then to 2024 and maybe beyond.[467/468] This act could easily be considered a violation of democracy because a population that grows from 106 million to 331 million in ninety-five years cannot be a democracy if the United States has the same number of seats in the House and keeps the Electoral College at the same at 538 from ninety-five years ago. This denies the principles of a democracy by creating unequal representation and therefore does not give Americans a one person, one vote theory that every vote is equal.[469]

Table 10.1 below clearly demonstrates how the size of our districts, versus the size of the House and the Electoral College, showing the extent of discrepancies from 1910 to 2020.

Table 10.1: Actual Expansion of the House of Representatives and Electoral College 1790–2020

Census Year	Avg Pop / House Member	Total House Members	Electoral College
1790	34,436	105	138
1800	34,609	142	235
1810	36,377	182	261
1820	42,124	213	288
1830	49,712	240	296
1840	71,338	223	294
1850	93,020	234	296
1860	122,614	241	303
1870	130,533	292	352
1880	151,912	325	401
1890	173,901	356	444
1900	193,167	386	447
1910	210,583	**435**	**531**
1920	243,728	**435**	531
1930	280,675	**435**	531
1940	301,164	**435**	531
1950	334,587	**435**	531
1960	410,481	**435**	538*
1970	469,088	**435**	538*

1980	510,818	**435**	**538***
1990	571,477	**435**	**538***
2000	646,946	**435**	**538***
2010	709,760	**435**	**538***
2020	761,169	**435**	**538***

**=only additions were Alaska and Hawaii*

These numbers in Table 10.1 are not what our founders envisioned when they wrote out Constitution, in Article 1, Section 2, where it clearly states that "the number of representatives shall not exceed one for every thirty thousand people, and each state shall have at least one US Representative, while the total size of a state's delegation to the House depends on the population of each state." Also, the Constitution did not limit how many members there could be in the House of Representatives. Many members of the first Congress in 1789 assumed the words in the Constitution sufficiently expressed the number of House members would be directly related to the apportionment of the population of the US Census every ten years, but it does not.[470]

Another portion of Article 1, Section 2 states that the "direct election of the House members will be done by the People of the several states." However, because our Constitution gave state legislatures the freedom of how this would be done and what they consider *a direct election by the people* differed from one state to the next. This legislative branch portion of the Constitution also said House members should be accountable by "conducting frequent elections every two years for the purpose of requiring an actual enumeration of the people (how many members in the House of Representatives) to be apportioned every ten years, with each state having no less that one US House member."[471]

Instead of following what our founders wanted, for over a century the United States Congress has restricted our representation in the House because of the Reapportionment Act of 1929.[472] In 1941, Congress adopted the Method of Equal Proportions for apportionment, giving each state one electoral vote per state, then redistributing the 385 remaining members of the House. The mathematical goal of this method minimizes the relative percentage differences in representation by the number of people per representative among each state. Mathematical staff members at the US Census Bureau determine the number of seats each state receives while redistributing the remaining 385 every ten years.[473/474]

If we chose to abolish the Electoral College completely, it would require a constitutional amendment to move toward a nationwide popular vote. However, that amendment requires a two-third vote by both the House (290 votes) and the Senate (67 votes), then it must be ratified by a three-quarter (38) vote of the state legislatures.[475] Because of our present day ugly partisan politics, obtaining that two-third vote in both the House and the Senate would most likely be impossible. Also, on the state level those same political partisanships in different state legislatures would be just as difficult. This creates an additional hurdle because in our world of the 2020s bipartisanship is an unheard proposition.

However, enlarging the House of Representatives does not require a constitutional amendment. All that would be required is a repeal of the Reapportionment Act of 1929 with an act for Congress to continue to make new decennial apportionments after every census as was done from 1790 to 1920. Naturally, if we enlarge the House, it automatically increases the total electoral votes, bringing it more in line with the population that has tripled since 1920. During most of the twentieth century, several presidential elections were landslides, both in the popular vote and the Electoral College votes, making the number of electors irrelevant. However, since 1992, only two winning presidential candidates have received more than 52 percent of the nationwide popular vote, and those are President Obama in 2008 and President Biden in 2020. On the Electoral College side, Obama received the most electoral votes this century in 2008 with 365. Another fact is since the beginning of the twenty-first century, two of the last six elections were lost by the candidate who won the nationwide popular vote. That is 33 percent of the elections in the twenty-first century.

The first was the thirty-five-day debacle in 2000 when Al Gore won the popular vote by 500,000 but lost the electoral vote by the slimmest possible margin of 271 to 266 to President George Bush. Then eight years ago in 2016 Hillary Clinton won the nationwide popular vote over former President Trump by over three million votes (over 2 percent) but lost the Electoral College vote by 304 to 227 with seven faithless electors who abandoned the Clinton slate. To put those elections in perspective, from 1789 to 1996 we had fifty-three presidential elections and only three of those elections were won by the candidate who lost the popular vote.[476] While some political analysts deem this coincidental, the prospects continue to grow today for it to happen more often in the future unless we fix, reform, or abolish the Electoral College. This is where the partisan politics problems reside.

Most observers and political analysts concur that it cannot be coincidental that all five of those elections since 1789 ended with a Democrat losing all of those Electoral College elections while winning the nationwide popular vote. Even if we can assume it was simply coincidence, it has become obvious that there undoubtedly will be possible nightmares of it reoccurring many more times with the potential contingent election by the United States House of Representatives because no candidate reaches the 270 majority. That has happened only one time in our entire history, and that was in 1824, exactly 200 years ago. That happened when Andrew Jackson won both the popular and electoral vote. However, he did not reach a majority of the electoral votes needed for a victory probably due to the fact that five candidates from the same party, the Democratic-Republicans, split those votes requiring a contingent election in the House of Representatives.

Another factor that must be considered in apportionment is the shift to urbanization in state populations would have moved more House seats in that direction. America has continued urbanization steadily to 80 percent of the population in the 2020 US Census while the rural population shrunk to only 20 percent. According to that 2020 census, there are approximately 274 million people living in urban areas with only fifty-seven million remaining in rural areas. These astounding differences in numbers are real problems affecting the current redistribution of our Electoral College votes, which do not reflect the properly apportioned increase in urbanization.

The debates surrounding the growth of the United States population as it expands every ten years is the redistribution of the Electoral College votes, which is totally out of line with the actual populations of the states involved. Examples of this show the fact that although the state of California gained 2.3 million people since the 2010 Census it is losing one electoral vote in the upcoming 2024 election. That same inequality continues with the states of New York, Pennsylvania, Illinois, Ohio, and Michigan, also losing one electoral vote while their populations increased since the 2010 Census. The apportionment of 2020 leaves these states with their smallest congressional delegation in history: New Jersey since 1900, New York since 1800, Ohio since 1820, Pennsylvania since 1790, Massachusetts since 1800, Illinois since 1860, Indiana since 1830, and Iowa and Missouri since 1850. This is all despite increases in their populations. This negative apportionment leads to lesser populated states making gains the larger populated states diminish with the impact of gerrymandering.

A larger chamber decreases the disparity between presidential performance and partisan politics. It also makes minority districts easier to maintain because it increases the difficulty of drawing compact groups in the population.[477]

The case for enlarging the House, and therefore expanding the Electoral College, is noted in a recent report from the American Academy of Arts and Sciences stating "the chamber's lack of growth over the last ninety years has had serious and harmful consequences for both the representatives and the voting public. One result has been the connection between constituents and their congress people has attenuated (lessened or weakened the magnitude), leading to worse representation and bolstering the feeling among voters that their voices does not matter."[478] And again, James Madison in his Federalist 55 addressed the important issue of a proper size in the House aids the role of representation in a democracy, and the importance of civic republican virtues. He stated, "No political problem is less susceptible of a precise solution than that which relates to the number most convenient for a representative legislature."[479]

The 2020 Census has seen more northern states finding themselves drawing more minority districts while southern states have House members districts underrepresenting the minority shares of their population. Mississippi with a 37 percent African Americans population has only one of its four members who is black. Louisiana minorities are 32 percent with only one out of six represented. Alabama has a 27 percent black population with only one out of seven represented, and Florida with 16 percent minorities will have only one black member out of its twenty-seven members due to its latest gerrymandering of drawing ridiculously proportioned non-representative districts.

Another fact is the continued national urbanization should make rural small-town districts smaller fractions in Congress, but the continuous gerrymandering does the opposite. All of these reasons for increasing the overall number of members in the House and Electoral College will help align urban and rural districts properly.[480]

We can all agree that the nation has representation inequality at this time, so the question is not whether we need to expand the House, but it is how we need to do it that will best fit the one person, one vote theory where every vote is equal. To overcome the problems resulting from our undersized House and Electoral College, there are several plans that are frequently suggested as the basis for correctly reapportioning the total number of House members we should have, which also increases the Electoral College to a similar increase in numbers. The way they get to their numbers differ, but they all bring the Electoral College to look more like a population that has tripled since 1913.

The American Academy of Arts and Sciences in its report *The Case for Enlarging the House of Representatives* presented several options to enlarge the House and the Electoral College. When the *Reapportionment Act of 1929* froze the house in 1929, the only way for a state to gain any seats comes at the expense of another state losing a seat. During the last ten apportionments done between 1930 and 2020, twice as many times states lost at least one electoral vote and a member in the House as there were from 1790 to 1910. Also, in the last ninety-five years 86 percent of the times that a state lost at least one electoral vote, it did so while the state population was either the same or increased.

Since 1930, the redistribution of House seats shifted 149 Electoral votes by taking them away from states in order to redistribute them to other states in order to maintain the same 435 seats.[481] Table 10.2 shows during how many of those 149 House seats were lost in each census, and of course, this cost those states presidential electors, and they were redistributed to other states to maintain the same 435 seats. According to their report, the academy shows what would happen if these seats were restored, plus one to keep an odd number, allocating the districts more evenly. This would bring the total to 584 House members, making the Electoral College 687. According to the 2020 US Census report, each seat in the House of Representatives would represent 568,145 constituents, which is better representation of our government than the present day 762,000 constituents per House seat. This expansion would restore the representation lost over the last ninety years.[482]

Table 10.2: Electoral Votes Lost due to the Reapportionment Act of 1929

Census	Number of Year Reapportioned Seats
1930	27
1940	9
1950	14
1960	21
1970	11

1980	17
1990	19
2000	12
2010	12
2020	7
TOTAL	**149**

Source: The Case for Enlarging the House of Representatives—Part III (https://www.amacad.org/sites/default/files/publication/downloads/2021_ Enlarging-the-House.pdf)

The American Academy of Arts and Sciences report shows that the House should have grown as the population grew. Their viewpoint is that moving forward no state should lose a representative as it did before, unless that state had a population decrease from the previous decennial census or their population dropped below that of another state that may have had less House seats. It also adds the necessary additional seats as needed to ensure the House has the proper number of seats in relationship to the other states and the overall nationwide population.[483]

America needs to get our politics working again on a bipartisanship basis. The system needs energy to get things done, republican safety of our rights, sovereignty to the will of the people, and finally inclusion of the voices in the House of Representatives. The proximity of House members to their constituents is essential. For those reasons, we need a larger and continuously growing House of Representatives, which will also increase the Electoral College votes, having smaller districts representing each representative.[484]

These are all the good "what ifs" of the past to prove the necessity of enlarging the House of Representatives. The study by the American Academy of Arts and Sciences showed us historical information all the way back to 1930 and how it would have changed the number of seats in the House, which of course effects the Electoral College. The only problem is we unfortunately cannot undo what happened in past elections, but we can certainly fix the future.

We must start with the 2020 US Census and get the proper apportionment of how many members there should be in the House of Representatives today. This apportionment will give us the number of seats each state should have for the foreseeable future in the 2024, 2026, 2028, and 2030 congressional elections until the next decennial census report in 2030. The proper reapportionment also affects the Electoral College in the 2024 and 2028 presidential elections.

In Chapter 5, we discussed the many opponents versus the advocates of the Electoral College. We reviewed many reasons why some people see this present form of elections as some indispensable law of the land that our founding fathers created. That is untrue. Then others oppose it because it has become old and antiquated in the last one hundred years and needs to be replaced; otherwise, every vote will never be equal.

Let us look at what we need to do first, and that is there is no doubt that our House of Representatives must be expanded. There cannot be any possible objections to the plain fact that constant apportionment of our House seats needs to happen every ten years so that it coincides with the growth of the country as it clearly did from 1790 to 1930. When our population reached 106 million in the 1920 census, we chose to do nothing, ignored apportionment, and we decided it was no longer a good idea and created the Reapportionment Act of 1929, which has kept the House of Representatives frozen at 435 for one hundred years without any regard for the facts that our population tripled to over 331 million constituents in 2020.

Another fact that has been crystal clear that our founding fathers consistently spoke about the need to make the House of Representatives the "people's house". However, over time it has become clear that the House quite obviously has been claimed by extraordinary political power led by the lobbyists who offer constant quid pro quos that are nothing more than for selfish interests that are not usually what "the people" want or need. Therefore, it leaves us no other choice other than to take the advice of our founding fathers and expand this sacred "people's house" as they instructed us to do. Many groups can have opinions but none of those opinions hold water in comparison to the intentions of Madison and Jefferson.

Now, the only decision that must be made that does not need any amendment to the Constitution is to (1) repeal the awful Reapportionment (Permanent Apportionment) Act by a majority vote by the House and Senate; (2) find the best plan that will take us into the future expansion of our population for decades to come; (3) make a decision on what method to use to split the electoral votes, winner-take-all, fractional, or by district such as Maine and Nebraska have; and (4) go back the decennial apportionment that is needed every ten years as was done from 1790–1920. It is also crystal clear that this expansion should never stop as long as our population keeps growing. We must make use of the 2020 US Census plus us the projections for the next four decades ahead by enlarging the House at a pace that is conducive to what equalizes every state population will have in 2030, 2040, 2050, and 2060.

Then, after we complete this, we can start discussions of reforming the Electoral College with something like the NPVIC that will not need a constitutional amendment to achieve. It is truly the closest we will get to having a direct nationwide popular vote (see Chapter 9 for more NPVIC details). Otherwise, we will have no choice but to go the route of most difficulty with an amendment that could take months or more likely years due to political greed, which will only put us further behind, if we choose to completely abolish the Electoral College. Now that we know what comes first, enlarging the House, we can move into ideas of how that takes place. After one hundred years, the House of Representatives and its effects on the Electoral College should be top priority before the upcoming elections turn into constant repeats of what has happened in 2000 and 2016.

According to the US Census Bureau, the projected population of the United States will reach somewhere around 425 million by 2060, with a steady growth rate every ten years. That projected growth goes from 331 million in 2020 to 359 million in 2030, 381 million in 2040, 402 million in 2050, and

425 million by 2060. This population growth is a change of ninety-five million over the next thirty-six years, representing a 28.70 percent change.[485]

This leaves the United States of America with an important decision that will affect the democracy of this nation. Enlarging the House of Representatives must be done, and the only questions remaining are only when and how.

CHAPTER 11

What is the Wyoming Rule and the Cubic Root Rule

Two Methods That Could Save the Electoral College by Expanding the House

Today we use the winner-take-all in forty-eight of fifty states, and we are closely following the progress and future of the National Popular Vote Interstate Compact (NPVIC). But none of these cures what has truly been the biggest problem for the last ninety-five years, the *Reapportionment Act of 1929,* which froze the House of Representatives at 435 while also freezing the Electoral College at 538. As we spoke of in Chapter 10 and prior to this act, apportionment from 1790 to 1910 continued to enlarge our House of Representatives consistently in accordance with the ever-growing population during that period.

Since 1920, our population has tripled, while using the *Method of Equal Proportions* (Chapter 7) that only redistributes the same number of total seats by taking seats away from some states in order to add them to others in order to maintain the same 435 magic number in the size of the House size. This method has created a situation where this redistribution of House seats has caused many districts to average 760,000 or more constituents per representative, leaving representation in California and Texas at a fraction of what a person in Wyoming has because their single district only represents 577,000.

Historical documents from our founding fathers proved their intention was to be meant to continuously increase the number in the House of Representatives every ten years in order to keep pace with an ever-growing population. Founding fathers, such as Thomas Jefferson, eloquently wrote, "When the people fear their government there is tyranny, when the government fears the people there is liberty." And in Federalist 58, James Madison supported this theory with "as the population census increases, we must augment (add to) the apportionment of representatives to the number of inhabitants in each state ... so the number of representatives should be left to the people, not the discretion of the government." These great founding fathers' ideas, which were used for our first 130 years to properly implement the shifting of the political power to the people by ending incumbent domination of reelections, diminish lobbyist influences, overcome any single political party control of our government, and maximize our individual liberties while at the same time increasing the size of our government in accordance with its total population.[486] Let us also be perfectly clear that our Constitution does not determine the size of the House of Representatives.

The 1920 census created the greatest controversy in Congress over which states should receive new seats. At that time, we had to consider the weight of the political powers of the rural states that were no longer in the majority of America. The rural and more conservative areas dipped from 72 percent in 1880 to only 45 percent by 1920, while the more moderate urban states increased from 28 percent to 55 percent in that same period. What happened? A law was enacted in 1929 called the Reapportionment (or better known as the Permanent Apportionment) Act of 1929 that obviously did not allow any more apportionments to happen. The fact is our nation has become even more closely in line with a population that has 80 percent urbanization to 20 percent rural population in 2020.

Another significant factor that was conveniently overlooked was the actual first section of the Bill of Rights from 1790, which became known as simply "Article the First," would have insured that the number of representatives would forever increase in accordance with the growth of our population. Unfortunately, as mentioned in previous chapters, it was never ratified and as time went on it completely disappeared from our history.[487]

Many plans were discussed to improve and determine our Electoral College; however, they were always based on the same total of 538. There was the district plan that is similar to what is used in Maine and Nebraska—the fractional proportionate plan that suggested we split the Electoral votes based on a candidate's percentage of the popular votes to the third decimal point, and the whole number approach that rounded off the electoral votes to the nearest whole number and splitting them accordingly. None of these plans, which all had their good ideas and intentions to save our democracy, ever addressed enlarging the House and how that would also automatically increase the current Electoral College system, splitting the votes in accordance with the ever-growing national population.

Finally, let us not forget about all the serious discussions about abolishing the Electoral College altogether; however, this method would have required the most difficult means of accomplishment, an amendment to the Constitution. Because this would require a two-thirds vote by both the House (290 votes) and Senate (67 votes) and be ratified by a three-quarters (38) vote of the state legislatures. An amendment as discussed in the last chapter, would be nearly impossible because of constant partisanship of political powers influenced by outsiders, rather than the citizens themselves.[488]

In this chapter and for the remaining chapters in this book we will discusses how the following two methods, the Wyoming rule and the cubic root rule, for enlarging the House that is available and simple in order to increase the Electoral College without the need for a constitutional amendment. These methods would both move us forward to a place where the House of Representatives should be after this one-hundred-year frozen sabbatical. They would both enlarge the House to create equally proportioned districts according to their populations because voters living in larger populated states have been at a huge disadvantage in comparison to those living in smaller populated states. The absolute conclusion is we have to enlarge the House if we are to create equally populated districts based on individual state populations. Then we can automatically resolve the inequality of our Electoral College system of representation.

According to the 2020 US Census, seven states are losing one House seat each while they are added to other states even though those states losing a seat had a gain in their population. It also relates to a loss of seven electoral votes. That is why apportionment every ten years needs to be put in effect in order to have continuous growth in the size of the House and we can stop the continuous game of musical chairs where some states gain representation at the expense of others based on the current Reapportionment Act of 1929 that redistributes those same 435 members. This causes many states to end up with significantly more people per representative than others.[489]

With this unequal representation of states under the current system of redistribution instead if reapportionment makes it very difficult to understand how anybody could resist the simple fix that the Wyoming rule or the cubic root rule gives all the states.

State and national populations are very important in selecting the correct number of people to represent every House district in America. But it is this electoral side of the equation that is our priority because that is the one that will elect all future presidents. The only problem is it will be impossible to implement before the upcoming 2024 election. The law would need both houses of Congress to pass a majority vote that will (1) repeal of *the Reapportionment Act of 1929,* and (2) institute the Wyoming rule or cubic root rule. Both will have to be dealt with separately and considering how fast our Congress acts on important legislation, add to that the partisanship that exists in our current Congress because two different parties control the House (Republicans) and the Senate (Democrats). The last time I looked, both parties have acted like hypocrites refusing to get their act together and get the work done on a bipartisan basis across the aisles as they should because that is why the people of America put them there. The major reason this happens is both political parties want to take credit for anything good that happens. But that is a subject for another book.

The Wyoming Rule

The Wyoming Rule was introduced by Rep. Sean Casten (D-Illinois) and has the makings of practicality because is based on the state with the lowest population that has the minimum of only one representative as our Constitution mandates. It will also amount to slower, more gradual growth over the next few decades. The Wyoming rule calls for increasing the size of the House to create a consistent representative-to-constituent ratio based on the least populous state, Wyoming since the 1990 US Census. Then as previously occurred every ten years, the apportionment is based on the population of the least populated state, which should continuously increase the size of the House based on projections of 2020 to 2060.[490]

The Wyoming Rule uses as its benchmark the size of the least-populous state with only a single House member, currently Wyoming, which now has a 577,419 total population according to the 2020 US Census. This would increase the number of members in the House by 139 to 574. Wyoming has been the least populated state since the 1990 census, hence the reason for which this method is named.[491] That is 180,000 less people than the average of the 435 House districts currently, which is 762,000. The only drawback to this rule is the use of Wyoming as the constant smallest population, which could change in the future. Some political analysts have envisioned using a method that would use a constant of 580,000—that creates a problem because by earmarking the population number with a permanent number leads us back to the present ongoing problem of apportionment that we experience now.[492]

There was an attempted resolution that addressed increasing the House members problem that is directed all the way back to the *1911 Apportionment Act,* which said that Congress "shall be elected by districts composed of a contiguous and compact territory, and containing as nearly as practical an equal number of inhabitants," which is easily interpreted that we needed to continue to apportion Congress based on equal population of every congressional district.[493] This act was meant to challenge gerrymandering districts. Then *the Reapportionment Act of 1929* took this language out, leading to states gaining the ability to utilize gerrymandered districts again, which has become an ongoing issue. Many states have some wacky shaped representative districts to help gerrymander the political powers of a given state. This results in House members who do not necessarily represent their home locations. Part of the language in the so-called Wyoming rule would reinsert the original language of the *1911 Apportionment Act* to protect against this continuous gerrymandering.

The adoption of a larger House size to a more equitable district size as was the case in 1910 before the *Reapportionment Act of 1929.* By increasing the size of the House and adding new member districts, it would simultaneously increase the Electoral College by that same amount. The use of the additional required presidential electors per the Constitution, Article 1, Section 2, would need to first repeal the antique *Reapportionment Act of*

1929, then pass by majority in both the House and Senate to be enacted and become law. One of the best advantages of this plan is it can be accomplished without a constitutional amendment. As *Crystal Ball* editor in chief, Larry J. Sabato, wrote in his book *A More Perfect Constitution,* "there was every indication that the founders believed the House would continue to grow with population, yet it has not done so for more than a century."[494]

Under Article 1, Section 2 of the Constitution each state must have a minimum of one House member. Based on that section of the constitution, each state's House members can be compared as a ratio to Wyoming with the smallest population, which in the 2024 presidential election has the minimum of three electoral votes. That calculates to 192,573 people per Electoral College Votes, whereas California has the largest population of 39,576,757 people representing fifty-four electoral votes, an average of 732,902 people per electoral vote. That gives each a vote in Wyoming has a four-to-one population per elector weight ratio over the state of California.[495]

By instituting the Wyoming Rule, these ratios will become more equitable because California would gain seventeen new House members, for a total Electoral College of seventy-one, reducing the ratio of one electoral vote per 573,576 people. This decreases the ratio to a more equitable margin but still favors Wyoming by a three-to-one margin. Although it is not a perfect one person, one vote, it is more equitable than our present Electoral College. The expansion of the House would align states with their current populations, making representation more accurate. Increasing the House by 139 members to 574 will increase the Electoral College to 677 votes. We cannot achieve the perfect one-to-one ratio because the Constitution awards each state the same two bonus electoral votes for the US senators.[496]/[497]

On the negative side, as equitable and reasonable the Wyoming rule population apportionment seems there is always the possibility that the House may become too large at some point in the future. In fact, if we look back to the 1930 US Census, the use of the smallest populated state rule would be Nevada, which had only 91,058 constituents then. According to Table 11.1 below, this rule would have resulted in a House of 1,418 members. At that time, the population was 123 million with 435 House members, so each House member averaged 282,382 constituents.[498] If you use Wyoming as the standard with 225,5656 population the House would have totaled a more reasonable increase to 545 seats. Wyoming became the smallest state in 1990, preceded by Nevada (1920 to 1950), then Alaska (1960 to the 1980) census. Another angle would be to use the apportionment method used before the *Reapportionment Act of 1929*, which would have increased the House to 583 seats.[499]

Passage of the Wyoming Rule would make the reapportionment laws based on the US Census every decennial (recurring every ten years) population. Also, the Wyoming Rule can be done without a constitutional amendment because from the constitutional standpoint the only mention of the House size is there "can be at most one representative per 30,000 people, and no state has two or more representatives with a population below 60,000."[500]

This is where the Wyoming Rule ironically works and gives America more equal representation while it decreases Wyoming's share of representation in relation to the national population to a more equal 1/574 (0.17 percent), down from 1/435 (0.23 percent), where it should be. It also represents more parity in relationship with the overall population representation by equally raising the number of seats in forty states while the other ten remain the same as they are now, and no state losing any seats at all. They will only lose a seat if their state population decreases, or the national census decreases over a ten-year period. This is a major improvement over our stymied, antiquated Electoral College of 538 that has not had any apportionment for one hundred years. The method prioritizes fairness between districts.[501] The necessity for expanding the size of the House enables representatives to serve their constituents better, brings them closer to their people, minimizes lobbyist infiltration, while at the same time spreads their huge committee workloads in the present House amongst more representatives.[502]

The final piece of the puzzle is the consideration of the effects of the Wyoming rule to the Electoral College. With this method, the electoral would more closely align with the current populations of the states, making its representation more accurate for future elections. The elections of 2000 and 2016 created a disparity between the popular vote versus the electoral vote. In both of those elections, as previously discussed extensively in Chapter 4, "Controversial Elections or Wrong Winners," the winner of the popular vote by 500 thousand in 2000 and three million in 2016 lost the presidency due to an inadequate Electoral College. The probability of this happening more often increases every election if we continue to stay stuck at 538 electoral votes due to inadequate population distribution.[503]

For analytics, let's look at what future population changes mean with regards to House members and Electoral College votes. For the naysayers who feel the Wyoming rule will not protect the possibility that the House may become too large in the future, the US Census Bureau disproves that theory with their future population projections. Using this Wyoming rule along with US Census projections, the 28.70 percent increase in the population from 2024 to 2060 translates into an increase of 212 electoral votes by the 2060 elections. The increases would translate to 707 in 2030, 725 in 2040, 740 in 2050, and 750 in 2060.

Analyzing a couple of states relative to their present Electoral situations, the Wyoming rule act takes away the ugliness of today's Electoral College. For instance, let's take the state that has its name. Based on US Census projections for Wyoming's population will go from present day 577,719 up to the 2060 US Census projection of 668,000, which will still leave them with the lowest state population with a minimum of three electoral votes, keeping them as the benchmark for the lowest population, therefore, remaining the Wyoming rule basis to determine our total Electoral College votes.

Using this Wyoming Rule for the four largest populations, from 2020 to 2060, here is an example of what this new method will do. California would go from fifty-four Electoral College votes now to eighty by 2060, Texas with forty electoral votes would have seventy by 2060, Florida which has thirty electoral votes will have fifty-one in 2060, and New York will move from twenty-eight electoral votes to thirty-seven in 2060. Texas has the greatest change by gaining thirty House seats as their population will grow from twenty-nine million to forty-five million by 2060. The state with the most people, California with thirty-nine million will grow to fifty-two million and add twenty-six more electoral votes to eighty by 2060. This equal apportionment brings us as closer to one person, one vote.

Opponents offer three objections that this plan is not logical. First, it costs nearly $2 million per Congressman each year to cover health benefits, pensions, and travel. This could be offset by moving some of this cost back to the state they are from. Also, do not forget, retiring and tenured members who leave the House still get some of these benefits for life. The second and most ridiculous reason is the current configuration of the House chamber not having the ability to create enough seats. Not true because it has been redesigned many times and if needed could be improvised again to fit the additional members. And finally, this plan may change the number of seats in the House every ten years. So what? It creates more equal representation, which is not a problem, but it is an asset.

There could be a reverse effect in states such as Pennsylvania, Illinois, Ohio, and Michigan where the projected populations are expected to decrease over the next three decades; however, meaning they could possibly lose seats as in the past because in which the Wyoming Rule is structured.

On the other hand, states such as Georgia, North Carolina, Arizona, and Colorado will make the biggest gains as those states experience millions of people during that same period as people are moving to the suburbs at the expense of the large inner-city populations.

This Wyoming Rule will therefore be tied to every decennial US Census in the coming years. That equates to the states gaining significant amounts of House members with Texas leading the pack by adding thirty in the next thirty-six years. This would bring the overall average for each of the 637 representative districts in 2060 to an average of 668,837 constituents, bringing Congress closer to the ideal of one person, one vote as our population grows.[504]

Table 11.1 also identifies the number of House seats that would be given to the respective states if the Wyoming Rule was implemented in 2024 based on the 2020 US Census. The states with the largest increases in House seats would be California (17), Texas (13), Florida (9), and New York (9). The population per district range would be 577,719 (using Wyoming) per district nationally. On the reverse, South Dakota with two, would have the lowest average district of only 443,885, giving it the most seats per capita, while North Dakota, with one seat for 779,702, would have the fewest seats per capita. Delaware would add a seat for a district size of 495,419 (versus the actual one seat of 989,948 now), and Montana with its newly added second seat averages 542,704 per seat (versus one seat for 1,085,407). This Wyoming rule leaves only North Dakota, Alaska, Vermont, and Wyoming with one House seat and keeps the District of Columbia at three electoral votes with zero representation for its 689,575 constituents as they continue their fight to become a state. Six states will have two House members, New Hampshire, Maine, Rhode Island, Delaware, South Dakota, and Montana. Another item shown in Table 11.1 that you will notice is implementing the Wyoming rule would not take away any House seats as always happens in every reapportionment method that we use today. Therefore, forty states would receive additional House seats while ten remain the same.[505]

One observation can be made in the comparison of our present-day Electoral College versus what it would be today using the Wyoming rule is the fact that it comes close to the American Academy of Arts and Sciences study in Chapter 10 that reveals a total of 149 seats were redistributed (lost to other states) from 1930 to 2020. The "lost reapportioned seats" method they used came very close to using the Wyoming rule today. This simple actual mathematical explanation gives the Wyoming rule significant credibility and reliability from now and moving forward.

If this rule were introduced to Congress it might have a better chance of passing than the NPVIC because (1) it retains all the presidential electors which in turn, (2) gives the Electoral College significantly more credibility than it has today, (3) provides more equality in representation across the country, (4) and gives the proponents of the Electoral College a different perspective that the Electoral College would bring us up to date.

It rewards the Republicans who view the Electoral College as some sort of "indispensable object."

The Wyoming rule reduces the average disparities that dominate the current electoral system while reducing the differences in average populations between the small and large districts. Before it was granted its second House member this year, Montana had the largest individual district that was over 76 percent larger than the smallest district, Wyoming. Thus, this would be a huge advantage to this rule.[506]

The Cubic Root Rule

Before we move ahead with the Cube Root Rule (CRR), we need a better explanation and understanding of what is "cube rooting"? The basis for this comes from the theory that the House of Representatives works best when it has the proper representation.[507] The model for this was first devised by Estonian political scientist Rein Taagepera in his 1972 paper "The Size of National Assemblies" and later endorsed by the *New York Times's* editorial board in 2018.[508]

The cube root of a number is the number multiplied three times to get the cube results, which in this case would be the national population number. The cube for the number (x) represents "x-cubed." For example, using the number 5, we know that if x = 5, then 5 x 5 x 5 = 125. Therefore, 125 would be called the Cube Root of 5. So how do we need to find a starting point for applying this rule to our House of Representatives to determine how many members it should have? There are several mathematical formulas used to get the answer we need, but for this purpose, we will use a simpler experimental method as explained by the formula in "CUEMATH: What Is Cube Root?"[509] Many political experts view the Cube Root Rule as the best way to accomplish true apportionment if it was done properly from 1930 to 2020 when achieving the correct size of the House and the Electoral College.

In moving forward, we have found significant research done about the Cube Root Rule and there are many political scientists who come up with two different end results. They both use the same math to get to the cube root of our population, but the difference comes after that, on what the actual size of the House and Electoral College should be. There may be two answers to how many House seats there should be and because this is still in only discussion stages the use of either one still concludes that the House of Representatives needs to be enlarged. Either way the increases in the number of districts will lead us to where we should be to have any chance of getting to the one person, one vote theory so that every vote is equal.

If we use the formula that Rein Taagepera used in 1972, the Cube Root Rule would have the national legislature always be the cube root of the total population of the nation. The House would be the cube root of the population minus one hundred (the one hundred US senators).[510] Many political scientists support this formula because it automatically prioritizes the responsiveness to our population changes. As our population grows, Congress grows.[511]

The number we start with is the 2020 Census population, which is what is represented by our House members. So, our population is 331,792,120, which reveals a *cube root* of 692, which will be the closest come to our population. Using the formula, 692 x 692 x 692 = 331,373,888, making the 692 our Electoral College. Then we take the 692 minus 100 (that represents the number of senators there are), and we will have 592 seats in our House of Representatives. If the Electoral College was changed to the cubic root rule, there would be 692 Electoral Votes. This formula will have an average of 560,468 per House seat.

As we go forward into the future with the decennial Census every ten years starting with 2030 to 2060 this Cube Root Rule will accomplish the ultimate purpose of equal representation with continuous increases every ten years with apportionment based on the US Census.[512]

The second method of Cube Root Rule uses this same 692 number; however, some political advocates want to use that number as the size of the House of Representatives then adding one hundred (for the senators) to come up with an Electoral College of 792.[513]/[514] This formula will have an average of 479,476. This puts it below the Wyoming rule, and also going back to 1930 to 1950, the numbers would actually be less than 435. My personal opinion on this is to use the more logical method, which is the cube root of 692 minus one hundred Senators, giving us 592 House seats.

Most political scientists have discovered that national legislatures in many countries all over the world have often used the cube root method to configure the size of their lower legislative body across global democracies. Fact is, the United

States has one of the largest gaps in the world between our House chamber size and the cube root population. For that reason, the use of this cube root rule would prioritize a real responsiveness to population changes.[515]

Opponents of the rule point to very few issues other than its implementation would add too many seats at once if we add another 157 House seats using the first formula, or adds another 257 House seats using the second formula.[516] Of course, the forever argument has always been if we have not made any changes for one hundred years, and it is working, why change it now. Of course, like so many other changes, the initial shock of expansion may not look good, but over the last one hundred years and ten US Census Bureau reports of continuous population growth shows that going from only 435 House members to 592 (692 with the second formula) is a gradual growth with the cubic root rule (CRR). As with any enlargement theory, it will obviously be based on an ever-growing population to determine the variations in district sizes.[517]

The most impressive aspect of the Cubic Root Rule is it assigns the House of Representatives based on the reality today instead of one hundred years ago. The overall increase in the number of seats will result in two important outcomes. First, it balances the weight of each state's voting power, whether you are voting in Wyoming or California. The other and more important point is the seats in the House means elected congressmen will represent a smaller group of constituents, giving them a closer relationship with those voters.[518]

This Cube Root Rule should silence those defenders of the Electoral College because it functions by assigning each state electoral votes that are aligned using equality to get the total number of representatives and senators. It gives those advocates the protection it wants for the republic that guarantees a more significant voice of the voters.[519]

With a continuous expansion of the population, the Cube Root Rule will also change proportionately to provide the best fit between population and the total size of the House. Either way, both the Cube Root and the Wyoming Rule have strengths and weaknesses that gives voting power across the various states more equal. And that is what the expansion of the House and Electoral College will do for America.

The Cube Root Rule, using that 2020 census report giving us a new House size of either 592 (or 692 using the second formula), with an Electoral College of (695 or 795 using the second formula). It apportions additional seats to thirty-six states while eight remain the same and six lose one seat, and those are all states that have at least two House seats but also have extremely low populations.

Although both the Wyoming Rule and the Cubic Root Rule algorithms would increase the size of the House, we need to assess the extent to which of these increases would mitigate the problems of an increasing House that could become too large. The Wyoming rule simply determines the number of Representatives by dividing the nation's total population by the state with the smallest population, while the cube root rule asserts the ideal size of the House should be the cube root of the total population.[520]

Is the Cube Root Rule or the Wyoming Rule Best for Our Democracy?

This is a close-up of what a comparison of what would have occurred had we used the Cube Root Rule versus the Wyoming Rule. As Table 11.1 shows, the Cube Root Rule gives a continuous enlargement of the House from 1790 to 2020.

The amazing statistic is the fact that if you multiply the Cube Root of our population three times, you get a number that is closest to our actual national population. Cube rooting the 2020 Census of 331,797,124 would equal the 692 Electoral College, then minus 100 Senators gives us the 592 House members. The calculation is 692 x 692 x 692 = 331,373,888 giving us the closest formula to our actual 2020 Census. And the 592 House members equals our total population divided by 592 = 560,468 people per House member, a much more representative number than the 762,000 we have today. It also clearly represents the proper Electoral College votes that would be the most representative of the people, making every vote equal.

Using Table 11.1 as a reference to make a judgement on what is the best way moving forward to enlarging the House of Representatives, you only need to start with the time of the Reapportionment Act of 1929 and look at the numbers moving forward after that act. Of course, we cannot go back and change the past, but it clearly supports any initiative for using the cube root rule for enlarging the House and Electoral Votes that have been frozen at 435 for the last one hundred years. Yes, the Wyoming rule also shows continuous gains, but it also shows some out of character numbers for 1920, with 1,370 House members, compared to only 793 in 1960, then 549 in 1990, because it uses the smallest states of Nevada from 1920 to 1940, Alaska from 1960 to 1980, and finally Wyoming from 1990 to 2020. These up and down irregularities of the House members would create political havoc.

Therefore, in my opinion the Cubic Root Rule would help us catch up and move forward with a more constant gradual increasing trend all the way until 2060. Why? Because it is strictly based on the national population every ten years, meaning only significant negative changes in the population would result in any possible decrease. And another reason is the clear facts that our current political landscape does not show any potential for us to reach the majority needed to enact the NPVIC, the only method nearest to a straight up popular vote.

NOTE: The Wyoming Rule uses the smallest state which would be as follows:

- 1920–1950: Nevada would have been the smallest state.
- 1960–1980: Alaska would have been the smallest state.
- 1990–2020: Wyoming is the smallest state.

The Cube Root Rule uses the cube number of the population.

Ex: 2020 is 692 x 692 x 692

692 = Electoral College

592 = House Members

Table 11.1 – Cube Root vs Wyoming Rule vs Actual vs Continuous Apportionment

Census Year	Cubic Root Rule	Wyoming Rule		Actual
	EC Votes	EC Votes	Smallest State Rule	EC Votes
1790				138
1800				176
1810				218
1820				261
1830			*Wyoming Rule uses population of smallest state for all House Seat sizes.*	288
1840				294
1850				296
1860				303
1870				366
1880				401
1890				444
1900				447
1910				**531**
1920	475	1,466	NV	**531**
1930	500	1,514	NV	**531**
1940	512	1,287	NV	**531**
1950	534	1,036	NV	**531**
1960	564	893	AK	**537**
1970	588	775	AK	**538**
1980	610	670	AK	**538**
1990	629	652	WY	**538**
2000	655	674	WY	**538**
2010	676	646	WY	**538**
2020	692	677	WY	**538**

CHAPTER 12
The National Popular Vote Plan for the Future
NPVIC is Already in Progress

There is a plan to replace the Electoral College that your state may already be a part of the plan. It is called the National Popular Vote Interstate Compact, otherwise referred to as the NPVIC. So, what is this National Popular Vote Interstate Compact (NPVIC)? In its simplest terms, it is a compact, or contract, agreement between several states to award all their presidential electors to the winner of the national popular vote instead of the statewide vote.[521] If this NPVIC becomes law, it will guarantee the election of the president to the candidate who receives the most popular votes nationally, which truly applies the one person, one vote principle to presidential elections and makes every voter equal.[522]

The first person who offered the idea of states changing their laws to award their electors to the national popular vote winner was made by an attorney by the name of Dale Read Jr. He wrote a law review titled "Direct Election of the President without a Constitutional Amendment: A Call for State Action." At the time, even he thought the idea was radical and virtually nobody in the general public paid any attention.[523]

Then in 2001, a northwestern law professor, Robert Bennett suggested that the states could pressure Congress to pass a compact clause where the electors pledge their electoral votes to the winner of the national popular vote which would not require a constitutional amendment.[524]

A few months later, Yale law Professors Akhil Amar and his brother Vikram Amar from U-Cal Hastings suggested that the states should coordinate their efforts by passing uniform legislation under the Presidential Electors Clause and the Compact Clause in the Constitution. The structure would be the electors would join a compact where they would guarantee their vote for the national popular vote winner guaranteeing he/she be elected president. Bennett and the Amar brothers are generally credited as the intellectual godparents of the NPVIC.[525]

These two brothers wrote a three-part report on "How to Achieve Direct National Election of the President without Amending the Constitution," where they claimed, "Imagine this: Americans could pick the president by direct national election, in 2004 and beyond, without formally amending our Constitution." At that time, it only took eleven key states, which are also the eleven most populous states in 2004, to secure 271 electoral votes, or one more than the 270 needed to win. Those were California (55), Texas (34), New York (31), Florida (27), Pennsylvania (21), Illinois (21), Ohio (20), Michigan (17), New Jersey (15), Georgia (15), and North Carolina (15).[526]

John Koza, an inventor and computer scientist from northern California who was a longtime critic of the Electoral College, built on the writings of Bennett and the Amar brothers, and designed and created the National Popular Vote Interstate Compact (NPVIC) in 2004.[527] The NPVIC would be a compact building support one state at a time and be a legal method of enforcing states electors to commit to the goal of accepting the popular vote winner as the president when they reach the 270 majority. Koza began working with an election's attorney, Barry Fadem, to promote a publication *Every Vote Equal,* an over 1,000-page detailed explanation advocating the NPVIC that would eventually be announced in Washington, DC, on February 23, 2006.[528]/[529] Koza is now the chairman of the National Popular Vote nonprofit organization.

Koza's first edition of *Every Vote Equal* ran around 500 pages. Now in its fourth edition the book has taken on the methodical dismantling of every imaginable myth and misconception about the Electoral College and the popular vote. There are myths ranging from presidential elections, the Constitution, the privileges and immunities clause in the Fourteenth Amendment, small states versus big cities, mob rule, recounts, campaign spending and the current winner-take-all system we use today state-by-state. The book currently addresses 131 different myths. Koza claims, "the myths are the way legislators work. They are used to being in a battle with arguments thrown at them and throwing arguments back."[530]

As time went on, Koza realized that the more time he spent making his case to legislators, the more success he brought to his side. His political persuasion theory is "we convert people when we can sit down with them and talk about it as a policy issue and not a shouting match about ending civilization. Usually, we convert almost everybody because the facts support it. Of all the myths (131), there is not one you can say is convincingly true. Most are factually and demonstrably false."[531]

This NPVIC can only take effect when the "compact" is joined and the law is enacted by states representing a total of 270 electoral votes which represents a majority guaranteeing the candidate who wins the popular vote nationally will become the president. At this time, in 2024, the NPVIC has been adopted by eighteen states totaling 209 electoral votes, with Minnesota and Maine being the most recent states to join the compact. That puts the compact at 77.4 percent of the needed 270 electoral votes the states need to enact the NPVIC into law. The states have agreed that approved legislation to join the compact could not take effect until this threshold is reached. Once it does, those states will have the power to use their Electoral College votes to elect a winner according to the national popular vote. Obviously to be the winner the candidate who wins the popular vote also needs the winner-take-all basis in those NPVIC states to reach the 270 or more needed to be elected. So, in a sense, it preserves the Electoral College system functionally.[532]/[533]

In his book *Let the People Pick the President,* Jesse Wegman dedicates a major portion to the NPVIC. Wegman talks about how the "National Popular Vote Interstate Compact works as a contract among the states in which states join it and agree (with a firm commitment that eliminates faithless electors) to award all of their electors to the winner of the most states in the country, not to the winner of the most votes in their state. Once states representing 270 or more electoral votes join the compact, it automatically takes effect and awards 270 or more electors to the candidate that wins the popular vote in the country, thereby implementing a national popular vote and eliminating winner-take-all rules."[534]

The campaign that passed this compact started in 2006 with the first victory in Maryland in 2007, with ten electoral votes. Since then, seventeen more states have enacted the same law, for a grand total of 209 Table 12.1 below:

Table 12.1: Jurisdictions Who Have Enacted the Contract to Join the NPVIC

No.	Jurisdiction	Date adopted	Current Electoral Votes (EVs)
1	Maryland	April 10, 2007	10
2	New Jersey	January 13, 2008	14
3	Illinois	April 7, 2008	19
4	Hawaii	May 1, 2008	4
5	Washington	April 28, 2009	12
6	Massachusetts	August 4, 2010	11
7	District of Columbia	October 12, 2010	3
8	Vermont	April 22, 2011	3
9	California	August 8, 2011	54
10	Rhode Island	July 12, 2013	4
11	New York	April 15, 2014	28
12	Connecticut	May 24, 2018	7
13	Colorado	March 15, 2019	10
14	Delaware	March 28, 2019	3
15	New Mexico	April 3, 2019	5

16	Oregon	June 12, 2019	8
17	Minnesota	May 24, 2023	10
18	Maine	April 16, 2024	4
		Total	**209**
		Percentage of the 270 EVs needed	**77.4%**

Reference: https://en.wikipedia.org/wiki/National_Popular_Vote_ Interstate_Compact

Multiple editorials and journalists argue that the NPVIC encourages equality of voting power. At the present time in 2024, most of the states that have enacted the NPVIC are presently Democratic strongholds that also control state legislatures and governorships. There were some bipartisan efforts by Republicans until the recent political battles of the last eight years has widened the gap between the two parties. The work accomplished in the first ten years stalled after the 2016 election, and further deeper splits followed between the in the parties since Election Day in the 2020 election. Therefore, without bipartisanship the probability of the enactment of the NPVIC before the 2024 election is impossible.[535]

The following Table 12.2 illustrates states that have introduced legislation to their state legislatures through April 2024. The table lists all the state bills to join the NPVIC introduced in the state's most current legislative session. This includes all bills that are law, pending or have failed. The EV column indicates the number of electoral votes each state has.

These states total another 147 electoral votes, of which two states totaling fourteen electoral votes has already become law, while there are four states totaling fifty-four where it has failed. That leaves eight states totaling seventy-nine electoral votes still pending. If those state enacted the law, it would bring the grand total to 288, which would surpass the 270.[536] As of April 24, 2024, only Nevada, with another six electoral votes has passed both chambers and are only pending signature. That would bring the total to 215 electoral votes. Most NPVIC advocates now believe that the total remaining sixty-one electoral votes needed are well within reach, however, not enough time to be secured prior to the 2024 presidential election.[537] The hugest factor slowing down the process is the fact that in four states with fifty-four electoral have already failed, three states with eighteen electoral votes are Republican strongholds, three are battleground states totaling forty-two electoral votes, and only one, Virginia, with thirteen electoral votes is considered a Democratic state. With the ongoing partisan political turmoil, the best possible scenario would be a total of 235 by the end of 2024.

Table 12.2: Jurisdictions in the Process of Enacting the NPVIC

State	EVs	Latest action	Status
Alaska	3	May 3, 2023	Failed
Arizona	11	February 6, 2024	Failed
Florida	30	March 8, 2024	Failed
Kansas	6	April 30, 2024	Failed
Kentucky	8	January 4, 2024	Failed
Michigan	15	June 6, 2023	Pending

Mississippi	6	March 5, 2024	Failed
Nevada	6	May 22, 2023	Pending
North Carolina	16	February 27, 2023	Pending
South Carolina	9	25-Jan-23	Failed
Virginia	13	February 9, 2024	Pending
Wisconsin	10	April 15, 2024	Failed
TOTAL Evs	**133**		
Need to Pass	**61**		
TOTAL Enacted	**209**		

Reference: https://en.wikipedia.org/wiki/National_Popular_Vote_Interstate _Compact

How will this NPVIC work? Currently, the Electoral College is supposed to award the electors in each state all its electors on a winner-take-all basis until the presidential candidate has won at least 270 of the 538 electoral votes. The Constitution gives the states exclusive rights to control the way each state awards their electoral votes. Right now, forty-eight of the fifty states plus the District of Columbia the electoral votes are awarded on a winner-take-all to the popular vote winner of those states. The two exceptions since the nineteenth century are Maine and Nebraska who award their state popular vote winners only two electoral votes, then the winner of each congressional district gets one additional electoral vote. For example, if a candidate wins the Maine popular vote they would get two electoral votes. Then the two congressional districts would be split individually to the winner of each of those districts. So, the winner could get at least three or possibly four.[538]

Some of the motivation to enact the NPVIC is the fact that winner-take-all laws encourage candidates to focus disproportionately on the swing states because small changes in the popular vote in those areas produce large changes in the Electoral College vote. However, state winner-take-all laws can lead to decreases in voter turnout in the states without close races. Although polls are not always correct, they sometimes lead voters to choose whether to vote or not. There are also those that contend that the winner-take-all is unconstitutional because if you vote for the loser of the popular vote in your state your votes are ignored by the Electoral College.[539]

The problem with the current winner-take-all system is its responsibility of five of our forty-six presidents who came into office while losing the popular vote. Two of those, in 2000 and 2016, have occurred in the last six election cycles. This is in total constitutional contrast to the one person, one vote principle of democracy.[540] The bigger problem is if we do not make some changes this wrong winner theory will happen more frequently over and over in the upcoming future presidential elections.

Let us first look at the 2000 election where Al Gore won by over 500,000 in the popular vote. However, he lost the election because of only 537 votes out of six million in Florida. Had he turned those votes around he would have won the Electoral College to a 291-246 win. Another major factor takes Florida out of the picture, and that is New Hampshire and its four electoral votes. Gore is the only Democrat since 1988 to lose the state. Had he won New Hampshire, he would have won the election and reversed the Electoral College to 271-267.

Then in 2016, Clinton won by 2.9 million (2 percent) of the popular votes but lost the election because by a 304-227 winner-take-all Electoral College. Had she received 10,704 (0.23 percent) in Michigan, 44,292 (0.72 percent) in Pennsylvania and 22,748 (0.76 percent) in Wisconsin, she would have won by a 273 to 265 margin in the Electoral College.[541]

To compound this even more, two more elections since 2000 could have easily experienced the same fate. In 2004, if 59,393 voters, out of a total of over five million in Ohio voted for Kerry, Bush would have lost the election. Another debacle could have happened in 2020, if 5,229 in Arizona, 5,890 in Georgia, and 10,342 in Wisconsin equal to half of the total margin +1, changed their vote to Trump rather than Biden. Those 21,461 would have made the Electoral College vote a 269-to-269 tie that would have sent the vote to the House of Representatives for a contingent election. Because the incoming House votes in this contingent election, and the Democrats has control, the outcome would have still favored President Biden.[542] Those 21.461 votes were 326 times more important than the seven million voters elsewhere.

Supporters of the NPVIC compact contend that a national popular vote would encourage candidates to campaign equally for votes in both the competitive and noncompetitive states, while critics argue that candidates would have less incentives to focus on states with small populations where rural issues may not be addressed.

One of the many questions is whether the compact meets the test of constitutionality. According to the Supreme Court, there has been several rulings agreeing that "a compact is a contract." In this case, compacts are subject to the same principles of contract law and are protected by the constitutional prohibition against laws that may impair the obligations to contracts.[543]

According to Supreme Court findings, once a state enters an interstate compact, the state—like any individual, corporation, or any other entity—is bound by the compact's terms. In most cases, states do not engage in interstate compacts unless certain other states simultaneously agree to abide by the same compact. That would be the case with the NPVIC, as several interstate compacts have been made to define boundaries between two or more states. Another obligation would be on the part of the candidates themselves, who would also have to pledge their acceptance of the nationwide popular vote, making this part of the compact more difficult than the state-by-state commitments.[544]

One of the most vocal opponents is Tara Ross, the famously acclaimed author of *The Indispensable Electoral College: How the Founders' Plan Saves Our Country from Mob Rule*, contends that "the National Popular Vote (NPVIC) legislation that has proposed presents difficult legal issues that deserve careful, thoughtful consideration. Moreover, including NPV in an omnibus bill is a disservice to a constitutional institution that has served the country well for decades. These issues deserves independent evaluation."[545]

Detractors of the NPVIC list several objections to the idea. At the top of that list is the argument that the NPVIC Bill violates the Compact Clause of the US Constitution. An unconstitutional compact is one that "authorizes member states to exercise powers they could not exercise in its absence." Allocating electoral votes to the winner of the overall popular votes rather than the winner of a particular state gives those states more powers than they would not usually have, making the NPVIC unconstitutional. They also argue that this is the same as the faults of the current winner-take-all rule that ignores the votes of the people who voted for the Electoral College losing candidate.[546]

Another major problem would be how to handle a national recount since the states run the elections? The differences in state laws could potentially create huge issues that could last months to resolve only to end up at the steps of the Supreme Court. They argue that the thought of additional *Bush v Gore* incidents could create substantial disasters. They argue this is the reason that if we are looking for an alternative or reform of the Electoral College, we would need a constitutional amendment.[547]

A problem that the GOP has is the fact that all the states that have enacted or that are close to enacting the NPVIC are Democratic strongholds. Whereas all except four of the states that have partially passed this NPVIC or others that have not even considered passing it are Republican strongholds. On the state legislature level this could create problems of states joining then leaving the compact at will as the two major parties control certain states, which could change from one election to another. This could cause many states to withdraw from the NPVIC. However, the NPVIC has addressed this issue by administrating a clause that each state contract forbids any state from withdrawing from the compact without the voice of all fifty states. That may have its limitations that could rule the compact unenforceable both legally and practically at certain state levels.[548]

Article 2 of the Constitution empowers the state legislatures to decide how presidential electors are selected, and that power exists regardless of whether it is used or not. Sure, the attempted pre- or post-election withdrawals would violate the terms of the NPVIC, but the Constitution trumps any interstate compacts and does so whether Congress ratifies the NPVIC or not. States who do not comply or attempt to withdraw could face lawsuits pushing the Supreme Court to choose between two states.[549]

Although the detractors oppose the method of the NPVIC, the majority of those opponents believe that the use of a national popular vote in presidential elections must come sooner than later. Most of them agree that "if we were to rewrite the Constitution today, we would not adopt the Electoral College system that we have. However, our presidential elections are the byproduct of historical forces and political compromises made in 1787 that no longer have contemporary relevance or political resonance. Therefore, today the relevant question before us is not whether the Electoral College is the best way to elect the President, but whether the NPVIC is the right way to reforming our Presidential system, which it may not be. The only correct way to jettison the Electoral College is to adopt an amendment to the Constitution abolishes the EC and provides for the direct election of the president based on the national popular vote." Yes, that would be politically difficult; however, it is far preferable.[550]

The problem with a constitutional amendment is the requirement of getting ratification by three-quarters (38) of the states and the governor's certification signature even after passing both the House and the Senate by a two-thirds vote in each. This has always been the single largest hurdle to overcome. Although the Constitution has been amended twenty-seven times, reaching the thirty-eight states needed is nearly impossible due to partisan politics in the nation today.[551]

Supporters of the NPVIC look at our Electoral College in 2024 and realize that the winner only needs to win twelve states by one single vote to be elected president. Those states would be California (54), Texas (40), Florida (30), New York (28), Pennsylvania (19), Illinois (19), Ohio (17), Georgia (16), Michigan (15), North Carolina (15), New Jersey (14), plus any single state with three electoral votes to total the necessary 270 electoral votes to be the winner. Grant it five of these states are Democratic strongholds, two are Republican strongholds with the other five being battleground swing states. This makes the possibility nearly impossible due to push back by partisan politics. However, for this example let us imagine there was a candidate who could make this happen. That means that a candidate who was able to win twelve states by one single popular vote in only twelve states while ignoring the other thirty-eight completely and still become president of the United

States. This is a major issue and hurdle that both the Electoral College and the NPVIC must address before it can be enacted into law nationally.[552]

One of the biggest proponents of the NPVIC is *New York Times* journalist and author of *Let the People Pick the President,* Jesse Wegman, who makes his case for abolishing the Electoral College. He argues that the winner-take-all method causes millions of voters to become irrelevant, especially in battleground states. He brings up a major fact that the "winner-take-all electors is nowhere in the Constitution, which only addresses the number of electors each state gets." In his book *Let the People Pick the President,* he states that "if you are okay with the way the Electoral College works right now, with a statewide winner-take-all rule in almost every state, I just don't see what the argument is against using the winner-take-all rule, but for the whole country. The winner-take-all is assumed that it is in the Electoral College. It's purely extra-constitutional. States adopt it because it gives politicians extra clout in the election."[553]

In his book, Wegman tackles the problem that all of the battleground states use the winner-take-all method, putting them into a safe category where a candidate may not pay attention to these states. We all know that California will continue to be a Democratic stronghold while Texas will continue as a Republican stronghold, but because of their size and number of electoral votes, they will always be in play for candidates to campaign vigorously. That leaves ten or twelve states in each presidential election that become the battleground or "swing" states that determine the presidency. The states deciding the most recent elections are Wisconsin, Pennsylvania, Michigan, Arizona, North Carolina, Georgia, and Florida. Because these states are winner-take-all is the major reason the idea of holding a national popular vote election is treated differently by the two major parties.[554]

The idea of this NPVIC concludes that since our Constitution gives the states nearly total authority to decide how to award the electors to candidates, states either (1) give all their electors to the candidate who wins the popular vote in that state, (2) allocate them by congressional districts as Maine and Nebraska do, or (3) have the state legislators decide how to allocate them. The compact uses its power in a different way. Rather than the states giving their presidential electors to the candidate who wins the state popular vote, the NPVIC instead awards all the electors to whomever wins the national popular vote.[555]

In the beginning, it was not clear that the NPVIC would gain any support. Then Congressman Jamie Raskin, a Democrat from Maryland, fought tooth and nail until he got his state to enact the law. That was the first ten electoral votes in April 2007. During the next eight years 150 electoral votes from eleven states and the District of Columbia joined, bringing the total to 162 and that represented 60 percent of what was needed to get to 270. Over time all the work began to pay off and throughout the Obama presidency and especially after 2012, Republican lawmakers grew more open minded. Believe it or not, New York who is the pillar of liberalism, was a hard sell.[556]

The problem Koza saw was that he was a lifelong Democrat, and he knew he needed to get conservative Republicans on board, or he may never get to 270. He found Saul Anuzis, Pat Rosenthal and Ray Haynes, all Republicans who had worked with George W. Bush in 2000 and developed a plan to pitch the compact that was fundamentally conservative. Hayes said that "basically we are trying to change the minds of people who do not like change. It became a burden to persuade a very large jury that this is a good idea." But they remained confident and Anuzis believed it was a very deep dive, but he still had the conversations with his fellow Republicans.[557]

From 2018 to 2019, another five states and thirty-three electoral votes joined and in 2023, Minesota and its ten electoral votes joined to bring us to the 205 where we stand today, 75.9 percent of the 270 needed. All of this is completely speculation until there are enough states enacting the NPVIC to get to that magical 270 before we can talk about adoption and putting it in place. Today it is the only pending legislation that could affect the future of the Electoral College.

CHAPTER 13

One Person, One Vote: Making Every Vote Equal

Why the Electoral College Is Not a Democracy

"That this nation, under God, shall have a new birth of Freedom—and that government of the people, by the people, for the people, shall not perish from this earth."

-Abraham Lincoln, Gettysburg Address, November 1863[558]

The "One Person, One Vote" (OPOV) Doctrine Is Democracy

The OPOV Doctrine expresses the principle of equal voting representation by establishing that one person's voting power should be equivalent to another person, meaning no vote should carry more weight than others. Therefore, one could say the One Person, One Vote Rule slogan is used by advocates of democracy and political equality, especially regarding electoral reforms like universal suffrage and proportional representation.[559]

The fundamental core of democracy is simple, all votes should count equally. It does not matter whether you are black, white, rich, poor, from Rapid City, SD, or New York, NY, every voter should be counted equally. Today, that principle of a one person, one vote democracy is being challenged and violated by how we elect the president.[560] The word *democracy* comes from Greek words that means "rule by the people." President Lincoln captured this meaning best at Gettysburg by stating we are a "government of the people, by the people, and for the people."[561]

Beginning with the 1962 case of *Baker v Carr,* the Supreme Court established that redistricting is justifiable because "citizens are entitled to equal protection of the laws under the Fourteenth Amendment's Equal Protection Clause." Then again in the court's 1964 decision in *Reynolds v Sims* the one person, one vote (OPOV) doctrine that requires every state legislative district should be of equal populations. When each representative district has the same amount of people, all voters have equal opportunity. The same year in *Westberry v Sanders*, the Court extended OPOV to all US congressional districts. The court also made clear and defined "total population" means of all persons in a district, not just the registered voters.[562] Finally, in the 2016 case of *Evenwel v Abbott,* the Supreme Court was challenged again with the definition of "total population" and ruled 8-0 to uphold the OPOV doctrine that all legislative districts will be based on the total population of everyone in their districts, not the total number of voters. Now, virtually every jurisdiction in the country draws congressional districts using total populations.[563]

When the founding fathers designed the system of choosing the president in Article 2, Section 1, Clause 2 of the US Constitution, they gave the states exclusive authority to "appoint, in such manner as the legislature of that (state) directs, a number of electors equal to the number of senators and representatives to which that state is entitled, and those electors shall meet and vote for president."[564] This clause is the reason that the people of the United States do not have a nationwide popular vote directly for the president. Instead, it only gives the people the ability to choose the president indirectly through the elected presidential electors of that are committed to each candidate, and even that is not true in all fifty states, as many electors are predetermined by each political party long before Election Day.

Were they right? Yes, at least in 1787 when it made sense for a new nation with a new government, as the people did not have access to the information to make a credible decision as news took days or weeks to get to people instead of a split second like today. However, our founding fathers were vehemently opposed to allowing Congress to choose the president, which today would become a partisan political disaster.

According to what Jesse Wegman reported in *Let the People Pick the President,* that "one person, one vote are four words that sound like common sense today. So, if we apply one person, one vote for congressional and state legislative elections, why don't we hold the presidential elections to the same standards? One person, one vote represents what a democracy is and proves that the Electoral College is the most undemocratic element of our political system." He also makes it abundantly clear that "for the most part democracy has always won, except when it comes to the Electoral College."[565] OPOV is not just a principle of a democracy, but it should also be the constitutional law.

Stop Corrupt Voter Suppression and Expand Voting Opportunities

Voter suppression has a long history in America traced back to 1865. However, over the past few years it has been roaring back with vengeance and 2021 was a banner year for putting up barriers to stop the people's right to vote. These are not just anti-democratic, but they also border on violating our constitutional voting rights. We must stop these laws from continuing or we will lose our democracy[566]

These voter suppression laws have become a strategy used to influence the outcome of an election by discouraging or preventing certain groups of people from voting, more specifically blacks, Latinos, Asians, and other minority groups. They are used as antidemocratic tactics known as authoritarianism, which encourages political systems to reject democracy. These tactics range from suppressing voter fatigue through intimidations that are harming prospective voters at the polls. They are also used as a tactic to discourage the senior citizens who are fearful of election workers retaliation just because they are exercising their constitutional rights to vote.[567]

This has become a major issue facing our democracy today because there are groups of political extremists who have been pushing both the federal and state governments to create more and more voter suppression laws. Just since 2021, states have enacted hundreds of local and state laws creating more obstacles, making mail voting more difficult with more restrictions, making it harder to register to vote as well as the ability to stay on those voting rolls, empowering partisan poll watchers whose function is to harass voters and election workers, and extreme voter ID requirements. They have also enacted laws, like some states restricting same day registration to vote. Laws like this are dangerous, discriminatory, and racist.[568]

Other states have opened the doors to partisan interference that threatens election workers with criminal and civil penalties for aiding voters, and empowering supervisory election officials to pursue criminal action as more states are joining the parade of voter ID suppression.[569]

In 2023 alone, states enacted restrictive laws by interfering with election officials trying to send out legitimate mail ballots, empowering partisan state board of election officials to conduct voter registration audits, and empowering various board of election officials to go as far as determining changes to the actual vote counts. All these allow them to remove people from their constitutional right to vote.[570] The more we allow the government to restrict our eligibilities to vote by any means, especially elected officials themselves, the more we get further away from every vote being equally counted. This will eventually destroy our democracy.

Whether they are right, left, or center on the political spectrum, it is completely against the (small *d*) democratic process to allow the politicians to pick who their voters are, when it should be the other way around where it the voters rule the outcome of elections by choosing their elected representation, especially when it comes to who should be the president of the United States.[571] If we are truly going to be a nation of a one person, one vote democracy, there is no place for this type of political hypocrisy. The following are some of those laws and their states that are responsible for this continuous attempt to suppress the vote.

Let us start with doing away with Florida Senate Bill 90 that imposes restrictions on mail voting by severely limiting availability and accessibility and creating difficult ID requirements without alternatives for voters who lack certain information. This is another anti-senior citizen suppression because these older voters who have gone to the polls for 60–75 years should not have to succumb to this voter intimidation because they want a mail ballot. This is antidemocratic and violates a person's first amendment constitutional rights.[572]

The most embarrassing and disgraceful law is Georgia S. B. 202, which places a ban on food and water for voters who have waited for hours in long lines to vote. This is mostly due to individuals having to travel excessive distances to vote because of poll closures in nearby local districts are made to discourage higher voter turnout. If this is not unconstitutional, I do not know what is, and it must be overturned.[573]

Iowa Senate File 413 criminalizes election officials for protecting voters. They are imposing penalties and even criminal prosecution if election officials do not implement aggressive voter-roll purging. It must be reversed.[574]

Then Montana House Bill 176 ended a popular policy for simply partisan reasons. It eliminated same day voter registration because a politically powerful state representative said the law only helps young people who are "not on our side of the aisle." Really? Talk about unconstitutional, this one is blatant racism.[575]

Of course, who cannot forget Texas S. B. 1 that targets election workers and restricts mail voting by threatening election officials and workers with criminal penalties and jail time if they try to expand voter access, eligibility, and empowers partisan poll watchers to harass voters and election workers.[576]

On the side of democracy, some states along with Washington, DC, are counteracting these issues by gaining power with groups vigorously working to make it easier for mail ballot voting by expanding it to be legitimate if the ballot is post-marked by midnight on Election Day in every time zone, also creating more automatic registration policies that will increase same day voting and also extended days and hours of early in-person voting. Another bill being enacted in several places will open reserve parking spaces designated for curbside voting ballot drop-offs.[577] Afterall, the purpose of voting is to give every American who turns eighteen years old by Election Day a right to vote and exercise their political preferences. This will also increase the nationwide turnout of the younger generation. When an American registers to vote, they should stay on the voting rolls for life and should not be subjected to removal because of partisan voting roll audits.

States are restoring voting rights to people upon their release from prison, which is a big win for democracy. These former prisoners of non-violent crimes, who have been released from prison by midnight the day before election day, should be allowed to qualify for the same day registration policies of others and the right to vote that day. This group includes individuals who may have outstanding warrants, individuals in halfway houses, and any non-convicted person awaiting trial for nonviolent crimes, who also deserve that same right to vote because Americans are innocent until proven guilty in a court of law. Restoring these rights will encourage higher voter turnout, which should always be the goal of every legitimate politician.

Presidential Election Day should be expanded nationally so all voting precincts open no later than 6:00 a.m. and close no earlier than 9:00 p.m. in each time zone. This will give us larger turnouts, allowing people with odd working hours more time to vote. We also need to make Presidential Election Day a national holiday in all fifty states. There needs to be expanded early in-person voting that requires every state to begin at least fifteen days prior to Election Day for the same hours as mentioned above and shall not end until the Sunday night before Election Day at 9:00 p.m. in each time zone.

Another problem with voter turnout on Election Day is the news media giants wanting to be the first to release early projections based on exit polling while voters in other time zones still have time to go to the polls in zones other than the East. Polls closing at 9:00 p.m. eastern time when it is still only 6:00 p.m. on the West Coast could be leaving millions of people nationwide who may choose to stay home and not vote because they think their vote does not matter.

We should expand voting precincts to include public schools, municipal buildings, fire stations, police stations, local sports arenas and venues, churches, senior citizen centers, assisted living facilities, nursing homes, and hospitals. It is time to move voting precincts as close as possible to eligible voters instead of forcing people to make ridiculous travel plans because there may only be one polling place in any town, city, or county. That is a tactic used 200 years ago when we only had a horse and buggy. We must stop allowing towns, cities, or counties from having only one voting precinct, no matter how small that population may be in that area.

Many states have taken steps to provide more protection for election workers who are doing a thankless job as patriotic Americans while receiving threats on their lives as well as their families due to partisan radicalized campaign workers. These antidemocratic groups impose terror and fear on these workers to the extent they sometimes needing bodyguards.

All these enhanced laws and regulations should be enforced by the FEC (Federal Elections Commission), an independent regulatory agency tasked with administering and enforcing federal campaigns. These regulations should apply to the election of the president of the United States in all fifty united states and cannot be ignored by state or local governments. Remember we are a government of the people, for the people, and by the people, not an oligarchy that completely ignores the rule of law by representing their self-interests for personal and political power.

Some states have started making Election Day a holiday, so there is the potential for maximizing voter turnout. All of these policies are big wins for a more (small *d*) democratic society on the side of equal voting. The time is here to stop the unconstitutional antidemocratic restrictions and interference.

Why the Winner-Take-All Electoral College System Is Anti-Democratic

The use of the winner-take-all electoral votes is an antidemocratic procedure. Most people assume that the winner-take-all is part of the Electoral College in our Constitution. Both of those theories are *false*. Neither the winner-take-all nor Electoral College have ever appeared anywhere in the Constitution. There is evidence that supports reasons why winner-take-all is considered unconstitutional. It was never discussed by the framers of our Constitutions, which sufficiently shows it is an unconstitutional way to award the electors the electoral votes in each state because it ignores the people's votes for the loser in their state.[578]

Most Americans simply think since "we did it this way for centuries" makes it right and assume it is legal and in in the Constitution. The winner-take-all defenders rely on this "we've always done it that way" argument. The other arguments of "it's in the Constitution"(which it is not), or "states can choose presidential electors however they want" (which they can't because it does not comply with one person, one vote in the Equal Protection Clause), makes these theories unconstitutional.[579]

Looking ahead, we need to see that maybe the reality of the inequality of the Electoral College is created by the winner-take-all (WTA) rule for allocating electoral votes. The WTA says the person who wins the popular votes in a state gets all of the Electoral College votes for that state. This is how it is done in forty-eight out of fifty states, with the exceptions being Maine and Nebraska. And this WTA was a state creation, nothing to do with the federal government whatsoever.[580]

Originally states adopted the winner-take-all (WTA) because it seemed to amplify the power of their votes. This method makes absolutely no sense in the battleground states because those are where we have the closest elections.[581] The major flaw of the WTA Electoral College is the fact it allocates electoral votes only to the winner of the popular vote in each state. So, if you voted for the loser in your state, your votes are ignored completely, so basically, they did not count. That is not an encouraging fact for those promoting more people get out and vote to have the highest possible turnouts.

In the 2016 presidential election, fifty-five million voters were ignored simply because they voted for the candidate who lost their state. That was 42 percent of the total electorate, and that is not even counting the seven million people who voted for third-party candidates.[582] These wasted votes violate the constitutionally protected voting rights of the Fourteenth Amendment that established the principle of one person, one vote. This causes a lower turnout of voters because people will simply stay home and not vote at all because they feel their votes are not counted in states that are dominated by one party or the other.

An example we can use is to go back to 2016 and use the Maine and Nebraska methods of one of our "wrong winner" elections. Trump won 230 House district to only 206 for Clinton, which makes the election appear extremely close. But when you award the two bonus electoral votes each state gets under the Constitution, Trump won 30 states x 2 = 60, while Clinton takes only 20+DC x 2 = 42. Even though it makes it appear closer, the margin would still be Trump 290 and Clinton 248. This is slightly closer than his actual 304-227 (does not include the seven faithless electors) victory that was the winner-take-all. However, his 304 electoral total represented approximately forty million votes in the states he won, or just 30 percent of the nationwide 134 million, leaving approximately seventy-four million (55 percent) people of the nationwide voters being ignored because they voted for whoever lost their home state.[583]

Because the winner-take-all process gives the states the power to award electors any way they want, the people are stripped of any constitutional rights to be involved in the election of our presidents. In fact, we are not only unable to cast a direct vote for our choice for president, we also cannot even vote for our state's electors in most states where their legislature doesn't allow us to do. The state legislature's exclusive powers allow them to hand pick their electors according to how they will vote, even to the extent of ignoring the popular vote winners in certain states. It stands to reason that the states of Maine and Nebraska probably use the only structural way of awarding electors in a much more equal manner. At least they recognize the voters of each congressional district as viable voters with the right to choose who is awarded those electors.[584]

Imagine your governor announces that you may as well stay home because "we won't be counting your direct popular vote in our state." This happened in Colorado in 1876 when they were a new state that simply appointed three electors and awarded them to Rutherford Hayes without having a statewide popular vote by the people. That year gave us one of our five wrong winners, electing Hayes, who lost the nationwide popular vote by 3 percent but won the Electoral College over Sam Tilden 185-to-184. If Colorado had a popular vote and Tilden won it, he would have won those three electors and would have been elected president by the Electoral College vote 187-to-182.

Nowhere in our United States Constitution can you find the words "Electoral College," or "winner-take-all." Yet, the consequences of this WTA Electoral College allows a candidate to become president of the United States by winning a simple plurality of the votes in only twelve states in 2024. Those states would be California (54 electoral votes), Texas (40), Florida (30), New York (28), Pennsylvania (19), Illinois (19), Ohio (17), Georgia (16), North Carolina (16), Michigan (15), New Jersey (14), plus Washington, DC, with three electoral votes for a total of 271. This, as unlikely it could be possible, could happen without the candidate on the ballot in the other thirty-eight states.

Also, there are no federal election laws or constitutional statutes binding an elector's vote, which is why we have faithless electors. Therefore, if a candidate can form some sort of coup of faithless electors, he/she can gain additional electoral votes in a state that they did not win. The reason is the Constitution only calls for these presidential electors to "vote their conscience," leading to even more of the people's votes being ignored, tossed aside, which is the same as not even being counted. The probability of these things happening is highly unlikely, but not impossible. This is clearly another violation of the one person, one vote doctrine that every vote is equal. It also violates our Declaration of Independence that "all men (persons) are created equal."

According to Atlanta political attorney Jerry Sims, "a reasonable argument can be made that the allocation of state presidential electors on a winner-take-all basis is an unconstitutional denial of the equal protection law of the principle of one person one vote."[585] The Supreme Court and Congress need to end the winner-take-all along with the Electoral College because neither are in our Constitution. There is no reason for this inequality and there is no democratic justification for it. It has literally made our presidential elections the least democratic of any election in America.[586]

How the WTA causes the "Wrong Winner" Debacles

Then there is the case of the wrong winner syndrome that is far from being something new, and even further from being over. In the 1991 book *Wrong Winner: The Coming Debacle in the Electoral College,* the writers, David Abbott and James Levine, predicted that emerging political and demographic trends would lead to an increasing number of elections in which the candidate with the most popular votes nationwide would not win the election due to the Electoral College. They called these elections *wrong winners.*[587] Around half of all American presidential elections have been landslides, which are those having winners of the popular vote by a margin of more than 10 percent. However, in five presidential elections the popular vote winner lost the election to the Electoral College vote. That is a ratio of one out of six presidential elections that were not a landslide going to the loser of the popular vote, but winning the Electoral College, thus commonly referred to as the wrong winner.

There is the entire Chapter 4—Controversial Elections or Simply Wrong Winners—in this book totally dedicated to those senseless five elections, including two in the last six cycles (2000 and 2016), where we experienced presidents elected by the minority of the people. However, they were able to capture the necessary majority of electoral votes needed to be the winner.

Given the relative closeness and the ever-increasing divided political environment that exists in all nine of the presidential elections between 1988 and 2020, we can expect more and more problems with the winner-take-all rule in the future. The biggest supporters of the current winner-take-all that worship the Electoral College are the same partisan political groups that are the cause of candidates who lost the nationwide popular vote becoming an Electoral College wrong winner at the rate of 33 percent in this current twenty-first century. That percentage is not acceptable and must be corrected to save our democracy, giving the power of the vote back to the people not the politicians.

The abuse of this WTA can be traced to a hundred-year-old mistake which has become a major issue, as we continue to lockdown the nation at the same 538 electoral votes forever, which gives politicians more and more power over the American people's wishes by stealing elections and their political freedoms. That is not how democracy works.

Table 13.1 demonstrates those consequences caused by the five presidential elections won by the loser of the nationwide popular vote.

Table 13.1: Election Results Which the Popular Vote Winner Lost

1824		Votes	Pct	EC	Difference	
Andrew Jackson	D	151,309	40.5%	99	10.5%	+44,419
J.Q. Adams	R	122,440	32.7%	84		Winner

1876		Votes	Pct		Difference	
Samuel Tilden	D	4,286,808	50.9%	184	3.0%	+254,235
Rutherford Hayes	R	4,034,142	47.9%	185		Winner

1888		Votes	Pct		Difference	
Grover Cleveland	D	5,534,488	48.6%	168	0.8%	+90,596
Benjamin Harrison	R	5,443,892	47.8%	233		Winner

2000		Votes	Pct		Difference	
Al Gore	D	50,999,897	48.4%	266	0.5%	+543.895
George W. Bush	R	50,456,002	47.9%	271		Winner

2016		Votes	Pct		Difference	
Hillary Clinton	D	65,853,514	48.2%	227	2.1%	+2,868,686
Donald Trump	R	62,984,828	46.1%	304		Winner

The Inequality of the Contingent Election by the House of Representatives

The most frightening part of all this is the fact when no candidate reaches that 270 magic number of electors, the Constitution states that House of Representatives would choose the president. Although our founding fathers were against Congress choosing the president, they ratified the Twelfth Amendment in 1804 with this contingent election by the House of Representatives that still remains part of our Constitution. This is where the powers of partisan politics take over the outcome of the elections. Considering the extremely large political divide of our political parties today, partisan politicians could possibly elect a president that not only lost the popular vote, but a candidate who was less favorable to their chosen presidential electors even in the Electoral College voting. And that happened exactly 200 years ago in 1824.

At that time there was only one party, the Democratic-Republicans, who ran 4 candidates (see Chapter 2). As you see in Table 13.1, John Quincy Adams lost the national popular vote by 10.5 percent to Andrew Jackson. But that's not all, Jackson also won the electoral vote over Adams 99 to 84. However, due to the votes and states the other two candidates won no candidate reached the required 131 Electoral College majority. So, we had our one and only contingent election in the House of Representatives, where Adams formed a political back door alliance with Henry Clay to gain the necessary thirteen states (we only had twenty-four states then) to get him elected. Adams also was the beneficiary of the Twelfth Amendment that stated only the top three candidates would be considered in a contingent election, and because of the failing health of William Crawford who finished third, it gave fourth placer Henry Clay an opportunity to make his move. And that he did by establishing quid pro quo with Adams for him to get the Secretary of State position in exchange for Clay pledging his states that he won to Adams. This major back door political corruption ended the single party, and in 1828, we had our two-party system, the Democratic Party and the National Republican Party. The election of 1824 is one of the major reasons that advocates for abolishing the Electoral College hang their hats.

This contingent election in the House creates the furthest thing from being representative of the population as each state gets only one vote each. Today that would help the least populated state, Wyoming, with less than 600,000 people and only one House seat, to have more power than the largest most densely populated state, California which has 40,000,000 people and fifty-two House seats. That single Wyoming House member gets to cast the single vote for their state while a candidate needs a majority of the fifty-two members in the California House in order to gain that same single vote in the contingent election. That makes the one vote in Wyoming worth sixty-six times more than the California vote, proving its total violation of democracy as one tiny vote state gets the same power as fifty-two in a larger state. Obviously, this is not one person, one vote.

We can go on forever with these ridiculous comparisons of how one vote per state no matter what your population is, but I think you get the point.

"Gerrymandering" Is Political Corruption Regulating the House of Representatives

What is gerrymandering? In any republic voters are supposed to democratically choose their representatives, but *gerrymandered* districts allow politicians to choose their voters though *gerrymandering,*[14] which is a corrupt practice by powerful politicians and their political parties use to establish "safe seats" by reshaping their districts favorably. They create twisted, contorted districts shaped like the ones below to help a candidate predetermine election outcomes. Corrupt political consultants with sophisticated software regularly engage in this kind of manipulation.[588] Tables 13.2, 13.3, and 13.4 show us where *gerrymandering* got its name and what it looks like today. Table 13.5 shows two different districts in North Carolina. District 1 is somewhat closer to what a district of equality might look, but District 12 demonstrates the sins of gerrymandering at its best with totally contorted and twisted boundaries.

---

[14] *Gerrymandering* is a political species known by its varied and grotesque shapes with its monstrous size making it a particularly fierce predator of democracy.

Table 13.2: Where Did the Name Gerrymandering Come From?

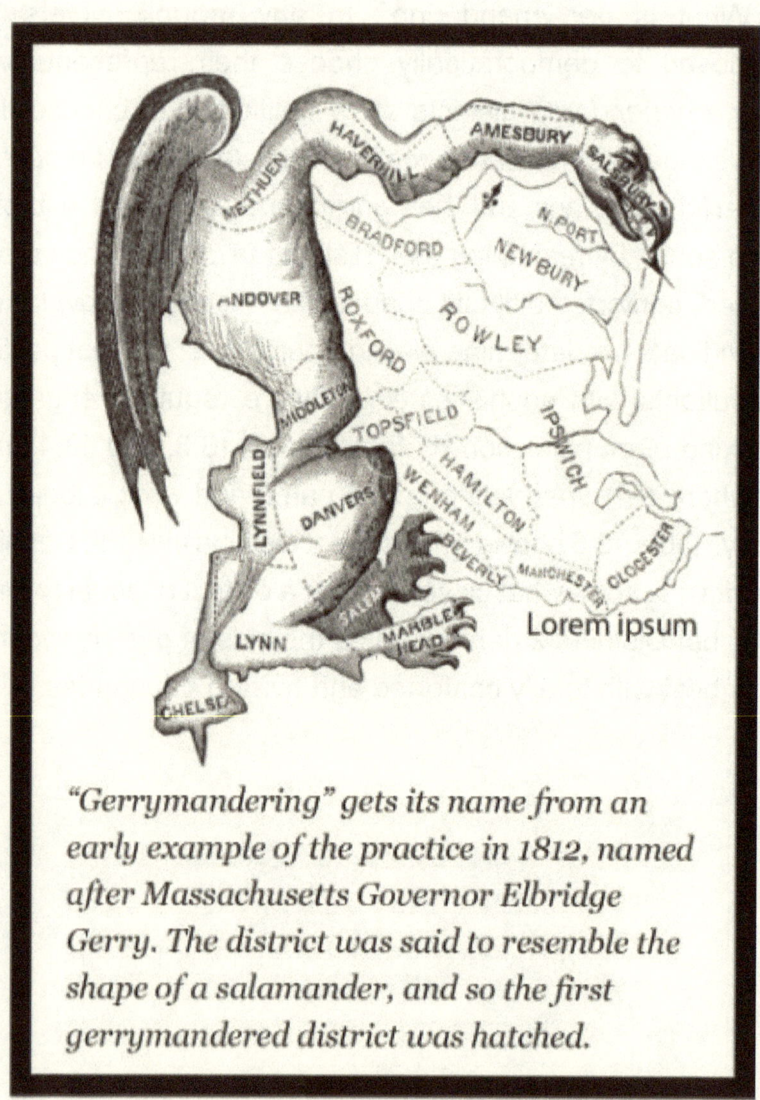

"Gerrymandering" gets its name from an early example of the practice in 1812, named after Massachusetts Governor Elbridge Gerry. The district was said to resemble the shape of a salamander, and so the first gerrymandered district was hatched.

Source: https://thirty-thousand.org/end-gerrymandering/

Table 13.3: What Gerrymandered Districts Look Like

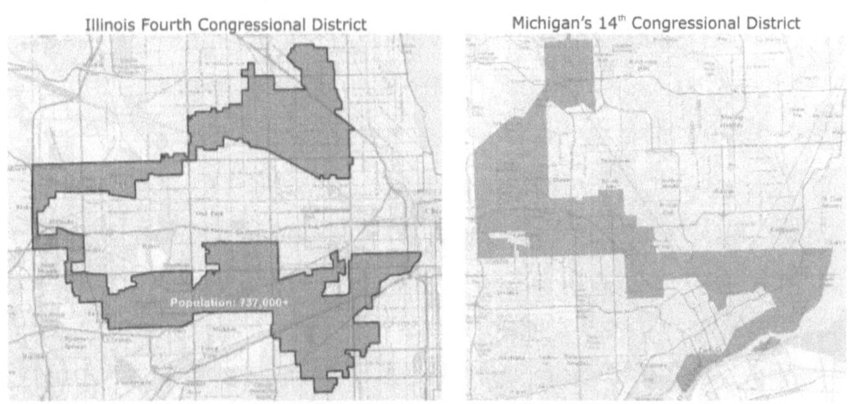

Source: https://thirty-thousand.org/end-gerrymandering/

Table 13.4: Another Look at What Gerrymandering vs. Democracy Can Look Like

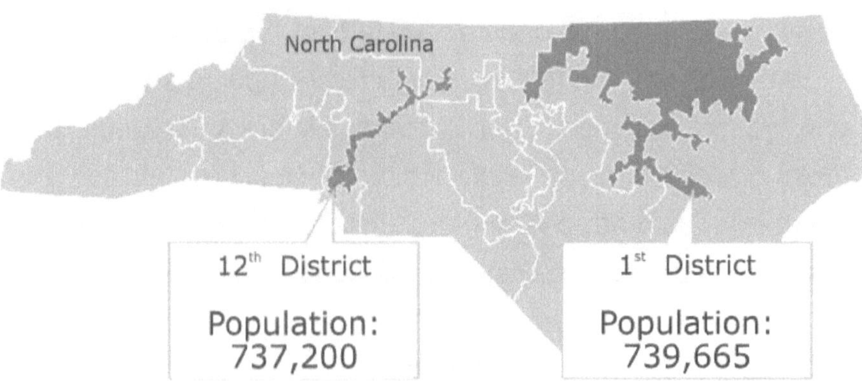

Source: https://thirty-thousand.org/end-gerrymandering/

How politicians and their powerful political parties achieve this is by keeping the average population of the US Congressional Districts as close to 760,000 people as possible.

Also, the larger the district the easier it is to be gerrymandered. Thomas Mann once said, "Redistricting is a deeply political process, with incumbents actively seeking to minimize the risk to themselves via bipartisan gerrymanders or to gain additional seats for their party via partisan gerrymandering."[589]

You might ask, "What does congressional districts have to do with presidential elections?" The mission of these congressmen who represent these districts is by controlling voter turnout in contorted drawn districts, which can cause a small swing in votes from these districts causing an overall affect in a particular state. This can assist the manner which can affect the winner-take-all method of assigning electoral votes. In states such as Maine and Nebraska, who do not use winner-take-all, it may be used by a political party to win maybe one or two additional congressional districts, possibly tipping a very close election to one candidate over the other.

Although you might think that this will become a moot point if we go to a nationwide popular vote, it is still a very important topic to representation in the House of Representatives, who ultimately could affect any presidential election that is sent to them in any potential contingent election in the House. This can be demonstrated in an extremely close presidential election, such as 2000, where a two electoral vote swing would have resulted in a 269-to-269 Electoral College outcome that would have sent the election to a contingent election in the House of Representatives for president. This most likely would give the Republican majority the states single votes needed to elect

Bush, even with Gore winning the nationwide popular vote by over 500,000.

Congress choosing the president is exactly what our founding fathers vehemently opposed. However, it remains a possibility of these contingent election disasters becoming more frequent in the future because of improper distribution of the electoral votes. Due to our "we could care less what our people think" attitude of partisan politicians in Congress, the matter of contingent elections becomes a partisan vote along party lines as House members can totally ignore who the people of their own states chose in the popular vote in their state. These gerrymandered district representatives will be part of the tally of each state leading to an unconstitutional inequality toward properly drawn districts. This can give an opportunity to use this unfair weight of their votes to obstruct that one contingent vote for a state.

Consider that there are questionable ways for political parties to use their own state constitutions to assist in drawing gerrymandered districts to favor one political party over another. If these actions seem fraudulent, it's because they are. When challenged in higher courts, over 90 percent of the time, these unfairly drawn districts lost. The questions surrounding the use of this method of drawing district lines that make absolutely no sense is one of the most partisan means of holding power in Washington, DC. Remember it only takes a one vote majority to elect a Speaker of the House or the congressional and Senate majority leaders. Imagine one of these disastrous gerrymandered districts is held by a representative who goes on to have the power of becoming the Speaker of the House of Representatives. With the power that person can use in their gerrymandered district can be used to do whatever it takes to hold that power in the nation's capital while giving orders to their political cronies and other party leaders and taking order from the high powered lobbyists and the billionaire donors instead of committing themselves to the needs of the people who elected them.

The answer to stopping gerrymandering is easy to look at and decide want should be; however, each individual state legislature is the only one responsible for making it happen. The only solution we can offer is to work vigorously to defeat incumbents who are abusing these powers because they have usually been there too long and usually stopped working "for the people" long ago. So it is up to a government "by the people and of the people" to send a message to these overzealous politicians that it is time to leave your office to a person who will represent the people by doing the only thing we can do, VOTE them OUT!

CHAPTER 14
The Final Word

How America Can Keep Its Democracy

"as we speak, there are those who are preparing to divide us, the spin master's and negative ad peddlers who embrace the politics of anything goes. Well, I say to them tonight, there's not a liberal America and a conservative America— there's the United States of America. There's not a black America and white America and Latino America and Asian America; there's the United States of America. The pundits like to slice-and-dice our country into Red States and Blue States, Red States for Republicans, Blue States for Democrats. But I've got news for them too … we are one people, all of us pledging allegiance to the same Stars and Stripes, all of us defending the United States of America"- **Barack Obama, DNC Keynote Speech, July 27, 2004**[590]

Excessive Rural State Power Has Ignored Expanding Urbanization for One Hundred Years

As we discussed in Chapter 7, after the Constitution was proposed in 1787, James Wilson, a prominent founder, believed "the House of Representatives in a century would have more than six hundred members." These numbers seem exaggerated, yet here we are two centuries later, and the House has been frozen at 435 for the last one hundred years. In 1789, James Madison stated, "The sense of the people of America that the number of representatives ought to be increased, but should not be left at the discretion of the government to diminish them below that proportion which certainly is in the power of legislatures as the constitution now stands ... and I confess I always thought this part of the Constitution to be defective, referencing Article 2 using presidential electors instead of the people's vote."[591]

One of the major problems can be traced to a part of the very first amendment in our Bill of Rights of 1789 was never ratified. It was called *Article the First*—which would have ensured the number of the House of Representatives would forever increase equally along the lines of the total population of each state. For some strange reason, this proposal was never sent to the states for ratification but instead was replaced with a defective version that sabotaged our democracy.[592]

The first *Apportionment Act of 1792* in accordance with the Fourteenth Amendment established that Congress would pass Apportionment Acts following each decennial census, apportioning the number of House seats granted to each state proportionately to their respective total populations. Prior to the 1910 Census, Congress consistently abided by the methods of apportionment that adequately enlarged the House of Representatives every ten years from 105 in 1790 to 433 in 1910. Table 14.1 shows the consistent increase in the House seats every ten years. The size of the congressional districts also increased accordingly from 34,436 to 210,583. Of course, as the House continued to enlarge so did the Electoral College increase from 138 to 531. This consistency not only brought the voters closer to their representatives, but it also automatically increased the Electoral College to make that number more in line with the vote by the people.

Table 14.1: Apportionment of the House and the Electoral College 1790–1910

Starting Year	Census Year	House Size	Electoral College	Average Pop/District
1793	1790	105	138	34,436
1803	1800	142	176	34,609
1813	1810	181	218	36,377
1823	1820	213	261	42,124
1833	1830	240	288	49,712
1843	1840	223	294	71,338
1853	1850	234	296	93,020
1863	1860	241	303	122,614
1873	1870	292	366	130,533
1883	1880	325	401	151,912
1893	1890	356	444	173,901
1903	1900	386	447	193,167
1913	1910	433	531	210,583

Source: https://en.wikipedia.org/wiki/United_States_congressional_apportionment [593][594][595]

Then on August 8, 1911, a law was passed to determine how many members the House would have "permanently" called *An Act Fixing the Size of the House of Representatives (a.k.a. Apportionment Act of 1911),*[596] which caused a population paradox[15], which is a counterintuitive result of some procedures of apportionment.[597] A good example is 1900 when a larger more rapidly increasing population of Virginia lost a seat to the smaller slower growth of Maine.

Changes in our population were due to our increased immigration with primarily Europeans flocking to America and shifting the population from smaller rural states to the larger urban states from 1900 to 1930. During that period both chambers of Congress were controlled by a Republicans majority. Also, lobbyists with lifelong political connections to rural states caused Congress to simply do nothing with apportionment in 1920. The reason was primarily due to the fact that a reapportionment would have shifted the political power away from the less populated rural states to the more populated urban states.[598] This failure to ignore the urban population growth allowed Congress to control the voters instead of the people controlling the fate of their democracy.

By 1930, there still were no new apportionments except one House seat added for each new state, New Mexico and Arizona, even though the population increased 33 percent. The major cause for this population increase was the growth of the urban population to 56 percent, while the rural population decreased to 43 percent as shown in Table 14.2 below.

---

[15] Population paradox is a counterintuitive result of some procedures for apportionment; for example, a rapidly growing state can lose seats to a slower growing state.

Table 14.2: The Urbanization of America 1790–2050[599]

Year	Urban	Rural
1790	5.13%	94.87%
1810	7.26%	92.74%
1830	8.77%	91.23%
1850	15.41%	84.59%
1870	25.68%	74.32%
1890	35.42%	64.58%
1910	45.85%	54.15%
1930	56.16%	43.84%
1950	64.15%	35.85%
1970	73.60%	26.40%
1990	75.30%	24.70%
2010	80.77%	19.23%
2030*	84.84%*	15.14%*
2050*	89.16%*	10.84%*

* = Projected

Source: https://www.statista.com/statistics/269967/urbanization-in-the-united-states/

The urbanization of America was taking place coast to coast as states such as California grew by 147 percent from 2.3 million in 1900 to 5.7 million people by 1930 while New York grew 74 percent from 7.2 million to 12.5 million and Pennsylvania grew 52 percent from 6.3 million to 9.6 million over the same period. That resulted in a 76 percent increase in just three states over those thirty years while the entire country grew 61 percent over the same time frame. If Congress did an apportionment in as it had done after every decennial census since 1790, it would have added seventy-seven seats to the House, giving it 463 members after the 1930 Census, which would have been 559 electoral votes. But it never happened because Congress violated both the one person, one vote equality and the rules of democracy, as every vote was no longer equal. If we factor in projected population increases to 2050, the urban and suburban communities will outweigh the rural areas 89.16 percent to only 10.84 percent.

How Continuation of the Reapportionment Act of 1929 Could Destroy Our Democracy

After Congress passed the *Act Fixing the Size of the House of Representatives on August 8, 1911,* it set the size of the House at 433. It allowed for one member each for the soon-to-be states of Arizona and New Mexico, making it 435. What happened next created the most nondemocratic law imaginable with the passing of *The Reapportionment Act 1929,* permanently freezing the maximum number of seats in the House of Representatives at 435. This act has been referred to by other names such as *The Permanent Apportionment Act of 1929* or *The Redistribution Act* because it only adds electoral votes to states by taking them away from other states.

The act has predetermined procedures for automatic reapportionment, which only means a redistribution of the same House seats after each census, discontinuing proper apportionment forever. Meanwhile, the Electoral College remains stuck at 538 since 1929 due to this act. This was done by a Congress dominated by rural politicians who stood to lose their power in a quickly growing urbanization, so they failed to reapportion seats following the 1920 census.

Reapportionment takes effect in the elections beginning three years after the last census. For instance, the 2020 Census will affect the presidential elections in 2024, 2028, and 2032, without any regard to increases in the populations of any state. This makes it a potentially unconstitutional way of apportioning our Electoral College because it does not take into consideration how many states have increased their population since the prior census without additional electoral votes. It also does not account accurately the population increases taking place in some of the fastest growing states, such as Nevada, Arizona, and North Carolina, by ignoring the three years of changes after the census.

This cannot be demonstrated any more than in the upcoming 2024 presidential election, which has unjustly removed one electoral vote from the State of California, which has never done before in our history even though their 2020 US Census revealed increased by over two million (2,232,801 to be exact) from the last census in 2010. Other states losing one electoral vote in 2024 are New York, Pennsylvania, Illinois, Ohio, Michigan, and West Virginia. On the reverse side of the redistribution are Texas gaining two electoral votes, while Florida, North Carolina, Colorado, Oregon, and Montana each gained one. The other thirty-seven states remained the same and did not lose any electoral votes for 2024. This does not follow the constitutional principle that one person, one vote makes every vote equal. These redistributions that started in 1930 have cost states a total of 149 redistributed House seats and electoral votes while the same amount was added to other states as constant redistribution does not consider increases in populations from 1930 to 2020. All this because of the *Reapportionment Act of 1929.*

Table 14.2, it clearly shows the urbanization of America increased to 80.77 percent in 2020, while rural population fell to 19.23 percent. There is also a substantial amount of proof that urbanization in America will continue up to the 2050 projections. This will happen without rewarding these states for their equal share of increases in the Electoral College unless changes in the apportionment are made properly, or this will be a mockery of our principles of democracy.

Moving to Table 14.3, we look at what the apportionments of the House of Representatives and Electoral College should have been from 1790 to 2020. The portion on the left shows the lack of reapportionment of the House from 1910 to 2020, because the House was frozen at 435. On the right side, the numbers starting with the 1910 Census shows what the normal apportionment of the seats in the House and Electoral College would have been with proper decennial apportionments from 1910 to 2020. It would have increased the Electoral College votes from 531 in 1910 to 680 in 2020. Those 149 redistributed House seats represent the difference caused by the unfair redistribution of House seats and Electoral College votes because the *Reapportionment Act of 1929* discontinued the principles of one person, one vote.

The formula used in Table 14.3 is like the formula used by the *cubic root rule* if it were used in 2020 for the House of Representatives and Electoral College because it relates to a steady increase that is more closely proportionate and representative of the actual increases in the census every ten years.

These fatal inadequacies must be fixed to bring the House and the electoral vote to where it should be. Congress must repeal and replace the *Reapportionment Act of 1929* and add the House seats and electoral votes to where they should be for the 2028 presidential election and continue this apportionment after the 2030 Census and every decade to come.

Table 14.3: Actual vs. Expansion of the House of Representatives and Electoral College Using Prior Formula 1790–2020

Start Year	Actual Apportionment				Proper Apportionment if Prior Methods were used		
	Census Year	House Size	EC Votes	Avg Pop / District	House Size	EC Votes	Avg Pop/ District
1793	1790	105	138	34,436	105	138	34,436
1803	1800	142	176	34,609	142	176	34,609
1813	1810	181	218	36,377	181	218	36,377
1823	1820	213	261	42,124	213	261	42,124
1833	1830	240	288	49,712	240	288	49,712

1843	1840	223	294	71,338	223	294	71,338
1853	1850	234	296	93,020	234	296	93,020
1863	1860	241	303	122,614	241	303	122,614
1873	1870	292	366	130,533	292	352	130,533
1883	1880	325	401	151,912	325	401	151,912
1893	1890	356	444	173,901	356	444	173,901
1903	1900	386	447	193,167	386	447	193,167
1913	1910	**433**	**531**	**210,583**	**433**	**531**	**210,583**
1923	1920	**435**	**531**	**243,728**	**446**	**542**	**237,716**
1933	1930	**435**	**531**	**280,675**	**463**	**559**	**265,300**
1943	1940	**435**	**531**	**301,164**	**464**	**560**	**284,837**
1953	1950	**435**	**531**	**334,587**	**483**	**579**	**313,304**
1963	1960	**435**	**537**	**410,481**	**485**	**585**	**369,738**
1973	1970	**435**	**538**	**469,088**	**517**	**620**	**393,060**
1983	1980	**435**	**538**	**510,818**	**520**	**623**	**435,665**
1993	1990	**435**	**538**	**571,477**	**547**	**650**	**454,680**
2003	2000	**435**	**538**	**646,946**	**548**	**651**	**513,544**
2013	2010	**435**	**538**	**709,760**	**571**	**674**	**540,710**
2023	2020	**435**	**538**	**761,169**	**577**	**680**	**575,038**

This number crunching determines what our House of Representatives should look like with proper apportionment from 1910 to 2020. Table 14.3 represents those changes and makes every vote equal. Later we will show how these numbers could have affected some of the closer elections between 1960 and 2020 and changed the final results.

America Must Repeal and Replace the Reapportionment Act of 1929

For America to save its democracy, it must first regain control of the House of Representatives. The only way this can be done is to repeal and replace *The Reapportionment Act of 1929* that stopped all future apportionments of the House of Representatives at the same 435 members since the Census of 1920. Many people believe that the repeal and replacement of *The Reapportionment Act of 1929* would need a constitutional amendment. The answer to this question is simple, "No, it does not need an amendment." This act was created by a Congress that was dominated by rural politicians who would have lost their power to the urbanization of America.[600] From 1900 to 1930, urban population grew from 35 percent to 56 percent as rural populations dipped from 65 percent to 44 percent. Contrary to the people's beliefs, apportionment and "Reapportionment is NOT in the Constitution," those changes are done at the discretion of Congress.

During the past one hundred years, according to a study done by the American Academy of Arts and Sciences, shows that the lack of apportionment since 1920 displaced and redistributed 149 House seats and electoral votes to maintain a continuous House at 435 seats. This displacement created districts of over 761,000 constituents each in 2020, and if this displacement continues, we will see districts in the future with populations exceeding one million people.[601] The actual amount today should be closer to the 575,000 reflected below in Table 14.4. This table demonstrates what the proper House of Representatives would have been if we continued apportionment from the 1910 to 2020 Census, which adds an additional 149 electoral votes to a Congress that restricted our representation in the House to this oligarchy of 435 while the population tripled from 106 million in 1920 to over 331 million in 2020.

Table 14.4: Actual vs Proper Expansion of the House and Electoral College since 1900

Start Year	Actual Apportionment				Proper Apportionment if Prior Methods were used After Each Census		
	Census Year	House Size	EC Votes	Avg Pop/ District	House Size	EC Votes	Avg Pop/ District
1903	1900	386	447	193,167	386	447	193,167
1913	1910	433	531	210,583	433	531	210,583
1923	1920	435	531	243,728	446	542	237,716
1933	1930	435	531	280,675	463	559	265,300
1943	1940	435	531	301,164	464	560	284,837
1953	1950	435	531	334,587	483	579	313,304
1963	1960	435	537	410,481	485	585	369,738
1973	1970	435	538	469,088	517	620	393,060
1983	1980	435	538	510,818	520	623	435,665
1993	1990	435	538	571,477	547	650	454,680
2003	2000	435	538	646,946	548	651	513,544
2013	2010	435	538	709,760	571	674	540,710
2023	2020	435	538	761,169	577	680	575,038

Source: The Case for Enlarging the House of Representatives
https://www.amacad.org/sites/default/files/publication/downloads/2021_Enlarging-the-House.pdf

Table 14.5 gives us the state-by-state results based on what apportionment would have been had Congress continued apportionment after every census since 1920 and what it should be in the upcoming elections of 2024 and 2028. This would be based on proper apportionment if it was done regularly every ten years as it had been done from 1790 to 1910, giving us new Electoral College totals. The reason we are showing the changes in the Electoral College is to get a better view of the presidential elections of 2000 and 2016, and how these new Electoral College numbers if done correctly may not have produce the two wrong winners of the last six cycles. The final column shows the next two election cycles of 2024 and 2028, which is where the new Electoral College totals should be in those elections.

Table 14.5 – NEW Electoral College Properly Apportioned

State	Census Population 2000	EC Actual	Census Population 2010	EC Actual	Census Population 2020	EC Actual	NEW EC S/B
Alabama	4,447,100	9	4,779,736	9	5,030,053	9	11
Alaska	626,932	3	710,231	3	736,081	3	3
Arizona	5,130,632	8	6,392,017	11	7,158,923	11	14
Arkansas	2,673,400	6	2,915,918	6	3,013,756	6	7
California	33,871,648	54	37,253,956	55	39,576,757	55	71
Colorado	4,301,261	8	5,029,196	9	5,782,171	9	12
Connecticut	3,405,565	8	3,574,097	7	3,608,298	7	8
Delaware	783,600	3	897,934	3	989,948	3	4
Florida	15,982,378	25	18,801,310	29	21,570,527	29	40
Georgia	8,186,453	13	9,687,653	16	10,725,274	16	21
Hawaii	1,211,537	4	1,360,301	4	1,460,137	4	5

Idaho	1,293,953	4	1,567,582	4	1,841,377	4	5
Illinois	12,419,293	22	12,830,632	20	12,822,739	20	24
Indiana	6,080,485	12	6,483,802	11	6,790,280	11	14
Iowa	2,926,324	7	3,046,355	6	3,192,406	6	7
Kansas	2,688,418	6	2,853,118	6	2,940,865	6	7
Kentucky	4,041,769	8	4,339,367	8	4,509,342	8	10
Louisiana	4,468,976	9	4,533,372	8	4,661,468	8	10
Maine	1,274,923	4	1,328,361	4	1,363,582	4	4
Maryland	5,296,486	10	5,773,552	10	6,185,278	10	13
Massachusetts	6,349,097	12	6,547,629	11	7,033,469	11	14
Michigan	9,938,444	18	9,883,640	16	10,084,446	16	20
Minnesota	4,919,479	10	5,303,925	10	5,709,752	10	12
Mississippi	2,844,658	7	2,967,297	6	2,963,914	6	7
Missouri	5,595,211	11	5,988,927	10	6,160,281	10	13
Montana	902,195	3	989,415	3	1,085,407	3	4
Nebraska	1,711,263	5	1,826,341	5	1,963,333	5	5
Nevada	1,998,257	4	2,700,551	6	3,108,462	6	7
New Hampshire	1,235,786	4	1,316,470	4	1,379,089	4	4
New Jersey	8,414,350	15	8,791,894	14	9,294,493	14	18
New Mexico	1,819,046	5	2,059,179	5	2,120,220	5	6
New York	18,976,457	33	19,378,102	29	20,215,751	29	38
North Carolina	8,049,313	14	9,535,483	15	10,453,948	15	21
North Dakota	642,200	3	672,591	3	779,702	3	3
Ohio	11,353,140	21	11,536,504	18	11,808,848	18	23
Oklahoma	3,450,654	8	3,751,351	7	3,963,516	7	9
Oregon	3,421,399	7	3,831,074	7	4,241,500	7	9
Pennsylvania	12,281,054	23	12,702,379	20	13,011,844	20	25
Rhode Island	1,048,319	4	1,052,567	4	1,098,163	4	4
So. Carolina	4,012,012	8	4,625,364	9	5,124,712	9	11
South Dakota	754,844	3	814,180	3	887,770	3	4
Tennessee	5,689,283	11	6,346,105	11	6,916,897	11	14
Texas	20,851,820	32	25,145,561	38	29,183,290	38	53
Utah	2,233,169	5	2,763,885	6	3,275,252	6	8
Vermont	608,827	3	625,741	3	643,503	3	3

Virginia	7,078,515	13	8,001,024	13	8,654,542	13	17
Washington	5,894,121	11	6,724,540	12	7,715,946	12	15
West Virginia	1,808,344	5	1,852,994	5	1,795,045	5	5
Wisconsin	5,363,675	11	5,686,986	10	5,897,473	10	12
Wyoming	493,782	3	563,626	3	577,719	3	3
D.C.	572,509	3	601,723	3	689,575	3	3
TOTALS	281,422,356	538	308,745,538	538	331,797,124	538	680
House	513,544	435	540,710	435	575,038	435	577

How does this affect the election of the president? According to the executive branch in the Constitution, Article 2, Section 1, Clause 3, it states, "Each state shall appoint, in such manner as the (state) legislature may direct, a number of electors, equal to the whole number of senators and representatives to which the state may be entitled in Congress."[602] Because the number of presidential electors is tied to the total number of members in the House plus the Senate, it is that number that gives us the total electoral votes.

Let us talk a bit about these "presidential electors" that are in the Constitution. The abuse of this clause gave state legislatures the exclusive power to choose the presidential electors, who are the actual people doing our voting for president in forty-eight of our fifty states, who are mostly voting on a WTA basis but that is not etched in stone. It is the state legislatures who appoint these presidential electors as they see fit, who then elect the president by this WTA method that also is not found anywhere in our Constitution. This winner-take-all is simply another myth that people believe is in our Constitution. That is a myth because it is *not* in the Constitution. However, it is these electors who ultimately elect their choice for president, which in two in the last six elections cycles, has gone against the wishes of the voters of America, violating the one person, one vote, where every vote is not equal while abusing a government of the people, by the people, and for the people.

To further the effects of this inequality of electoral votes, all we need to do is make a few comparisons. First, let's look at where we are today with only 538 electoral votes. If we compare the population per voters in California is 732,903 per each of the fifty-four electoral votes while Wyoming has only 192,573 per electoral vote. Therefore, the weight of a voter in Wyoming is worth 3.81 times the power of a voter in California. The median population per voter is Maryland and Missouri whose votes are worth 617,000, which still gives Wyoming 3.18 times more power per voter. Another outrageous comparison is the percentage of the total population difference of California with 11.928 percent compared to only 0.174 percent in Wyoming, giving Wyoming voters 6.86 times the power over California. Another comparison of the Electoral College inequality is the population to electoral vote ratio. California with almost forty million people has sixty-eight times the number of people as Wyoming does with their 577 thousand; however, it gets only an eighteen times electoral votes than Wyoming, fifty-four to three.

Enlarging the House will reflect one person, one vote making every vote equal, would be accomplished by this increase in the Electoral College to 680, with a House of Representatives of 577. Using these numbers, go back to the comparison of Wyoming vs. California. Wyoming will still be 192,573 per electoral vote, but California is reduced to 557,419 per electoral vote, which decreases Wyoming to 2.89 times more power per voter. The reason for the difference closing by only 0.29 is our Constitution gives every state two bonus US Senators per state, without any regard to populations, which gives two bonus electoral votes per state. However, when we look at the 577 House seats, the gap is very close with Wyoming being 577,719 and California is 573,576, with the overall fifty state population per House seat being 575,038. This would be the place we need to be in 2024 in order to have equality for every voter.

All this considered, a repeal and replacement of The Reapportionment Act of 1929 with "an act providing for equal decennial apportionment following the U.S.Census Report every ten years with a formula that will continuously increase the House of Representatives and the Electoral College by no more than a 10 percent increase in any ten-year period and also will not lose any seats unless there is a 5 percent decrease or more in population during any ten-year period. The standard population used per House seat in 2020 will be 575,038 per district nationwide. The act will begin with the 2028 presidential election."

The formula we should adapt would be a sort of hybrid combination of both the Wyoming Rule and the Cubic Root Rule. Both can be used with projections all the way to 2060 ensuring this continuous increase in our Electoral College.

Many Illegal Presidential Electors Became Conspirators of the Insurrection

As discussed throughout this book, we know that changing the presidential electoral system is not a simple task because our founding fathers created Article 2, Section 1, Clause 2 of the Constitution which use the words "in such manner as their legislature thereof may direct," giving exclusive power to the states to choose our presidents indirectly through a system using presidential electors, which later took became known as the Electoral College. Contrary to the belief of most Americans the Electoral College is not part of the Constitution.

This indirect way presidential electors are chosen for the past 200 years created significant flaws that are absolutely in need of reform or abolishment. Otherwise, we will continue to have more and more "wrong winner" elections won by the loser of the national popular vote of the people because of a handpicked majority of the 538 presidential electors elected the president. Because the Constitution allows states to have exclusive power "to appoint their presidential electors by whatever means their state legislatures see fit," this system can also lead to more contingent elections when no candidate gets a majority of the electors and the president is chosen by the House of Representatives, which happened exactly 200 years ago in 1824.

Historically this meeting of these electors was always a simple formality that most people were not even aware of where each state did this voting and or on which date. The other meeting, on the infamous day of January 6, was formerly a simple joint meeting of Congress, with the Senate president (the vice president) simply reading the official count of the certified submission of each of the individual state slates of electors. This day was a simple exercise in every election from 1796 through 2016, with the exceptions being only 1824 and 1876. It became such a formality that the news media just announced to Americans an "oh by the way, Congress met today and completed its certification of the electoral votes confirming the election of candidate X as officially the president of the United States."

Of course, we remember what happened in 2020, when the results of the election were proven to ultimately be totally correct and the required majority of certified electors elected President Biden the president, we had the worst attack on America since 9/11. On January 6, 2021, the Insurrection of our United States Capital was an attack by domestic terrorists and white nationalist organizations associated with fascist far-right, authoritarian, ultranationalist political groups representing a contempt for electoral, political, and cultural democracy. Their mission was to form a coup that would attempt to overturn the legal election of the President with the use of "illegal" electors, demanding that the election was somehow "stolen" from the outgoing President Trump.[603]

This heavily armed mob of domestic terrorists not only attacked our US Capital, but they attacked our democracy and the rule of law. Conspiracy theories and outright lies still exist the 2020 election and has escalated to becoming very real threats of future extremist violence by traitors of our Constitution.[604]

The scary and sad part of this are the facts that there is an army of candidates in or trying to gain seats in Congress that are dedicated to a doctrine they are prepared to follow to deny and refuse to accept the legitimate outcomes of elections, no matter how conclusive these elections are. There are plans for them to use whatever criminal tactics are available to suppress the vote by terrifying Americans to stay away from the polls or face unjust intimidation. This is just another example of how the use of this indirect presidential elector system could be fraudulently manipulated and influenced in the future because the people's votes of America continue to be ignored time and time again by this Electoral College monster.

The problems of that famous January 6, 2021, caused such a concern that Congress created and passed the Electoral Count Reform and Presidential Transition Improvement Act (ECRPTIA) OF 2022 (see Chapter 3). It makes it completely clear that the vice president's role would be simply and solely ministerial with no power to determine, accept, reject, or adjudicate disputes over improper use of multiple versions of presidential electors from the same state.[605] The process will be as simple as reading the certifications while the clerks tabulate the slate of electors.

The National Popular Vote Is the People's Choice

We need to start this conversation by refreshing our opening page of the introduction that asks, "Do you remember voting for the president of the United States in a mock classroom election in your elementary, middle school, or high school days?" We use this example here again because it is the best place to start discussion why Americans should be choosing their president by a National Popular Vote because it will be the only direct vote by the people. This one person, one vote would equalize everyone's vote and award the election to the person who gets the most total popular votes in all fifty states combined. The obvious logic is the president of the United States should not be elected by each individual state with an indirect system known as the Electoral College, which is the total number of senators and House members. Presidential elections should be a combined total of all fifty states collectively voting as one United States of America. Unfortunately, that is not the case.

The Electoral College is discussed in detail throughout this book. It is the major problem in our political system and could endanger our democracy if left unchanged. We only need to look back at Chapter 2, "The Early Electoral College Failures and the Twelfth Amendment," that our earliest government realized that this plan of presidential electors electing the president hit a wall not once, but twice, in the elections of 1796 and 1800. First in 1796, the presidential electors chose a president and vice president from different parties, and then in 1800, the electors ended in a tie. Remember these were technically the first two presidential elections in our history, and it was very early in our new government. And what did our government do? It took a step back, analyzed the problems, and took the action quickly with the Twelfth Amendment that fixed the issue by creating the idea of a joint ticket where the president and vice president are jointly attached to the same electors on the same ballot.

The fact still remains that the way the Electoral College chooses a president is a 235-year-old antique that is in dire need of reform or abolishment. The problem is abolishment would require a constitutional amendment, which there are only twenty-seven amendments in history, and ten of those happened prior to 1791. There have been 11,000 unsuccessful attempts to amend the Constitution, of which 700 of those involved the Electoral College and they all failed. The reason for those failures is simple, the ratification of a constitutional amendment requires a two-thirds vote in the House (290 votes), followed by a two-thirds vote in the Senate (67 votes), and then a three-quarters (38 states) ratification by the states along with a signature of certification by each of those governors. It does not require the signature of the president.

Due to our current political atmosphere of partisan politics, opposition argues that the Electoral College is indispensable. They claim that our founding fathers created it as some sacred part of our Constitution, and if it is not broken, we do not need to fix it.[606] These arguments could not be furthest from the truth. However, the use of an amendment to change the Electoral College could drag on for years due to the power of political selfishness of the partisan politicians who oppose a nationwide popular vote.

Of those 700 failed attempts to amend the Constitution to abolish the Electoral College, none came closer to becoming law than the Bayh-Cellar Amendment of 1969. The Gallup polls showed bipartisan support for the direct popular vote for president reaching a high of 80 percent due to a very contentious 1968 election. Bayh-Cellar believed their plan would generate the highest voter turnouts because the election would be placed solely in the hands of the people with a nationwide direct popular vote of the people. In other words, presidential elections would be representative of one United States of America, not fifty different ideas by each individual states creating their own methods of electing a president for the entire country.

A national direct vote by the people is a plan that has been supported by many of our contemporary presidents, both then and now. The amendment overwhelmingly passed the House of Representatives by a 338-70 vote. But the Senate dragged their feet with a continuous filibuster causing only a 54-36 vote, and it died there a year later. At that time, it was not only one party in the Senate opposing this law, but it was both Democrats and Republicans who did not want to sacrifice their political power.[607]

A study done by the Pew Research Center in in Table 14.6 below in 2023, a study was done asking if you "think about the way the president is elected in this country, would you prefer to change the current system so a system that the candidate who receives the most votes wins, or would you prefer to keep the current Electoral College system?" The table shows that Americans prefer to change to the National Popular Vote by almost two to one, a 65 percent to 33 percent margin, over the current Electoral College system. Except for after the 2016 election, these numbers have remained consistent since 2000. Electing the president by who receives the most popular votes of the people gives everyone one person, one vote voting power.[608]

Table 14.6: A National Popular Vote Is What Americans Want

**By almost 2 to 1 Americans
want the Popular Vote,
Not the Electoral Vote, to decide
who is the President**
*Question: Electing who is the
president would you prefer?*

	Popular Vote	**Electoral Vote**
2000	58%	37%
2004	61%	35%
2008	61%	36%
2012	62%	35%
2016	55%	41%
2020	60%	37%
2024	65%	33%

Source: PEW RESEARCH CENTER

Source: https://www.pewresearch.org/short-reads/2023/09/25/majority-of-americans-continue-to-favor-moving-away-from-electoral-college/

When Pew Research Center asked that same question in Table 14.7, except changing the research to political party affiliation, the vote was more divided. Over 82 percent of those who identify as Democrats overwhelmingly want to change to a popular vote by the people while only 47 percent of Republicans favored that idea.

One of the most interesting pieces of information that is related to these numbers is explained in Chapter 4, "Controversial Elections or Simply Wrong Winners." Coincidentally, all five elections won by the candidate who lost the popular vote but were elected president by the Electoral College were all Republican candidates.[609] We cannot stake claim that this was necessarily the reason, but as recently as 2017, a year after the 2016 wrong winner debacle, only 27 percent of Republicans wanted the popular vote to 74 percent of the Democrats. The closest these numbers ever came since 2000 were in 2012 when it was a 69 percent Democrat to 54 percent Republican margin. Those numbers were the lowest percentage for Democrats, and the highest number for Republicans since 2000.

Table 14.7: Most Democrats support moving to a National Popular Vote for President while Republicans are more divided

Questions: What % say presidential elections should be changed so the candidate who receives the most nationwide popular vote wins?

	DEM	REP
2000	73%	46%
2004	75%	40%
2008	71%	50%
2012	69%	54%
2016	74%	27%
2020	84%	33%
2024	82%	47%

Source: PEW RESEARCH CENTER

The Current Status of the National Popular Vote Interstate Compact (NPVIC)

What many of us do not realize is we can go to a national popular vote without a constitutional amendment, and this is already in progress with the National Popular Vote Interstate Compact (NPVIC) discussed extensively in Chapter 12. The key to this NPVIC is the law will provide an equality of voting power directly to the people.

What is this NPVIC and what is a compact? According to the Supreme Court there has been several rulings agreeing that "a compact is a contract." In this case, compacts are subject to the same principles of contract law and are protected by the constitutional prohibition against laws that may impair the obligations to contracts.[610] So a compact is a contract by law according to the Supreme Court, which would become an agreement between the states to award all their presidential electors to the winner of the National Popular Vote.

The compact cannot take effect until the total of the electoral votes of the states enacting the NPVIC reaches 270 or more. Then it guarantees the winner of the NPVIC will be president, which automatically makes certain that the winner of the National Popular Vote is elected president. It is the best way to apply the one person, one vote principle to all future presidential elections. Supporters of the NPVIC compact believe a national popular vote will encourage candidates to campaign equally for votes in both the competitive and noncompetitive states because every vote will count equally across America. No more votes will be ignored by a controversial winner-take-all system.

By 2019, NPVIC legislation had been introduced in all fifty states. As of April 15, 2024, eighteen states and the District of Columbia had adopted the NPVIC, for a total of 209 electoral votes, leaving the plan sixty-one votes shy of the 270, as shown in Table 14.8. Most of the eighteen states that have enacted the law have been Democratic strongholds in most of the presidential elections since 1992, which shows in the last two columns how many times each of those states voted Democrat or Republican. As you can see, all except two have vote Democrat all eight times, whereas Colorado has gone Republican three times and New Mexico once. The fact those numbers exist is a sad thought for our democracy. This is proof that one party does not want to work together in bipartisanship to achieve one person, one vote, making every vote equal.

Then there is the issue of reapportionment as it is done now. This is one of the main problems because if the NPVIC is going to work it has to become law before the 2030 Census. Why? So that no political interests interfere with the electoral vote totals and make ridiculous deductions like it did after 2020 by taking electoral votes away from states like California, New York, Pennsylvania, and New Jersey. All these states grew in population from 2010 to 2020, yet they all lost an electoral vote.

There are currently nine states totaling eighty-seven electoral votes where legislation is pending. Those are Alaska (3), Arizona (11), Kansas (6), Kentucky (8), Michigan (15), Nevada (6), North Carolina (16), South Carolina (9), and Virginia (13). Any combination totaling sixty-one would reach the magic number of seven.

The state most likely to pass next before is Nevada, with six electoral votes, which has passed both legislative chambers and is pending final approval. Also, Michigan, with its fifteen electoral votes, has passed the lower chamber and is pending in the upper chamber. If both of these passes by the end of 2024, the total will reach 230.

That leaves Arizona, which is in committee with eleven electoral votes, but probably will not pass until 2025. Virginia with an additional thirteen electoral votes has been tabled to be continued to committee sometime in 2025, following the 2025 elections. If these can all pass by the end of 2025, the NPVIC should be a 254, 94.07 percent of the 270 needed.

If we judge where it goes next, we have to look at two states that have been heavily Democratic since 1992, New Hampshire (4) and Wisconsin (10). Those could give the NPVIC 268, just two shy of 270. This would leave twenty-six states left to get only three more electoral votes before the 2028 election and the NPVIC becomes a real thing. The most interesting of all those states is Pennsylvania and its nineteen electoral votes. A state that has voted Democrat in seven of the last eight elections has not even brought the NPVIC to committee?

Table 14.8 – The NPVIC and its future projections

The Future of the National Popular Vote Interstate Compact					
No.	Jurisdiction	Date adopted	Current EC Votes	VOTED Since 1992	
				Dem	Rep
1	Maryland	April 10, 2007	10	8	0
2	New Jersey	January, 13, 2008	14	8	0
3	Illinois	April, 7, 2008	19	8	0
4	Hawaii	May, 1, 2008	4	8	0
5	Washington	April, 28, 2009	12	8	0
6	Massachusetts	August, 4, 2010	11	8	0
7	District of Columbia	October, 12, 2010	3	8	0
8	Vermont	April, 22, 2011	3	8	0
9	California	August, 8, 2011	54	8	0
10	Rhode Island	July, 12, 2013	4	8	0
11	New York	April, 15, 2014	28	8	0
12	Connecticut	May, 24, 2018	7	8	0
13	Colorado	March, 15, 2019	10	5	3
14	Delaware	March, 28, 2019	3	8	0
15	New Mexico	April, 3, 2019	5	7	1
16	Oregon	June, 12, 2019	8	8	0
17	Minnesota	May, 24, 2023	10	8	0
18	Maine	April, 15, 2024	4	8	0
Total EV Enacted / % of 270			209	77.40%	
19	Michigan	Passed Committee	15	7	1
20	Nevada	Passed Committee	6	6	2
21	Arizona	In Committee-Pending	11	2	6
22	Virginia	Pending 2025	13	4	4
Most Likely to Pass by 2025			45		
Possible Total by 2025 / % of 270			254	94.07%	

23	New Hampshire	Failed in 2018, 2019	4	7	1
24	Wisconsin	Failed April 2024	10	7	1
Failed - Need to try again			**14**		
Percentage of 270 by 2028			**269**	**99.63%**	
25	Pennsylvania	Never Attempted	19	7	1

One of the issues today is the NPVIC will be impossible to put into law before the 2024 presidential election. A potential problem that exists is the fact most of the pending electoral votes are Republican strongholds who mostly oppose the NPVIC. There are another forty-two electoral votes who are considered battleground states that would be as difficult to win in an election year. Some hope is the fact there are those who have failed at the legislative level, Wisconsin (10) and New Hampshire (4), that need another legislative push to be the most likely to enact the NPVIC next.

However, the possibility of it passing without bipartisanship will be extremely difficult because our current partisan politicians are encouraging Americans to believe in conservative radical ideas. On the other hand, these same deniable politicians consider the NPVIC as some sort of liberal progressive idea that only benefits the Democrats. There is substantial evidence to prove these conservative radical ideas are wrong.

Even though there remains many obstacles to pass the NPVIC, it still appears to be the best road to a National Popular Vote for president for a few reasons. First, the NPVIC avoids the need for an amendment to the Constitution because it still retains the presidential electors that are mandated in the Constitution. Second, it can be done without increasing the size of the House of Representatives because every vote in every state is counted equally making the United States of America a single entity when we vote for president. Do we need to enlarge the House? Absolutely, but that could be secondary to the National Popular Vote. Finally, the NPVIC eliminates the atrocious winer-take-all that literally ignores the millions of people who have voted for the candidate that may have lost their state.

With all of these considerations I believe that we must work to convince our local state legislatures that it is time to pass the NPVIC, so every vote counts equally.

What Can We Expect in 2024?

Throughout this book, we have analyzed every aspect of the Electoral College system and how there is a need for reform, replacement, or abolishment. All of these can only be done with a constitutional amendment, which due to the political landscape we have is definitely impossible. Especially before the 2024 election. So let us look at what can happen in this cycle.

First, we have discovered that the true villain of this Electoral College is actually the winner-take-all in forty-eight states. This can be completely changed with immediate legislation in any state legislature who chooses to do so. We can start with what the Constitution, Article 2, Section 1, says about the presidential electors and break it down. It states "(a) each state shall appoint, (by whatever exclusive right the state chooses to do so without interference by Congress); (b) in such manner as the legislature thereof may direct, (by popular vote, vote by their legislature, or maybe even chosen by the governor); (c) a number of electors, equal to the whole number of senators and representatives to which the state may be entitled in the Congress," (this is simple to explain); and (d) but no senator or representative or person holding an Office of Trust or Profit under the United States shall be appointed an elector" (any registered voting citizen who is not an elected official).[611] Herein lies the problem because of this completely unconstitutional winner-take-all method that ignores any person who votes for the loser of their state.

Secondly, in 2020, more than fifty-two million people of the 151 million voters were basically votes that did not count. If states decide this year in a reasonable amount of time before the election that they want to use another method, such as the district plan or the fractional plan or the whole number plan, or any other proportional plan, they can do so. The Constitution does not say anything about every state using the same method; otherwise, Maine and Nebraska could not do what they do.

Third, the Constitution also states the actual enumeration of the electors cannot exceed one elector per every 30,000 people, with no mandate for a maximum amount of people. This is the part that would need an amendment and will not happen in 2024.

Taking this all of this in account, it is the right of every state legislature to vote to completely ignore their previous use of winner-take-all and choose individually how to distribute their presidential electors. Therefore, the elimination of the WTA could change the upcoming election in 2024, making the Electoral College as close to one person, one vote where every vote is equal. Here is how something like that may look:

1. Going back to Chapter 8, Table 8.2, it reveals the Republican and Democratic strongholds that are practically "certain" in every election since 1964. This would start with sixteen Democratic states plus Washington, DC, totaling 194 Electoral College votes, and twenty Republican states totaling 155 Electoral College Votes. That is thirty-six of the fifty states to begin with.

2. Next, we can review the potential outcomes in the so-called five battleground states. Again, looking at Chapter 8, Table 8.3, we know right now, those are Wisconsin (10 electors), Pennsylvania (19), Michigan (15), Georgia (16), and Arizona (11). If we use just 2016 and 2020 as examples, these states went all Democrat in 2020 and all Republican in 2016. They total another seventy-one Electoral Votes, if added to the Democrat stronghold states totaling 194 Electoral Votes you have a total of 265 (5 short of victory), or if you add these to the Republican stronghold states totaling 155 Electoral Votes, it gives you 226.

3. Another scenario is if the battlegrounds follow the normal characteristics from Table 8.3, the Democrats have won Wisconsin, Pennsylvania, and Michigan seven of the last nine cycles, and Republicans won Georgia and Arizona seven of the last nine cycles. That would give Democrat Kamala Harris a total of 238, and Republican Donald Trump a total of 182.

4. In addition to scenario #2, if the Republicans continue to rule Florida, which they won six out of the last nine with 30 electoral votes, and North Carolina that they won eight out of the last nine with 16 electoral votes, it would give Trump a 272, enough to win the election, no matter what the rest of the country did. This would be done by winning twenty-four states.

5. Democrats, on the other hand, have dominated Nevada with 6 electoral votes and New Mexico with 5 in seven out of last nine, totaling twelve electoral votes. Again, using scenario #2 this would give Harris 276, which would be enough to win with twenty-two states.

The importance of all this analysis and projections is the importance the five battleground states play, plus two more Republican and two more Democratic states with high winning percentages, meaning almost every election since 1988 has come down to what happens in nine states plus the Washington, DC, out of the total fifty states.

This is very significant going into an election cycle that could very easily end up 269 to 269, which would send the election coincidentally to a contingent election in Congress for the first time since exactly 200 years ago in 1824, with a popular vote winner becoming wrong winner #6. All this put aside in the grand scheme of things the most important advice we can give all registered voters or more specifically all eligible voters, VOTE! VOTE! VOTE! The people's voice must be heard or our 238 year old Democracy could be at stake.

INDEX

END NOTES

Chapter 1: How the Electoral College Was Created

1   William C. Kimberling, "Essays in Elections: The Electoral College" (1992), the Origins of the Electoral College, https://uselectionatlas.org/INFORMATION/INFORMATION/electcollege_history.php.

2   William C. Kimberling, "Essays in Elections: The Electoral College" (1992), the *Origins of the Electoral College,* https://uselectionatlas.org/INFORMATION/INFORMATION/electcollege_history.php.

3   Harry Searles, (Oct 2015), "First Continental Congress–1774," R. Squared Communications, LLC, American History Central, https://www.americanhistorycentral.com/entries/first-continental-congress/; "Second Continental Congress–May 1775–1781," R. Squared Communications, LLC, American History Central, https://www.americanhistorycentral.com/entries/second-continental-congress/.

4   History.com Editors (Oct 2009) (updated Dec 2019), *Articles of Confederation*, A&E Television Networks, https://www.history.com/topics/early-us/articles-of-confederation.

5   Christopher H. Schroeder, Interactive Constitution, made by the National Constitution Center, *"Matters of Debate: The Most Compelling Reading of the Vesting Clause,"* https://constitutioncenter.org/interactive-constitution/interpretation/article-ii/clauses/347#the-vesting-clause-by-christopher-schroeder.

6   Deena C. Bouknight, *The Daily Herald*, Chicago, Illinois, Mar. 13–14 2017, "45 US Presidents or More?" https://www.columbiadailyherald.com/news/20170313/45-us-presidents--or-more.

7   History.com Editors, (2010),*Constitutional Convention Begins,* A&E Television Networks, https://www.history.com/this-day-in-history/constitutional-convention-begins; ConstitutionFacts.com, "The Constitutional Convention," https://www.constitutionfacts.com/us-constitution-amendments/the-constitutional-convention/.

8   Patti Wiginton, (2018), "What Was the Virginia Plan?" ThoughtCo., https://www.thoughtco.com/the-virginia-plan-4177329, American History from Revolution to Reconstruction and Beyond, http://www.let.rug.nl/usa/documents/1786-1800/the-anti-federalist-papers/the-virginia-plan-(may-29).php.

9   Patti Wiginton, (2018), "What Was the Virginia Plan?" ThoughtCo., https://www.thoughtco.com/the-virginia-plan-4177329, American History from Revolution to Reconstruction and Beyond, http://www.let.rug.nl/usa/documents/1786-1800/the-anti-federalist-papers/the-virginia-plan-(may-29).php.

10   Patti Wiginton, (2018), "What Was the Virginia Plan?" ThoughtCo., https://www.thoughtco.com/the-virginia-plan-4177329, American History from Revolution to Reconstruction and Beyond, http://www.let.rug.nl/usa/documents/1786-1800/the-anti-federalist-papers/the-virginia-plan-(may-29).php.

11   Robert McNamara, (2019), "What Was the New Jersey Plan?" https://www.thoughtco.com/new-jersey-plan-4178140, https://4.files.edl.io/0d10/01/28/19/032750-a7b5b372-0e50-4522-9568-3779603805dd.pdf, Leonard W. Levy, (1986), "New Jersey Plan." Encyclopedia of the American Constitution, https://www.encyclopedia.com/politics/encyclopedias-almanacs-transcripts-and-maps/new-jersey-plan.

12   James Madison, "Notes of the Debates in the Federal Convention of 1787," Teaching American History, https://teachingamericanhistory.org/library/document/notes-of-debates-in-the-federal-convention-of-1787-2/.

13   William C. Kimberling, *Essays in Elections: The Electoral College (1992), the Origins of the Electoral College,* https://uselectionatlas.org/INFORMATION/INFORMATION/electcollege_history.php.

14   Matt Riffe, "James Wilson, Popular Sovereignty, and the Electoral College," Constitution Daily—Smart Conversation from the National Constitution Center, Nov. 28,2016, https://constitutioncenter.org/blog/james-wilson-popular-sovereignty-and-the-electoral-college.

15   Jonathan Bernstein, *Favorite Sons Won't Be Fortunate Sons,* Feb. 3, 2011, *The New Republic Magazine,* https://newrepublic.com/article/82816/favorite-sons-wont-be-fortunate-sons.

16 Donald Applestein, Esq., "The Three-Fifths Compromise: Rationalizing the Irrational," Feb. 2, 2013, *Constitution Daily*, https://constitutioncenter.org/blog/the-three-fifths-compromise-rationalizing-the-irrational/.

17 Robert Yates, *Notes of the Secret Debates of the Federal Convention of 1787,* The Avalon Project: Yale Law School, Lillian Goldman Law Library, https://avalon.law.yale.edu/18th_century/yates.asp.

18 Alexander Hamilton, "The Mode of Electing the President" from *Federalist No. 68*, from the *New York Packet* (Mar. 14, 1788), RE: Electoral College, https://guides.loc.gov/federalist-papers/text-61-70#s-lg-box-wrapper-25493455.

19 Alexander Hamilton, "The Mode of Electing the President" from *Federalist No. 68*, from the *New York Packet* (Mar. 14, 1788), RE: Electoral College, https://guides.loc.gov/federalist-papers/text-61-70#s-lg-box-wrapper-25493455.

20 Eric Black, "Why the Constitution's Framers Didn't Want Us to Directly Elect the President," 10/17/2012, MINNPOST, a nonprofit, nonpartisan journal, https://www.minnpost.com/eric-black-ink/2012/10/why-constitution-s-framers-didn-t-want-us-directly-elect-president/.

21 Eric Black, "Why the Constitution's Framers Didn't Want Us to Directly Elect the President," 10/17/2012, MINNPOST, a nonprofit, nonpartisan journal, https://www.minnpost.com/eric-black-ink/2012/10/why-constitution-s-framers-didn-t-want-us-directly-elect-president/.

22 Eric Black, "Why the Constitution's Framers Didn't Want Us to Directly Elect the President," 10/17/2012, MINNPOST, a nonprofit, nonpartisan journal, https://www.minnpost.com/eric-black-ink/2012/10/why-constitution-s-framers-didn-t-want-us-directly-elect-president/.

23 Eric Black, "Why the Constitution's Framers Didn't Want Us to Directly Elect the President," 10/17/2012, MINNPOST, a nonprofit, nonpartisan journal, https://www.minnpost.com/eric-black-ink/2012/10/why-constitution-s-framers-didn-t-want-us-directly-elect-president/.

24 Eric Black, "Why the Constitution's Framers Didn't Want Us to Directly Elect the President," 10/17/2012, MINNPOST, a nonprofit, nonpartisan journal, https://www.minnpost.com/eric-black-ink/2012/10/why-constitution-s-framers-didn-t-want-us-directly-elect-president/.

25 Benjamin Franklin Quotes, "I confess there are several parts of this constitution which I do not at present approve, but I am not sure I shall never approve," https://www.goodreads.com/quotes/828906-mr-president-i-confess-that-there-are-several-parts-of.

26 Library of Congress, US Constitution, "Today in History–September 17, 1787," https://www.loc.gov/item/today-in-history/september-17/.

27 Library of Congress, US Constitution, "Today in History–September 17, 1787," https://www.loc.gov/item/today-in-history/september-17/.

28 Library of Congress, US Constitution, "Today in History–September 17, 1787," https://www.loc.gov/item/today-in-history/september-17/.

29 Library of Congress, US Constitution, "Today in History–September 17, 1787," https://www.loc.gov/item/today-in-history/september-17/.

30 Interactive Constitution, made by the National Constitution Center, "Article 2, the Executive Branch," https://constitutioncenter.org/interactive-constitution/article/article-ii.

31 Adam Levinson, Esq., "Statutes and Stories: Collections and Reflections of American Legal History," August 3, 2020, https://www.statutesandstories.com/blog_ html/presidential-election-day-act-of-1845-and-the-election-of-1840/.

32 Interactive Constitution, made by the National Constitution Center, "Article 2, the Executive Branch", https://constitutioncenter.org/interactive-constitution/article/article-ii.

33 David Roos, "Why was the Electoral College Created?" July 15, 2019: https://www.history.com/news/electoral-college-founding-fathers-constitutional-convention; Sarah Pruitt, "The History of the Electoral College Debate," Dec. 13, 2016, https://www.history.com/news/the-history-of-the-electoral-college-debate.

34 William C. Kimberling, "Essays in Elections: The Electoral College" (1992), *the Origins of the Electoral College,* https://uselectionatlas.org/INFORMATION/INFORMATION/electcollege_history.php.

35 Saikrishna B. Prakash, Interactive Constitution, made by the National Constitution Center, "Matters of Debate: The Significance of Executive Power", https://constitutioncenter.org/interactive-constitution/interpretation/article-ii/clauses/347#executive-power-clause

36   National Archives and Records Administration, "The Constitutional Amendment Process," Retrieved July 27, 2014, https://www.archives.gov/federal-register/constitution

37   National Archives, "Electoral College History," December 17, 2019, The Electoral College, https://www.archives.gov/electoral-college/history.

38   Bradley A. Smith and Daniel P. Tokaji, Interactive Constitution, made by the National Constitution Center, "Common Interpretation of Article 1, Section 2," https://constitutioncenter.org/interactive-constitution/interpretation/article-i/clauses/762.

39   Morgan Marietta, The Conversation, "The Right to Vote Is Not in the Constitution," https://theconversation.com/the-right-to-vote-is-not-in-the-constitution-144531.

40   Bradley A. Smith and Daniel P. Tokaji, Interactive Constitution, made by the National Constitution Center, "Common Interpretation of Article 1, Section 2," https://constitutioncenter.org/interactive-constitution/interpretation/article-i/clauses/762.

41   Alexander Keyssar, "The Right to Vote: The Contested History of Democracy in the United States," Basic Books, 2009, Harvard—Kennedy School, Ash Center for Democratic Governance and Innovation, https://ash.harvard.edu/publications/right-vote-contested-history-democracy-united-states.

42   Alexander Keyssar, "The Right to Vote: The Contested History of Democracy in the United States," Basic Books, 2009, Harvard—Kennedy School, Ash Center for Democratic Governance and Innovation, https://ash.harvard.edu/publications/right-vote-contested-history-democracy-united-states.

Chapter 2: Early Electoral College Failures And The Twelfth Amendment

43   D. Jason Berggren, "Presidential Election of 1789," Georgia Southwestern State University, written with Forrest McDonald, "The Presidency of George Washington," Lawrence, KS, University of Kansas,

1988, and William Michaelson, "Creating the American Presidency, 1775–1789," Lanham, MD, University Press of America, 1987, https://www.mountvernon.org/library/digitalhistory/digital-encyclopedia/article/presidential-election-of-1789/.

44 D. Jason Berggren, "Presidential Election 1792," Georgia Southwestern State University as written by Paul Boller Jr., *Presidential Campaigns,* New York, Oxford University Press, 1996.

45 Interactive Constitution, made by the National Constitution Center, "Article 2, the Executive Branch," https://constitutioncenter.org/interactive-constitution/article/article-ii.

46 William C. Kimberling, "Essays in Elections: The Electoral College" *(1992),* https://uselectionatlas.org/INFORMATION/INFORMATION/electcollege_choosing.php.

47 Richard Hofstadfer, *The Idea of a Party System: The Rise of Legitimate Opposition in the United States, 1780–1840,* Published by the University of California Press.

48 Richard Hofstadfer, *The Idea of a Party System: The Rise of Legitimate Opposition in the United States, 1780–1840,* Published by the University of California Press.

49 Richard Hofstadfer, *The Idea of a Party System: The Rise of Legitimate Opposition in the United States, 1780–1840,* Published by the University of California Press.

50 Jeffrey L. Pasley, *The First Presidential Contest: 1796 and the Founding of American Democracy,* Lawrence: University Press of Kansas, *Journal of American History,* Volume 101, Issue 1, June 2014, https://academic.oup.com/jah/article-abstract/101/1/249/748714?redirectedFrom=fulltext.

51 Jeffrey L. Pasley, *The First Presidential Contest: 1796 and the Founding of American Democracy,* Lawrence: University Press of Kansas, *Journal of American History,* Volume 101, Issue 1, June 2014, https://academic.oup.com/jah/article-abstract/101/1/249/748714?redirectedFrom=fulltext.

52 Jeffrey L. Pasley, *The First Presidential Contest: 1796 and the Founding of American Democracy,* Lawrence: University Press of

Kansas, *Journal of American History*, Volume 101, Issue 1, June 2014, https://academic.oup.com/jah/article-abstract/101/1/249/748714?redir ectedFrom=fulltext.

53 Jeffrey L. Pasley, *The First Presidential Contest: 1796 and the Founding of American Democracy,* Lawrence: University Press of Kansas, *Journal of American History*, Volume 101, Issue 1, June 2014, https://academic.oup.com/jah/article-abstract/101/1/249/748714?redir ectedFrom=fulltext.

54 Jeffrey L. Pasley, *The First Presidential Contest: 1796 and the Founding of American Democracy,* Lawrence: University Press of Kansas, *Journal of American History,* Volume 101, Issue 1, June 2014, https://academic.oup.com/jah/article-abstract/101/1/249/748714?redir ectedFrom=fulltext.

55 FairVote, "Controversial Elections," https://www.fairvote.org/ controversial_elections.

56 FairVote, "Controversial Elections," https://www.fairvote.org/ controversial_elections.

57 FairVote, "Controversial Elections," https://www.fairvote.org/ controversial_elections.

58 FairVote, "Controversial Elections," https://www.fairvote.org/ controversial_elections.

59 Jeffrey L. Pasley, *The First Presidential Contest: 1796 and the Founding of American Democracy,* Lawrence: University Press of Kansas, *Journal of American History*, Volume 101, Issue 1, June 2014, https://academic.oup.com/jah/article-abstract/101/1/249/748714?redir ectedFrom=fulltext.

60 Kenneth T. Walsh, *The Most Controversial Elections in History: Thomas Jefferson and the Election of 1800,* Aug. 18, 2008, US News and World Report, https://www.usnews.com/news/articles/2008/08/13/ the-most-consequential-elections-in-history-thomas-jefferson-and- the-election-of-1800.

61 Kenneth T. Walsh, *The Most Controversial Elections in History: Thomas Jefferson and the Election of 1800,* Aug. 18, 2008, US News and World Report, https://www.usnews.com/news/articles/2008/08/13/

the-most-consequential-elections-in-history-thomas-jefferson-and-the-election-of-1800.

62 William G. Morgan, *The Origin and Development of the Congressional Nominating Caucus,* Vol. 113, No. 2 (Apr. 17, 1969) p. 184–196 of *Proceedings of the American Philosophical Society,* American Philosophical Society, https://www.jstor.org/stable/985965?seq=1.

63 William G. Morgan, *The Origin and Development of the Congressional Nominating Caucus,* Vol. 113, No. 2 (Apr. 17, 1969), p. 184–196 of *Proceedings of the American Philosophical Society,* American Philosophical Society, https://www.jstor.org/stable/985965?seq=1.

64 William G. Morgan, *The Origin and Development of the Congressional Nominating Caucus,* Vol. 113, No. 2 (Apr 17, 1969), p. 184–196 of *Proceedings of the American Philosophical Society,* American Philosophical Society, https://www.jstor.org/stable/985965?seq=1.

65 Alexander Hamilton, *Letter from Alexander Hamilton, Concerning the Public Conduct and Character of John Adams, President of the United States,"* Oct. 24, 1800, National Historical Publications and Records Commission (NHPRC), https://founders.archives.gov/documents/Hamilton/01-25-02-0110-0001.

66 Jeffrey L. Pasley, University of Missouri–Columbia, *A Revolution of 1800 after All: The Political Culture of the Earlier Early Republic and the Origins of American Democracy,* http://www.pasleybrothers.com/jeff/writings/Pasley1800.htm.

67 Jeffrey L. Pasley, University of Missouri–Columbia, *A Revolution of 1800 after All: The Political Culture of the Earlier Early Republic and the Origins of American Democracy,* http://www.pasleybrothers.com/jeff/writings/Pasley1800.htm.

68 Interactive Constitution, made by the National Constitution Center, "Article 2, the Executive Branch," https://constitutioncenter.org/interactive-constitution/article/article-ii.

69 Kenneth T. Walsh, *The Most Controversial Elections in History: Thomas Jefferson and the Election of 1800,* Aug. 18, 2008, US News and World Report, https://www.usnews.com/news/articles/2008/08/13/

the-most-consequential-elections-in-history-thomas-jefferson-and-the-election-of-1800.

70   Kenneth T. Walsh, *The Most Controversial Elections in History: Thomas Jefferson and the Election of 1800,* Aug. 18, 2008, US News and World Report, https://www.usnews.com/news/articles/2008/08/13/the-most-consequential-elections-in-history-thomas-jefferson-and-the-election-of-1800.

71   Kenneth T. Walsh, *The Most Controversial Elections in History: Thomas Jefferson and the Election of 1800,* Aug. 18, 2008, US News and World Report, https://www.usnews.com/news/articles/2008/08/13/the-most-consequential-elections-in-history-thomas-jefferson-and-the-election-of-1800.

72   Bruce Ackerman and David Fontana, "How Jefferson Counted Himself In: Something was funny about the Georgia ballot in the 1800 election. Did Thomas Jefferson properly make himself President in 1801? A historical detective story," The Atlantic, Mar. 2004, https://www.theatlantic.com/magazine/archive/2004/03/how-jefferson-counted-himself-in/302888/.

73   Bruce Ackerman and David Fontana, "How Jefferson Counted Himself In: Something was funny about the Georgia ballot in the 1800 election. Did Thomas Jefferson properly make himself President in 1801? A historical detective story," The Atlantic, Mar. 2004, https://www.theatlantic.com/magazine/archive/2004/03/how-jefferson-counted-himself-in/302888/.

74   Jeffrey L. Pasley, University of Missouri–Columbia, "A Revolution of 1800 after all: The Political Culture of the Earlier Early Republic and the Origins of American Democracy," http://www.pasleybrothers.com/jeff/writings/Pasley1800.htm.

75   Cody Carlson, "This Week in History: The Presidential Deadlock of 1801," *Deseret News*, Feb. 20, 2013, https://www.deseret.com/2013/2/20/20514703/this-week-in-history-the-presidential-deadlock-of-1801.

76   Cody Carlson, "This Week in History: The Presidential Deadlock of 1801," *Deseret News*, Feb. 20, 2013, https://www.deseret.com/2013/2/20/20514703/this-week-in-history-the-presidential-deadlock-of-1801.

77   Robert Longley, "Twelfth Amendment: Fixing the Electoral College—Because the President and Vice President Really Should Get Along," ThoughtCo, Feb. 11, 2020, https://www.thoughtco.com/12th-amendment-4176911.

78   Robert Longley, "Twelfth Amendment: Fixing the Electoral College—Because the President and Vice President Really Should Get Along," ThoughtCo, Feb. 11, 2020, https://www.thoughtco.com/12th-amendment-4176911.

79   William C. Kimberling, "Essays in Elections: The Electoral College" *(1992), the Origins of the Electoral College,* https://uselectionatlas.org/INFORMATION/INFORMATION/electcollege_history.php.

80   Robert Longley, "Twelfth Amendment: Fixing the Electoral College—Because the President and Vice President Really Should Get Along," ThoughtCo, Feb 11, 2020, https://www.thoughtco.com/12th-amendment-4176911.

81   Robert Longley, "Twelfth Amendment: Fixing the Electoral College—Because the President and Vice President Really Should Get Along," ThoughtCo, Feb 11, 2020, https://www.thoughtco.com/12th-amendment-4176911.

82   William C. Kimberling, "Essays in Elections: The Electoral College" (1992), *the Origins of the Electoral College,* https://uselectionatlas.org/INFORMATION/INFORMATION/electcollege_history.php.

83   Robert Longley, "Twelfth Amendment: Fixing the Electoral College—Because the President and Vice President Really Should Get Along", ThoughtCo, Feb. 11, 2020, https://www.thoughtco.com/12th-amendment-4176911.

84   Robert Longley, "Twelfth Amendment: Fixing the Electoral College—Because the President and Vice President Really Should Get Along", ThoughtCo, Feb. 11, 2020, https://www.thoughtco.com/12th-amendment-4176911.

85   Jesse Wegman, *Let the People Pick the President: the Case for Abolishing the Electoral College,* St. Martin's Publishing Group and the *New York Times,* March 17, 2020, https://www.nytimes.com/2020/03/17/books/review/let-the-people-pick-the-president-jesse-wegman.html.

86   Robert Longley, "Twelfth Amendment: Fixing the Electoral College -Because the President and Vice President Really Should Get Along", ThoughtCo, Feb. 11, 2020, https://www.thoughtco.com/12th-amendment-4176911.

87   Jesse Wegman, *Let the People Pick the President: the Case for Abolishing the Electoral College,* St. Martin's Publishing Group and the *New York Times*, March 17, 2020, https://www.nytimes.com/2020/03/17/books/review/let-the-people-pick-the-president-jesse-wegman.html.

88   David W. Abbott and James P. Levine, *Wrong Winner: The Coming Debacle in the Electoral College*, New York, Praeger, 1991, https://products.abc-clio.com/abc-cliocorporate/product.aspx?pc=E2909C.

89   Interactive Constitution, made by the National Constitution Center, "Twelfth Amendment—Election of President and Vice President," https://constitutioncenter.org/interactive-constitution/amendment/amendment-xii.

Chapter 3: Electoral College Changes 1804–2022

90   United States Census Bureau, "Apportionment Legislation 1790–1840, 1890, Present," https://www.census.gov/history/www/reference/apportionment/apportionment_ legislation_ 1790_ -_ 1830.html, https://www.census.gov/history/www/reference/apportionment/apportionment_legislation_1840_-_1880.html, https://www.census.gov/history/www/reference/apportionment/apportionment_legislation_ 1890_-_present.html.

91   United States Census Bureau, "Apportionment Legislation 1840–1880", https://www.census.gov/history/www/reference/apportionment/apportionment_legislation_1840_-_1880.html.

92   National Archives, "America's Founding Documents: A Transcription of the Constitution of the United States, Article 1, Section 4," https://www.archives.gov/founding-docs/constitution-transcript#toc-section-4-.

93   National Archives, "America's Founding Documents: A Transcription of the Constitution of the United States," https://www.archives.gov/founding-docs/constitution-transcript#toc-section-1--2.

94   Statutes and Stories: Collections and Reflections on American Legal History, "Presidential Election Day Act of 1845 and the Election of 1840," August 3, 2020, https://www.statutesandstories.com/blog_html/presidential-election-day-act-of-1845-and-the-election-of-1840/.

95   Statutes and Stories: Collections and Reflections on American Legal History, "Presidential Election Day Act of 1845 and the Election of 1840," August 3, 2020, https://www.statutesandstories.com/blog_html/presidential-election-day-act-of-1845-and-the-election-of-1840/.

96   Statutes and Stories: Collections and Reflections on American Legal History, "Presidential Election Day Act of 1845 and the Election of 1840," August 3, 2020, https://www.statutesandstories.com/blog_html/presidential-election-day-act-of-1845-and-the-election-of-1840/.

97   Akhil Reed Amar and John C. Harrison, "The Common Interpretation of the Fourteenth Amendment: The Citizenship Clause," Interactive Constitution, made by the National Constitution Center, https://constitutioncenter.org/interactive-constitution/interpretation/amendment-xiv/clauses/700.

98   Akhil Reed Amar and John C. Harrison, "The Common Interpretation of the Fourteenth Amendment: The Citizenship Clause," Interactive Constitution, made by the National Constitution Center, https://constitutioncenter.org/interactive-constitution/interpretation/amendment-xiv/clauses/700.

99   Richard Pildes and Bradley Smith, "Common Interpretation of the Fifteenth Amendment," Interactive Constitution made by the National Constitution Center, https://constitutioncenter.org/interactive-constitution/interpretation/amendment-xv/interps/141.

100   Koger, Gregory, *The Origins of the 1887 Election Count Act: Mischiefs of Faction,* January 4, 2021, https://www.mischiefsoffaction.com/post/the-origins-of-the-1887-election-count-act.

101   Siegel, Stephen A, *The Conscientious Congressman's Guide to the Electoral Count Act of 1887,* 2004 Florida Law Review, Vol. 56, pp. 550–560, http://www.floridalawreview.com/wp-content/uploads/2010/01/Siegel-BOOK.pdf.

102 Siegel, Stephen A, *The Conscientious Congressman's Guide to the Electoral Count Act of 1887,* 2004 Florida Law Review, Vol. 56, pp. 550–560, http://www.floridalawreview.com/wp-content/uploads/2010/01/Siegel-BOOK.pd.f

103 Burgess, John W., (1888), *The Law of the Electoral Count, Political Science Quarterly,* Vol. 3, No. 4, pp. 633–653, Dec. 1888, https://www.jstor.org/stable/2139115?seq=1#metadata_info_tab_contents.

104 Schickler, Eric; Bimes, Terri; Mickey, Robert. "Safe at Any Speed: Legislative Intent and the Electoral Count Act of 1887, and *Bush v Gore,*" *Journal of Law and Politics*, 2000, https://escholarship.org/uc/item/2q38565q.

105 Supreme Court of the United States, *No. 20A98, Mike Kelly, United States Congressman, et al., Applicants v. Pennsylvania, et al.,* December 3, 2020, https://www.supremecourt.gov/search.aspx?filename=/docket/docketfiles/html/public/20a98.html.

106 McLaughlin, Dan, "Alternative Pro-Trump Slates of Electors Are a Dead End," National Review, Dec. 21, 2020, https://www.nationalreview.com/2020/12/alternative-pro-trump-slates-of-electors-are-a-dead-end/.

107 National Archives and Records Administration, July 2020, and retrieved November 19, 2020. "The 2020 Presidential Election: Provisions of the Constitution and the U.S. Code, Office of the Register," https://www.archives.gov/files/electoral-college/state-officials/presidential-election-brochure.pdf.

108 White, Michael, (Fall 2008). "The Electoral College: A Message from the Dean," *Prologue Magazine,* Vol. 40, no. 3, National Archives, https://www.archives.gov/publications/prologue/2008/fall/electoral.html.

109 "The 2020 Presidential Election: Provisions of the Constitution of the United States as Delivered in Amendment Twelve by the Office of the Federal Register," National Archives and Records Administration July 2020 and retrieved November 19, 2020, https://www.archives.gov/files/electoral-college/state-officials/presidential-election-brochure.pdf.

110   Watch Live, "Joint Session of Congress for Counting of the Electoral College Ballots," January 6, 2021, https://www.c-span.org/video/?507663-5/joint-session-congress-certifies-joe-biden-us-president&live=.

111   Siegel, Stephen A., (2004), *The Conscientious Congressman's Guide to the Electoral Count Act of 1887,* Florida Law Review, Vol. 56, p. 541, http://www.floridalawreview.com/wp-content/uploads/2010/01/Siegel-BOOK.pdf.

112   Siegel, Stephen A., (2004), *The Conscientious Congressman's Guide to the Electoral Count Act of 1887,* Florida Law Review, Vol. 56, p. 541, http://www.floridalawreview.com/wp-content/uploads/2010/01/Siegel-BOOK.pdf.

113   McLaughlin, Dan, (December 18, 2020), "Alternative Pro-Trump Slates of Electors Are a Dead End," National Review, Retrieved December 21, 2020, https://www.nationalreview.com/2020/12/alternative-pro-trump-slates-of-electors-are-a-dead-end/.

114   Siegel, Stephen A., (2004), *The Conscientious Congressman's Guide to the Electoral Count Act of 1887,* Florida Law Review, Vol. 56, p. 541, http://www.floridalawreview.com/wp-content/uploads/2010/01/Siegel-BOOK.pdf.

115   Foley, Edward, (2020), "Preparing for a Disputed Presidential Election: An Exercise in Election Risk Assessment and Management," https://lawecommons.luc.edu/cgi/viewcontent.cgi?article=2719&context=luclj.

116   National Archives Milestone Documents, "The Seventeenth Amendment to the US Constitution: Direct Election of US Senators (1913)," https://www.archives.gov/milestone-documents/17th-amendment#:~:text=Passed%20by%20Congress%20on%20May,were%20chosen%20by%20state%20legislatures.

117   National Archives, "Nineteenth Amendment to the US Constitution: Women's Right to Vote (1920)," https://www.archives.gov/milestone-documents/19th-amendment#:~:text=Passed%20by%20Congress%20June%204,women%20the%20right%20to%20vote.

118 History.com Editors, "Susan B. Anthony," History.com Editors, Original Mar 9, 2010, Updated Feb. 25, 2022, https://www.history.com/topics/womens-history/susan-b-anthony.

119 National Archives, "America's Founding Documents: A Transcription of the Constitution of the United States," https://www.archives.gov/founding-docs/amendments-11-27.

120 Mintz, Morton, "Arkansas Is First to Reject the District Voting Amendment," January 25, 1961, *The Washington Post.*

121 National Archives, "America's Founding Documents: A Transcription of the Constitution of the United States," https://www.archives.gov/founding-docs/amendments-11-27.

122 Vile, John R., (2003); *Encyclopedia of Constitutional Amendments, Proposed Amendments, and Amending Issues*, Santa Barbara, CA: ABC-CLIO, Inc., p. 480, April 14, 2014.

123 Vose, Clement, (1978), *When District of Columbia Representation Collides with the Constitutional Amendment Institution, Publius,* Oxford University Press, p. 105–125, https://academic.oup.com/publius/article-abstract/9/1/105/1937171.

124 Vose, Clement, (1978), *When District of Columbia Representation Collides with the Constitutional Amendment Institution, Publius,* Oxford University Press, p. 105–125, https://academic.oup.com/publius/article-abstract/9/1/105/1937171.

125 Jocelyn Benson and Michael Morley, "Common Interpretation of the Twenty-Sixth Amendment," Interactive Constitution by the National Constitution Center, https://constitutioncenter.org/interactive-constitution/interpretation/amendment-xxvi/interps/161.

126 Wendy Underhill, "What the Electoral Count Reform Act Means for States," NCSL (National Conference of State Legislatures), Jan. 16, 2023, https://www.ncsl.org/resources/details/what-the-electoral-count-reform-act-means-for-states.

127 Wendy Underhill, "What the Electoral Count Reform Act Means for States," NCSL (National Conference of State Legislatures), Jan. 16, 2023, https://www.ncsl.org/resources/details/what-the-electoral-count-reform-act-means-for-states.

128 Alan Wang and Liz Goodwin, *House Joins Senate in Passing Electoral Count Act Overhaul in Response to Jan. 6 Attack, The Washington Post,* published Dec. 23, 2022, https://www.washingtonpost.com/politics/2022/12/19/electoral-count-reform-omnibus/.

129 Alan Wang and Liz Goodwin, *House Joins Senate in Passing Electoral Count Act Overhaul in Response to Jan. 6 Attack, The Washington Post,* published Dec. 23, 2022, https://www.washingtonpost.com/politics/2022/12/19/electoral-count-reform-omnibus/.

130 Wikipedia, "The Electoral Count Reform and President Transition Improvement Act of 2022," Dec. 29, 2022, https://en.wikipedia.org/wiki/Electoral_Count_Reform_and_Presidential_Transition_Improvement_Act_of_2022.

131 GovTrack.us, "Text of H. R. 8824 (117th): Electoral Count Reform and Presidential Transition Improvement Act of 2022," March 26, 2023, https://www.govtrack.us/congress/bills/117/hr8824/text.

132 GovTrack.us, "Text of H.R. 8824 (117th): Electoral Count Reform and Presidential Transition Improvement Act of 2022," March 26, 2023, https://www.govtrack.us/congress/bills/117/hr8824/text.

Chapter 4: Controversial Elections or Simply Wrong Winners

133 David W. Abbott and James P. Levine, Wrong Winner: The Coming Debacle in the Electoral College, New York, Praeger, 1991, https://products.abc-clio.com/abc-cliocorporate/product.aspx?pc=E2909C.

134 Tyler Cowen, Feb. 2016, "Why Did the Federalist Party Collapse?" Marginal Revolution University, https://marginalrevolution.com/marginalrevolution/2016/02/why-did-the-federalist-party-collapse.html, History.com Editors, Oct. 2009, *The Federalist Party,* A&E Television Networks, https://www.history.com/topics/early-us/federalist-party.

135 The Hermitage: Home of the People's President, *A Controversial Election,* Andrew Jackson's Hermitage: Home of the People's

President, https://thehermitage.com/learn/andrew-jackson/president/candidacy/.

136 Donald Ratcliffe, *The One-Party Presidential Contest: Adams, Jackson and 1824's Five Horse Race,* Lawrence: University Press of Kansas, 2015, https://muse.jhu.edu/article/687330.

137 FairVote, "Controversial Elections," https://www.fairvote.org/controversial_elections.

138 FairVote, "Controversial Elections," https://www.fairvote.org/controversial_elections.

139 FairVote, "Controversial Elections," https://www.fairvote.org/controversial_elections.

140 Interactive Constitution made by National Constitution Center, "The Twelfth Amendment: the Election of President and Vice President as Passed by Congress Dec. 9, 1803, and ratified June 15, 1804," https://constitutioncenter.org/interactive-constitution/amendment/amendment-xii.

141 Christopher Marquis, *Andrew Jackson: Winner and Loser in 1824,* History Net, https://www.historynet.com/andrew-jackson-winner-and-loser-in-1824.htm.

142 Christopher Marquis, *Andrew Jackson: Winner and Loser in 1824,* History Net, https://www.historynet.com/andrew-jackson-winner-and-loser-in-1824.htm.

143 Christopher Marquis, *Andrew Jackson: Winner and Loser in 1824,* History Net, https://www.historynet.com/andrew-jackson-winner-and-loser-in-1824.htm.

144 Martin Kelly, *John Quincy Adams: Sixth President of the United States,* Mar 31, 2018, ThoughtCo.com, History and Culture, https://www.thoughtco.com/john-adams-6th-president-united-states-104763.

145 Christopher Marquis, *Andrew Jackson: Winner and Loser in 1824,* History Net, https://www.historynet.com/andrew-jackson-winner-and-loser-in-1824.htm.

146 Martin Kelly, *John Quincy Adams: Sixth President of the United States,* Mar. 31, 2018, ThoughtCo.com, History and Culture, https://www.thoughtco.com/john-adams-6th-president-united-states-104763.

147 Robert McNamara, (February 2020), "The Election of 1824 was decided in the House of Representatives," ThoughtCo, https://www.thoughtco.com/the-election-of-1824-1773860.

148 Martin Kelly, *John Quincy Adams: Sixth President of the United States,* Mar. 31, 2018, ThoughtCo.com, History and Culture, https://www.thoughtco.com/john-adams-6th-president-united-states-104763.

149 David Leip, "1828 Presidential Election Results," the US Presidential Elections, July 2005, and National Archives and Records Administration, *Electoral College Box Scores 1790–1996.*

150 Mark Cheathem, "Frontiersman or Southern Gentleman? Newspaper Coverage of Andrew Jackson during the 1828 Presidential Campaign," the Readex Report (2014).

151 Martin Kelly, Mar. 8, 2017, "Rutherford B. Hayes: Nineteenth President of the United States," ThoughtCo.com, History and Culture, https://www.thoughtco.com/rutherford-hayes-19th-president-united-states-104891.

152 A. M. Clancy and William Nelson, *Proceedings of the Republican National Convention—Cincinati, Ohio, June 14–16, 1876,* Concord, N. H. Republic Press Association, p. 83–117, Internet Archive, https://archive.org/details/proceedingsrepu00nelsgoog/page/n82/mode/2up.

153 Campaign Literature, 1876, *Official Proceedings of the National Democratic Convention Held in St. Louis, MO, Jun. 27–29, 1876,* St. Louis, Woodward, Woodward, Tiernan and Hale, Americana Collection, p. 129–197, https://archive.org/details/officialproceed03convgoog/page/n128/mode/2up.

154 "Samuel J. Tilden," the *New World Encyclopedia*, https://www.newworldencyclopedia.org/entry/Samuel_J._Tilden#Early_life_and_career.

155 Frank Freidel and Hugh Sidey, "Rutherford B. Hayes: The Presidents of the United States of America," White House Historical Association, https://www.whitehouse.gov/about-the-white-house/presidents/rutherford-b-hayes/.

156 Frank Freidel and Hugh Sidey, "Rutherford B. Hayes: The Presidents of the United States of America," White House Historical Association,

https://www.whitehouse.gov/about-the-white-house/presidents/rutherford-b-hayes/.

[157] 270towin.com, the 1876 Presidential Election Results, https://www.270towin.com/1876_Election/.

[158] N. R. Kleinfield, *Counting the Vote: the History; President Tilden? No, But Almost, in Another Vote that Dragged On,* Nov. 12, 2000, section 1, page 30, the *New York Times*, https://www.nytimes.com/2000/11/12/us/counting-vote-history-president-tilden-no-but-almost-another-vote-that-dragged.html.

[159] The *New York Times*, Nov. 12, 2000.

[160] The *New York Times*, Nov. 12, 2000.

[161] The *New York Times*, Nov. 12, 2000.

[162] Stephen M. Sheppard, *A Case for the Electoral College and for its Faithless Elector,* May 21, 2015, Wisconsin Law Review.

[163] N. R. Kleinfield, *Counting the Vote: the History; President Tilden? No, But Almost, in Another Vote that Dragged On,* Nov. 12, 2000, section 1, page 30, the *New York Times*, https://www.nytimes.com/2000/11/12/us/counting-vote-history-president-tilden-no-but-almost-another-vote-that-dragged.html.

[164] N. R. Kleinfield, *Counting the Vote: the History; President Tilden? No, But Almost, in Another Vote that Dragged On,* Nov. 12, 2000, section 1, page 30, the *New York Times*, https://www.nytimes.com/2000/11/12/us/counting-vote-history-president-tilden-no-but-almost-another-vote-that-dragged.html.

[165] The *New York Times*, Nov. 12, 2000.

[166] N. R. Kleinfield, *Counting the Vote: the History; President Tilden? No, But Almost, in Another Vote that Dragged On,* Nov. 12, 2000, section 1, page 30, the *New York Times*, https://www.nytimes.com/2000/11/12/us/counting-vote-history-president-tilden-no-but-almost-another-vote-that-dragged.html.

[167] The *New York Times*, Nov. 12, 2000.

[168] The *New York Times*, Nov. 12, 2000.

[169] The *New York Times*, Nov. 12, 2000.

[170] The *New York Times*, Nov. 12, 2000.

171 N. R. Kleinfield, *Counting the Vote: the History; President Tilden? No, But Almost, in Another Vote that Dragged On,* Nov. 12, 2000, section 1, page 30, the *New York Times,* https://www.nytimes.com/2000/11/12/us/counting-vote-history-president-tilden-no-but-almost-another-vote-that-dragged.html.

172 David W. Abbott and James P. Levine, *Wrong Winner: the Coming Debacle in the Electoral College,* New York, Praeger, 1991, https://products.abc-clio.com/abc-cliocorporate/product.aspx?pc=E2909C.

173 Interactive Constitution, made by the National Constitution Center, "The Twentieth Amendment: Common Interpretation," https://constitutioncenter.org/interactive-constitution/interpretation/amendment-xx/interps/153.

174 Edward B. Dickinson, "Official Proceedings of the National Democratic Convention," St. Louis, MO, June 5–7, 1888, Woodward, Tiernan Printing Co., Americana Collection, https://archive.org/details/officialproceed00dickgoog/page/n8/mode/2up/search/1888+democratic+national+convention?q=1888+democratic+national+convention.

175 Allen B. Spetter, Professor Emeritus of History at Wright State University, "Benjamin Harrison: the Campaign and Election of 1888," the Miller Center, UVA, https://millercenter.org/president/bharrison/campaigns-and-elections.

176 Andrew Glass, June 25, 2013, "Republicans nominate Benjamin Harrison, June 25, 1888," Source: www.Chicagohs.org/history/politics/1888.html, https://www.politico.com/story/2013/06/this-day-in-politics-093277.

177 Charles W. Johnson, "Official Proceedings of the Republican National Convention 1888," the Barkely Printing Co. 1888, Copyrighted by Charles W. Johnson 1903, https://books.google.com/books?id=XyldAAAAYAAJ&pg=RA1-PA5&lpg=RA1-PA5&dq=official+proceedings+of+the+republican+national+convention+of+1888&source=bl&ots=8OQByR4Bjk&sig=ACfU3U3srgbeYyxWz5btxwnX5W0UvY18SQ&hl=en&sa=X&ved=2ahUKEwiqk4W3zbTpAhWJHM0KHV0UCKEQ6AEwB3oECAoQAQ#v=onepage&q=official%20proceedings%20of%20the%20republican%20national%20convention%20of%201888&f=false.

[178] Allen B. Spetter, Professor Emeritus of History at Wright State University, *Benjamin Harrison: the Campaign and Election of 1888,* the Miller Center, UVA, https://millercenter.org/president/bharrison/campaigns-and-elections.

[179] Allen B. Spetter, Professor Emeritus of History at Wright State University, *Benjamin Harrison: the Campaign and Election of 1888,* the Miller Center, UVA, https://millercenter.org/president/bharrison/campaigns-and-elections.

[180] FairVote.org, *1888: Benjamin Harrison vs. President Grover Cleveland,* Controversial Elections, Fairvote Democracy, https://www.fairvote.org/controversial_elections, David Leip, *1888 Presidential Election Results,* Dave Leip's Atlas of US Presidential Elections, July 27, 2005, and *Electoral College Box Scores 1789–2016,* National Archives of Records Administration, July 31, 2005.

[181] David W. Abbott and James P. Levine, *Wrong Winner: the Coming Debacle in the Electoral College,* New York, Praeger, 1991, https://products.abc-clio.com/abc-cliocorporate/product.aspx?pc=E2909C.

[182] EDSITEment, "Like Father, Like Son: Presidential Families," NEH.GOV, https://edsitement.neh.gov/lesson-plans/father-son-presidential-families.

[183] Oyez—LII Supreme Court Resources, *"Bush v. Gore,"* Docket No 00-949, Rehnquist Court, Dec. 12, 2000, https://www.oyez.org/cases/2000/00-949.

[184] David Firestone, "The 2000 Campaign Crossover Voters: Democrats Drawn to McCain Are Unsettling Republicans," the *New York Times,* Feb. 10, 2000, https://www.nytimes.com/2000/02/10/us/2000-campaign-crossover-voters-democrats-drawn-mccain-are-unsettling-republicans.html.

[185] Gerhard Peters and John Woolley, *The Republican Party Platform–2000,* the *American Presidency Project,* July 31, 2000, https://www.presidency.ucsb.edu/documents/2000-republican-party-platform.

[186] Jennifer Preston, *Bradley Takes First Step toward Presidential Race,* the *New York Times,* Dec. 5, 1998, https://www.nytimes.com/1998/12/05/us/bradley-takes-first-step-toward-presidential-race.html.

187   *Dave Leip's Atlas of US Elections, LLV, 2019,* https://uselectionatlas.org/RESULTS/national.php?year=2000&f=0&off=0&elect=1.

188   Mike Ferullo, CNN, *Ford Appeals to Younger Voters in Keynote Address,* CNN Web posted, Aug. 16, 2000, https://web.archive.org/web/20070108024844/http://archives.cnn.com/2000/ALLPOLITICS/stories/08/16/ford.speech/index.html.

189   Gerhard Peters and John Woolly, *The 2000 Democratic Party Platform,* the *American Presidency Project,* August 14, 2000, https://www.presidency.ucsb.edu/documents/2000-democratic-party-platform.

190   James Campbell, *The Curious and Close Presidential Campaign of 2000,* Campbell-Crotty Chapter 4, https://www.acsu.buffalo.edu/~jcampbel/documents/CampbellCrottyChapter4.pdf.

191   Thomas E. Mann, *Reflections on the 2000 US Presidential Election,* Brookings Institute, Mon., Jan. 1, 2001, https://www.brookings.edu/articles/reflections-on-the-2000-u-s-presidential-election/.

192   Don van Natta Jr., *The 2000 Campaign: The Florida Vote; Democrats Tell of Problems at the Polls Across Florida,* the *New York Times,* Nov. 10, 2000, https://www.nytimes.com/2000/11/10/us/2000-campaign-florida-vote-democrats-tell-problems-polls-across-florida.html.

193   Emma Margolin, "Three Memorable Moments in Election Night History," from Hardball with Chris Matthews, 10/27/12, http://www.msnbc.com/hardball/watch-3-memorable-moments-election-night.

194   Dave Liep, "2000 Events Timeline-Post-Election," Dave Liep's Atlas of US Elections, Sources: CNN, ABC, CBS, AP, https://uselectionatlas.org/INFORMATION/ARTICLES/ElectionNight/pe2000elecnighttime.php.

195   CNN.com, "How We Got Here: A Timeline of the Florida Recount," Web posted, Dec. 13, 2000, https://web.archive.org/web/20080912012230/, http://archives.cnn.com/2000/ALLPOLITICS/stories/12/13/got.here/index.html.

196   CNN.com, "How We Got Here: A Timeline of the Florida Recount," Web posted, Dec. 13, 2000, https://web.archive.org/web/20080912012230/, http://archives.cnn.com/2000/ALLPOLITICS/stories/12/13/got.here/index.html.

197   Same as end note 196.

198 Same as end note 196.

199 Same as end note 196.

200 Same as end note 196.

201 Same as end note 196.

202 Same as end note 196.

203 Same as end note 196.

204 Same as end note 196.

205 David W. Abbott and James P. Levine, *Wrong Winner: The Coming Debacle in the Electoral College*, New York, Praeger, 1991, https://products.abc-clio.com/abc-cliocorporate/product.aspx?pc=E2909C.

206 Jordan Rudner, "All the Ways the 2016 Campaign Made History," Nov. 8, 2016, the *Dallas Morning News*, https://www.dallasnews.com/news/politics/2016/11/08/all-the-ways-the-2016-campaign-made-history/.

207 Jordan Rudner, "All the Ways the 2016 Campaign Made History," Nov. 8, 2016, the *Dallas Morning News*, https://www.dallasnews.com/news/politics/2016/11/08/all-the-ways-the-2016-campaign-made-history/.

208 History.com Editors, "The 2016 US Presidential Election," Nov. 29, 2018, A&E Television Networks, https://www.history.com/topics/us-presidents/us-presidential-election-2016.

209 History.com Editors, "The 2016 US Presidential Election," Nov. 29, 2018, A&E Television Networks, https://www.history.com/topics/us-presidents/us-presidential-election-2016.

210 Danielle Kurtzleben, *The Most Unprecedented Election Ever? 65 Ways It Has Been,* July 3, 2016, NPR, and April 19, 2016, *Washington Post*, https://www.npr.org/2016/07/03/484214413/the-most-unprecedented-election-ever-65-ways-it-has-been.

211 Hannah Johnson, *"Media Firsts in the 2016 Presidential Election,"* November 7, 2016, B2C, Business 2 Community, https://www.business2community.com/communications/media-firsts-2016-presidential-election-01700393.

212 Lauren Gambino and Madlhvi Pankhania, "How We Got Here: A complete Timeline of the 2016 Historic US Election," *The Guardian*, Nov. 8, 2016, https://www.theguardian.com/us-news/2016/nov/07/us-election-2016-complete-timeline-clinton-trump-president.

213 Polling by CNN, ABC, NBC, Quinnipiac, and *Huffington Post* according to Wikipedia, "Nationwide Opinion Polling for the 2016 Democratic Party Presidential Primaries," https://en.wikipedia.org/wiki/Nationwide_opinion_polling_for_the_2016_Democratic_Party_presidential_primaries.

214 Chris Cillizza and Aaron Blake, "Who's Most Likely to End Up as the Republicans Nominee in 2016 Presidential Race," Dec. 7, 2014, *The Washington Post*, https://www.washingtonpost.com/politics/whos-most-likely-to-end-up-as-republicans-nominee-in-2016-presidential-race/2014/12/07/b37cafca-7e3c-11e4-81fd-8c4814dfa9d7_story.html.

215 "The 2016 Republican Party Presidential Primaries," March 2020, https://en.wikipedia.org/wiki/2016_Republican_Party_presidential_primaries.

216 Danielle Kurtzleben, *The Most Unprecedented Election Ever? 65 Ways It Has Been,* July 3, 2016, NPR, and April 19, 2016, *Washington Post*, https://www.npr.org/2016/07/03/484214413/the-most-unprecedented-election-ever-65-ways-it-has-been.

217 Polling by CNN, ABC, NBC, Quinnipiac, and *Huffington Post* according to Wikipedia, "Nationwide Opinion Polling for the 2016 Republican Party Presidential Primaries," https://en.wikipedia.org/wiki/Nationwide_opinion_polling_for_the_2016_Republican_Party_presidential_primaries#Polls_conducted_in_2015.

218 Eli Stokols and Nolan McCaskill, "Rubio Urges Voters to Back Kasich in Ohio to Stop Trump," *Politico*, Mar 11, 2016, https://www.politico.com/blogs/2016-gop-primary-live-updates-and-results/2016/03/marco-rubio-ohio-kasich-220635.

219 Stephen Collinson, "Donald Trump: Presumptive GOP Nominee; Sanders Takes Indiana and Continues On," CNN Politics, May 4, 2016, https://www.cnn.com/2016/05/03/politics/indiana-primary-highlights/index.html.

220 Lauren Gambino and Madlhvi Pankhania, "How We Got Here: A Complete Timeline of the 2016 Historic US Election," *The Guardian*, Nov. 8, 2016, https://www.theguardian.com/us-news/2016/nov/07/us-election-2016-complete-timeline-clinton-trump-president.

221 Wikipedia, "2016 Republican National Convention," July 2016, https://en.wikipedia.org/wiki/2016_ Republican_ National_ Convention#Platform.

222 Lauren Gambino and Madlhvi Pankhania, "How We Got Here: A Complete Timeline of the 2016 Historic US Election," *The Guardian*, Nov. 8, 2016, https://www.theguardian.com/us-news/2016/nov/07/us-election-2016-complete-timeline-clinton-trump-president.

223 Wikipedia, "2016 Democratic National Convention," July 25–28, 2016, https://en.wikipedia.org/wiki/2016_Democratic_National_Convention#Platform.

224 History.com Editors, "The 2016 U.S. Presidential Election," November 29, 2018, History by A&E Television Networks, https://www.history.com/topics/us-presidents/us-presidential-election-2016#section_1.

225 History.com Editors, "The 2016 U.S. Presidential Election," November 29, 2018, History by A&E Television Networks, https://www.history.com/topics/us-presidents/us-presidential-election-2016#section_1.

226 Phillip Bump, *In the First Major Poll after Both Conventions, Trump's Bump Has Vanished,* Aug. 1, 2016, *The Washington Post*, https://www.washingtonpost.com/news/the-fix/wp/2016/08/01/in-the-first-major-poll-after-both-conventions-trumps-bump-has-vanished/.

227 History.com Editors, "The 2016 U.S. Presidential Election," November 29, 2018, History by A&E Television Networks, https://www.history.com/topics/us-presidents/us-presidential-election-2016#section_1.

228 Real Clear Politics, *General Election: Trump vs. Clinton vs. Johnson vs. Stein,* RCP, June–November 2016, https://www.realclearpolitics.com/epolls/2016/president/us/general_election_trump_vs_clinton_vs_johnson_vs_stein-5952.html.

229 Real Clear Politics, *General Election: Trump vs. Clinton vs. Johnson vs. Stein,* RCP, June–November 2016, https://www.realclearpolitics.com/epolls/2016/president/us/general_election_trump_vs_clinton_vs_johnson_vs_stein-5952.html.

230 Gregory King, "The Day That Changed Everything: Election Day 2016 as It Happened," Wed., Nov. 9, 2016, CNN Politics, https://www.cnn.

com/2017/11/08/politics/inside-election-day-2016-as-it-happened/
index.html.

[231] Gregory King, "The Day That Changed Everything: Election Day 2016 as It Happened," Wed., Nov. 9, 2016, CNN Politics, https://www.cnn. com/2017/11/08/politics/inside-election-day-2016-as-it-happened/ index.html.

[232] Gregory King, "The Day That Changed Everything: Election Day 2016 as It Happened," Wed., Nov. 9, 2016, CNN Politics, https://www.cnn. com/2017/11/08/politics/inside-election-day-2016-as-it-happened/ index.html.

[233] Nate Silver, "Final Election Update: There's a Wide Range of Outcomes and Most of Them Come Up Clinton," Nov. 8, 2016, FiveThirtyEight. com, https://fivethirtyeight.com/features/final-election-update-theres- a-wide-range-of-outcomes-and-most-of-them-come-up-clinton/.

[234] Gregory King, "The Day That Changed Everything: Election Day 2016 as It Happened," Wed., Nov. 9, 2016, CNN Politics, https://www.cnn. com/2017/11/08/politics/inside-election-day-2016-as-it-happened/ index.html.

[235] Same as 43.

[236] Same as 43.

[237] David W. Abbott and James P. Levine, *Wrong Winner: The Coming Debacle in the Electoral College*, New York, Praeger, 1991, https:// products.abc-clio.com/abc-cliocorporate/product.aspx?pc=E2909C.

[238] History.com Editors, "The 2016 US Presidential Election," Nov. 29, 2018, A&E Television Networks, https://www.history.com/topics/ us-presidents/us-presidential-election-2016.

[239] John Wagner, "Donald Trump Once Called the Electoral College a Disaster for Democracy. Now Says It's Far Better for the USA," *The Washington Post Democracy Dies in Darkness,* March 20, 2019, https://www.washingtonpost.com/politics/donald-trump-once- called-the-electoral-college-a-disaster-for-democracy-now-he-says- its-far-better-for-the-usa/2019/03/20/dc038b76-4af7-11e9-93d0- 64dbcf38ba41_story.html.

Chapter 5: Should the Electoral College Be Abolished? Yes or No?

240 Matt Riffe, "James Wilson, Popular Sovereignty, and the Electoral College," Constitution Daily—Smart Conversation from the National Constitution Center, Nov. 28,2016, https://constitutioncenter.org/blog/james-wilson-popular-sovereignty-and-the-electoral-college.

241 Jonathan Bernstein, "Favorite Sons Won't Be Fortunate Sons," Feb. 3, 2011, *The New Republic* Magazine, https://newrepublic.com/article/82816/favorite-sons-wont-be-fortunate-sons.

242 Michael McConnell, Law Professor at the Hoover Institution, "Should we Abolish the Electoral College," September/October 2016, *Stanford Magazine*, https://stanfordmag.org/contents/should-we-abolish-the-electoral-college.

243 Jack Rakove, Professor of American Studies and Political Science, "Should We Abolish the Electoral College," September/October 2016, *Stanford Magazine*, https://stanfordmag.org/contents/should-we-abolish-the-electoral-college.

244 National Constitution Center. "Article 2, Section 1 of the Executive Branch," https://constitutioncenter.org/the-constitution.

245 Tara Ross, *The Indispensable Electoral College: How the Founders' Plan Saves Our Country from Mob Rule*. Regnery Gateway Publishers, 2017, https://www.taraross.com/product-page/the-indispensable-electoral-college-how-the-founders-plan-saves-our-country-fr.

246 Trent England and Christopher Pearson, *Debating the Electoral College: Two Election Experts Argue for and against This Uniquely American Institution,* NCSL (National Conference of State Legislatures), March 24, 2020, https://www.ncsl.org/state-legislatures-news/details/debating-the-electoral-college.

247 Tara Ross, *"Founders created the Electoral College as a check to Tyranny"*, The Washington Times, Feb 2, 2021, https://www.washingtontimes.com/news/2021/feb/2/tara-ross-founders-created-electoral-college-check/.

248 Trent England and Christopher Pearson. "Debating the Electoral College: Two Election Experts Argue for and against this uniquely

American Institution," NCSL (National Conference of State Legislatures), March 24, 2020. https://www.ncsl.org/state-legislatures-news/details/debating-the-electoral-college.

249 Tara Ross, *The Indispensable Electoral College: How the Founders' Plan Saves Our Country from Mob Rule,* Regnery Gateway Publishers, 2017, https://www.taraross.com/product-page/the-indispensable-electoral-college-how-the-founders-plan-saves-our-country-fr.

250 Trent England and Christopher Pearson. "Debating the Electoral College: Two Election Experts Argue for and against this uniquely American Institution," NCSL (National Conference of State Legislatures), March 24, 2020, https://www.ncsl.org/state-legislatures-news/details/debating-the-electoral-college.

251 Tara Ross, *The Electoral College: Enlightened Democracy,* Heritage Foundation Legal Memorandum No. 15, November 1, 2004, https://www.heritage.org/the-constitution/report/the-electoral-college-enlightened-democracy.

252 Tara Ross, *Founders Created the Electoral College as a Check to Tyranny, The Washington Times,* Feb. 2, 2021, https://www.washingtontimes.com/news/2021/feb/2/tara-ross-founders-created-electoral-college-check/.

253 Tara Ross, *The Indispensable Electoral College: How the Founders' Plan Saves Our Country from Mob Rule.* Regnery Gateway Publishers, 2017, https://www.taraross.com/product-page/the-indispensable-electoral-college-how-the-founders-plan-saves-our-country-fr.

254 Trent England and Christopher Pearson. "Debating the Electoral College: Two Election Experts Argue for and against this uniquely American Institution," NCSL (National Conference of State Legislatures), March 24, 2020. https://www.ncsl.org/state-legislatures-news/details/debating-the-electoral-college.

255 William C. Kimberling, Deputy Director FEC National Clearinghouse on Election Administration, *The Pros and Cons of the Electoral College System: Essays in Elections,* (1992) Washington, DC, National Clearinghouse on Election Administration and Federal Election Commission, https://uselectionatlas.org/INFORMATION/INFORMATION/electcollege_procon.php.

256 Chris DeRosa and Steve Neumann, "The Good, the Bad, and the Ugly about the Electoral College," The Magazine of Monmouth University, Fall 2020, https://www.monmouth.edu/magazine/the-good-the-bad-and-the-ugly-about-the-electoral-college/.

257 Allen Guelzo, *In Defense of the Electoral College,* National Affairs, Winter 2018, https://www.nationalaffairs.com/publications/detail/in-defense-of-the-electoral-college.

258 Tara Ross, *Founders Created the Electoral College as a Check to Tyranny, The Washington Times,* Feb. 2, 2021, https://www.washingtontimes.com/news/2021/feb/2/tara-ross-founders-created-electoral-college-check/.

259 Tara Ross, *MSLF Forum: Author Tara Ross Explains Why We Need the Electoral College,* Mountain States Legal Foundation, May 19, 2020, https://mslegal.org/2020/05/tara-ross-why-we-need-the-electoral-college/.

260 Tara Ross, *Founders Created the Electoral College as a check to Tyranny, The Washington Times*, February 2, 2021, https://www.washingtontimes.com/news/2021/feb/2/tara-ross-founders-created-electoral-college-check/.

261 Tara Ross, *MSLF Forum: Author Tara Ross Explains Why we Need the Electoral College,* Mountain States Legal Foundation, May 19, 2020, https://mslegal.org/2020/05/tara-ross-why-we-need-the-electoral-college/.

262 Jesse Wegman, *Let the People Pick the President: the Case for Abolishing the Electoral College,* Copyright 2020, https://us.macmillan.com/books/9781250221971/letthepeoplepickthepresident.

263 Chris DeRosa and Steve Neumann, "The Good, the Bad, and the Ugly about the Electoral College," The Magazine of Monmouth University, Fall 2020, https://www.monmouth.edu/magazine/the-good-the-bad-and-the-ugly-about-the-electoral-college/.

264

265 Trent England and Christopher Pearson, "Debating the Electoral College: Two Election Experts Argue for and against this uniquely American Institution," NCSL (National Conference of State Legislatures), March 24, 2020. https://www.ncsl.org/state-legislatures-news/details/debating-the-electoral-college.

266 Trent England and Christopher Pearson, "Debating the Electoral College: Two Election Experts Argue for and against this uniquely American Institution," NCSL (National Conference of State Legislatures), March 24, 2020, https://www.ncsl.org/state-legislatures-news/details/debating-the-electoral-college.

267 Darrell West and Caitlinn Chin, *Its Time to Abolish the Electoral College*, Policy 2020 Brookings, https://www.brookings.edu/wp-content/uploads/2019/10/Big-Ideas_West_Electoral-College.pdf.

268 Elaine Kamarck and John Hudak, *How to Get Rid of the Electoral College*, Brookings, Dec. 9, 2020, https://www.brookings.edu/articles/how-to-get-rid-of-the-electoral-college/.

269 Robert Longley, *Five Ways to Change the US Constitution without the Amendment Process*, ThoughtCo, April 5, 2023, https://www.thoughtco.com/ways-to-change-the-us-constitution-4115574.

270 Trent England and Christopher Pearson, "Debating the Electoral College: Two Election Experts Argue for and against this uniquely American Institution," NCSL (National Conference of State Legislatures), March 24, 2020, https://www.ncsl.org/state-legislatures-news/details/debating-the-electoral-college.

271 Jesse Wegman, *Let the People Pick the President: the Case for Abolishing the Electoral College,* Copyright 2020, https://us.macmillan.com/books/9781250221971/letthepeoplepickthepresident.

272 John Koza, Barry Fadem, Mark Grueskin, Michael Mandell, Robert Richie, and Joseph Zimmerman, *Every Vote Equal: A State Based Plan for Electing the President by National Popular Vote,* Feb. 2013, National Popular Vote Press, https://www.every-vote-equal.com/.

273 Trent England and Christopher Pearson, "Debating the Electoral College: Two Election Experts Argue for and against this uniquely American Institution," NCSL (National Conference of State Legislatures), March 24, 2020, https://www.ncsl.org/state-legislatures-news/details/debating-the-electoral-college.

274 Jesse Wegman, *Let the People Pick the President: the Case for Abolishing the Electoral College,* Copyright 2020, https://us.macmillan.com/books/9781250221971/letthepeoplepickthepresident.

275 Jesse Wegman, *Let the People Pick the President: the Case for Abolishing the Electoral College,* Copyright 2020, https://us.macmillan.com/books/9781250221971/letthepeoplepickthepresident.

276 William C. Kimberling, Deputy Director FEC National Clearinghouse on Election Administration, *The Pros and Cons of the Electoral College System: Essays in Elections,* (1992) Washington, DC, National Clearinghouse on Election Administration and Federal Election Commission, https://uselectionatlas.org/INFORMATION/INFORMATION/electcollege_procon.php.

277 Chris DeRosa and Steve Neumann, "The Good, the Bad, and the Ugly about the Electoral College," The Magazine of Monmouth University, Fall 2020, https://www.monmouth.edu/magazine/the-good-the-bad-and-the-ugly-about-the-electoral-college/.

278 Jesse Wegman, *Let the People Pick the President: the Case for Abolishing the Electoral College,* Copyright 2020. https://us.macmillan.com/books/9781250221971/letthepeoplepickthepresident.

279 Chris DeRosa and Steve Neumann, "The Good, the Bad, and the Ugly about the Electoral College," The Magazine of Monmouth University, Fall 2020, https://www.monmouth.edu/magazine/the-good-the-bad-and-the-ugly-about-the-electoral-college/.

280 William C. Kimberling, Deputy Director FEC National Clearinghouse on Election Administration, *The Pros and Cons of the Electoral College System: Essays in Elections,* (1992) Washington, DC, National Clearinghouse on Election Administration and Federal Election Commission, https://uselectionatlas.org/INFORMATION/INFORMATION/electcollege_procon.php.

281 William C. Kimberling, Deputy Director FEC National Clearinghouse on Election Administration, *The Pros and Cons of the Electoral College System: Essays in Elections,* (1992) Washington, DC, National Clearinghouse on Election Administration and Federal Election Commission, https://uselectionatlas.org/INFORMATION/INFORMATION/electcollege_procon.php.

282 Jesse Wegman and Josh Chafetz, *Why We Should Abolish the Electoral College,* the *New York Times*, March 17,2020, https://

www.nytimes.com/2020/03/17/books/review/let-the-people-pick-the-president-jesse-wegman.html.

283 William Kimberling, Deputy Director FEC National Clearinghouse on Election Administration, *The Pros and Cons of the Electoral College System: Essays in Elections,* (1992) Washington, DC, National Clearinghouse on Election Administration and Federal Election Commission, https://uselectionatlas.org/INFORMATION/INFORMATION/electcollege_procon.php.

284 Megan Brenan, "61% of Americans Support Abolishing Electoral College," Gallup Politics, September 24, 2020, https://news.gallup.com/poll/320744/americans-support-abolishing-electoral-college.aspx.

285 Josh Chafetz, *Why We Should Abolish the Electoral College,* the *New York Times*, October 4, 2020, https://www.nytimes.com/2020/03/17/books/review/let-the-people-pick-the-president-jesse-wegman.html.

Chapter 6: Attempts to Abolish or Reform the Electoral College

286 Fair Vote, "Why James Madison Wanted to Change the Way We Vote for President," June 18, 2012, https://fairvote.org/why-james-madison-wanted-to-change-the-way-we-vote-for-president/.

287 John Koza, Barry Fadem, Mark Grueskin, Michael Mandell, Robert Richie, and Joseph Zimmerman, *Every Vote Equal: A State-Based Plan for Electing the President by National Popular Vote,* 4th Edition, February 2013, https://www.every-vote-equal.com/.

288 National Constitution Center, "Article II, the Executive Branch, Sections 1–4", https://constitutioncenter.org/the-constitution/articles/article-ii.

289 National Constitution Center, "Article II, the Executive Branch, Sections 1–4", https://constitutioncenter.org/the-constitution/articles/article-ii.

290 Fair Vote, "Why James Madison Wanted to Change the Way We Vote for President," June 18, 2012, https://fairvote.org/why-james-madison-wanted-to-change-the-way-we-vote-for-president/.

291 Fair Vote, "Why James Madison Wanted to Change the Way We Vote for President," June 18, 2012, https://fairvote.org/why-james-madison-wanted-to-change-the-way-we-vote-for-president/.

292 Fair Vote, "Why James Madison Wanted to Change the Way We Vote for President," June 18, 2012, https://fairvote.org/why-james-madison-wanted-to-change-the-way-we-vote-for-president/.

293 Fair Vote, "Why James Madison Wanted to Change the Way We Vote for President," June 18, 2012, https://fairvote.org/why-james-madison-wanted-to-change-the-way-we-vote-for-president/.

294 Thity-thousand.org, "Replace Career Politicians with Citizen Legislators and Return the House of Representatives to the People," https://thirty-thousand.org/overview/.

295 Fair Vote, "Why James Madison Wanted to Change the Way We Vote for President," June 18, 2012, https://fairvote.org/why-james-madison-wanted-to-change-the-way-we-vote-for-president/.

296 John Koza, Barry Fadem, Mark Grueskin, Michael Mandell, Robert Richie, and Joseph Zimmerman, *Every Vote Equal: A State-Based Plan for Electing the President by National Popular Vote,* 4th Edition, February 2013, https://www.every-vote-equal.com/.

297 Fair Vote, "Past Attempts at Reform," https://fairvote.org/archives/the_electoral_college-past_attempts_at_reform/.

298 Ruth Silva, *The Lodge-Gosett Resolution: A Critical Analysis,* American Political Science Review, Mar. 1950 and Cambridge University Press, Sep. 2013, https://www.cambridge.org/core/journals/american-political-science-review/article/abs/lodgegossett-resolution-a-critical-analysis/98DF1DCFC665D06C399A6D64C1DBBDB6.

299 Fair Vote, "Past Attempts at Reform," https://fairvote.org/archives/the_electoral_college-past_attempts_at_reform/.

300 Ruth Silva, *The Lodge-Gosett Resolution: A Critical Analysis,* American Political Science Review, Mar. 1950 and Cambridge University Press, Sep. 2013, https://www.cambridge.org/core/

journals/american-political-science-review/article/abs/lodgegossett-resolution-a-critical-analysis/98DF1DCFC665D06C399A6D64C1DBBDB6.

301 Stephen J. Wayne, *The Road to the White House 1996: the Politics of Presidential Elections,* Palgrave Macmillan Publishing, Jan 1, 1995, https://www.thriftbooks.com/w/the-road-to-the-white-house-1996-the-politics-of-presidential-elections_ wayne/2426929/# edition=45810193&idiq=40691269.

302 John Koza, Barry Fadem, Mark Grueskin, Michael Mandell, Robert Richie, and Joseph Zimmerman, *Every Vote Equal: A State-Based Plan for Electing the President by National Popular Vote,* 4th Edition, February 2013, https://www.every-vote-equal.com/.

303 Congressional Research Service, *Electoral College Reforms: 110th Congress Proposals, the National Popular Vote, and Other Alternative Methods,* February 9, 2009, https://crsreports.congress.gov/product/pdf/RL/RL34604/7.

304 John Koza, Barry Fadem, Mark Grueskin, Michael Mandell, Robert Richie, and Joseph Zimmerman, *Every Vote Equal: A State-Based Plan for Electing the President by National Popular Vote,* 4th Edition, February 2013, https://www.every-vote-equal.com/.

305 John Koza, Barry Fadem, Mark Grueskin, Michael Mandell, Robert Richie, and Joseph Zimmerman, *Every Vote Equal: A State-Based Plan for Electing the President by National Popular Vote,* 4th Edition, February 2013, https://www.every-vote-equal.com/.

306 John Koza, Barry Fadem, Mark Grueskin, Michael Mandell, Robert Richie, and Joseph Zimmerman, *Every Vote Equal: A State-Based Plan for Electing the President by National Popular Vote,* 4th Edition, February 2013, https://www.every-vote-equal.com/.

307 John Koza, Barry Fadem, Mark Grueskin, Michael Mandell, Robert Richie, and Joseph Zimmerman, *Every Vote Equal: A State-Based Plan for Electing the President by National Popular Vote,* 4th Edition, February 2013, https://www.every-vote-equal.com/.

308 John Koza, Barry Fadem, Mark Grueskin, Michael Mandell, Robert Richie, and Joseph Zimmerman, *Every Vote Equal: A State-Based*

Plan for Electing the President by National Popular Vote, 4th Edition, February 2013, https://www.every-vote-equal.com/.

309 John Koza, Barry Fadem, Mark Grueskin, Michael Mandell, Robert Richie, and Joseph Zimmerman, *Every Vote Equal: A State-Based Plan for Electing the President by National Popular Vote,* 4th Edition, February 2013. https://www.every-vote-equal.com/.

310 John Koza, Barry Fadem, Mark Grueskin, Michael Mandell, Robert Richie, and Joseph Zimmerman, *Every Vote Equal: A State-Based Plan for Electing the President by National Popular Vote,* 4th Edition, February 2013, https://www.every-vote-equal.com/.

311 Stephen J. Wayne, *The Road to the White House 1996: the Politics of Presidential Elections,* Palgrave Macmillan Publishing, Jan. 1, 1995, https://www.thriftbooks.com/w/the-road-to-the-white-house-1996-the-politics-of-presidential-elections_ wayne/2426929/# edition=45810193&idiq=40691269.

312 John Koza, Barry Fadem, Mark Grueskin, Michael Mandell, Robert Richie. and Joseph Zimmerman, *Every Vote Equal: A State-Based Plan for Electing the President by National Popular Vote,* 4th Edition, February 2013, https://www.every-vote-equal.com/.

313 Stephen J. Wayne, *The Road to the White House 1996: the Politics of Presidential Elections,* Palgrave Macmillan Publishing, Jan. 1, 1995, https://www.thriftbooks.com/w/the-road-to-the-white-house-1996-the-politics-of-presidential-elections_wayne/2426929/#edition=45810193&idiq=40691269.

314

315 John Koza, Barry Fadem, Mark Grueskin, Michael Mandell, Robert Richie, and Joseph Zimmerman, *Every Vote Equal: A State-Based Plan for Electing the President by National Popular Vote,* 4th Edition, February 2013, Chapter 4.1. https://www.every-vote-equal.com/.

316 David Nir, *Daily Kos Elections Presidential Results by Congressional District for 2020,* Daily Kos, November 14, 2022, https://www.dailykos.com/stories/2012/11/19/1163009/-Daily-Kos-Elections-presidential-results-by-congressional-district-for-the-2012-2008-elections.

317 Stephen Wolf, *Daily Kos Elections presents the 2016 Presidential Election Results by Congressional District,* Daily Kos, January 30, 2017, https://www.dailykos.com/stories/2017/1/30/1627319/-Daily-Kos-Elections-presents-the-2016-presidential-election-results-by-congressional-district.

318 John Koza, Barry Fadem, Mark Grueskin, Michael Mandell, Robert Richie, and Joseph Zimmerman, *Every Vote Equal: A State-Based Plan for Electing the President by National Popular Vote,* 4th Edition, February 2013, https://www.every-vote-equal.com/.

319 John Koza, Barry Fadem, Mark Grueskin, Michael Mandell, Robert Richie, and Joseph Zimmerman, *Every Vote Equal: A State-Based Plan for Electing the President by National Popular Vote,* 4th Edition, February 2013, https://www.every-vote-equal.com/.

320 Congressional Research Service, *Electoral College Reforms: 110th Congress Proposals, the National Popular Vote, and Other Alternative Methods,* February 9, 2009, https://crsreports.congress.gov/product/pdf/RL/RL34604/7.

321 Congressional Research Service, *Electoral College Reforms: 110th Congress Proposals, the National Popular Vote, and Other Alternative Methods,* February 9, 2009, https://crsreports.congress.gov/product/pdf/RL/RL34604/7.

322 The National Archives and Records Administration, "1968 Electoral College Results," https://search.archives.gov/search?utf8=&affiliate=national-archives&query=1968+electoral+college+results&sitelimit=archives.gov%2Felectoral-college.

323 Lawrence Longley and Alan Braun, *The Politics of Electoral College Reform,* Yale of University Press, 1972, https://www.journals.uchicago.edu/doi/10.2307/2129044.

324 David Ross, *How the Electoral College Was Nearly Abolished in 1970,* History published by A&E Television Networks, Aug. 3, 2020, https://www.history.com/news/electoral-college-nearly-abolished-thurmond.

325 Gillian Brockwell, "Of the 700 Attempts to Fix or Abolish the Electoral, This One Nearly Succeeded," *The Washington Post,*

Dec. 5, 2020, https://www.washingtonpost.com/history/2020/12/04/abolish-electoral-college-george-wallace-trump-bayh/.

326 Fair Vote, "Past Attempts at Reform", https://fairvote.org/archives/the_electoral_college-past_attempts_at_reform/.

327 Jesse Wegman, *Let the People Pick the President: the Case for Abolishing the Electoral College,* Copyright 2020, https://us.macmillan.com/books/9781250221971/letthepeoplepickthepresident.

328 Jesse Wegman, *What If We Just Counted Up All the Votes for President and Saw Who Won,* March 13, 2020, the *New York Times,* https://www.nytimes.com/2020/03/13/opinion/sunday/presidential-election-popular-vote.html.

329 John Koza, Barry Fadem, Mark Grueskin, Michael Mandell, Robert Richie, and Joseph Zimmerman, *Every Vote Equal: A State-Based Plan for Electing the President by National Popular Vote,* 4th Edition, February 2013, https://www.every-vote-equal.com/.

330 Stephen J. Wayne, *The Road to the White House 1996: the Politics of Presidential Elections,* Palgrave Macmillan Publishing, Jan. 1, 1995, https://www.thriftbooks.com/w/the-road-to-the-white-house-1996-the-politics-of-presidential-elections_wayne/2426929/#edition=45810193&idiq=40691269.

331 John Koza, Barry Fadem, Mark Grueskin, Michael Mandell, Robert Richie, and Joseph Zimmerman, *Every Vote Equal: A State-Based Plan for Electing the President by National Popular Vote,* 4th Edition, February 2013, https://www.every-vote-equal.com/.

332 John Koza, Barry Fadem, Mark Grueskin, Michael Mandell, Robert Richie, and Joseph Zimmerman, *Every Vote Equal: A State-Based Plan for Electing the President by National Popular Vote,* 4th Edition, February 2013, https://www.every-vote-equal.com/.

333 Gillian Brockwell, "Of the 700 Attempts to Fix or Abolish the Electoral, This One Nearly Succeeded," *The Washington Post,* Dec. 5, 2020, https://www.washingtonpost.com/history/2020/12/04/abolish-electoral-college-george-wallace-trump-bayh/.

334 Stephen J. Wayne, *The Road to the White House 1996: the Politics of Presidential Elections,* Palgrave Macmillan Publishing, Jan. 1,

1995, https://www.thriftbooks.com/w/the-road-to-the-white-house-1996-the-politics-of-presidential-elections_wayne/2426929/#edition=45810193&idiq=40691269.

335 Stephen J. Wayne, *The Road to the White House 1996: the Politics of Presidential Elections,* Palgrave Macmillan Publishing, Jan. 1, 1995, https://www.thriftbooks.com/w/the-road-to-the-white-house-1996-the-politics-of-presidential-elections_wayne/2426929/#edition=45810193&idiq=40691269.

336 Congressional Research Service, "Electoral College Reforms: 110th Congress Proposals, the National Popular Vote, and Other Alternative Methods," February 9, 2009, https://crsreports.congress.gov/product/pdf/RL/RL34604/7.

337 Stephen J. Wayne, *The Road to the White House 1996: the Politics of Presidential Elections,* Palgrave Macmillan Publishing, Jan. 1, 1995, https://www.thriftbooks.com/w/the-road-to-the-white-house-1996-the-politics-of-presidential-elections_wayne/2426929/#edition=45810193&idiq=40691269.

338 Stephen J. Wayne, *The Road to the White House 1996: the Politics of Presidential Elections,* Palgrave Macmillan Publishing, Jan. 1, 1995, https://www.thriftbooks.com/w/the-road-to-the-white-house-1996-the-politics-of-presidential-elections_wayne/2426929/#edition=45810193&idiq=40691269.

339 Gillian Brockwell, "Of the 700 Attempts to Fix or Abolish the Electoral, This One Nearly Succeeded," *The Washington Post,* Dec. 5, 2020, https://www.washingtonpost.com/history/2020/12/04/abolish-electoral-college-george-wallace-trump-bayh/.

340 Warren Weaver, "Senate Refuses to Halt Debate on Direct Voting," *The New York Times,* Sept. 18, 1970, https://www.nytimes.com/1970/09/18/archives/senate-refuses-to-halt-debate-on-direct-voting-plan-for-popular.html?auth=login-google1tap&login=google1tap.

341 Warren Weaver, "Senate Puts off Direct Vote Plan," *The New York Times,* Sept. 30, 1970, https://www.nytimes.com/1970/09/30/archives/senate-puts-off-direct-vote-plan-mansfield-acts-after-new-attempt.html.

342 Gerhard Peters and John Woolley, *Jimmy Carter Election Reform Letter to Congress, The American Presidency Project*, March 22, 1977, https://www.presidency.ucsb.edu/documents/election-reform-message-the-congress.

343 Warren Weaver, "Carter Proposes End of Electoral College in Presidential Elections," *The New York Times*, Mar. 23, 1977, https://www.nytimes.com/1977/03/23/archives/carter-proposes-end-of-electoral-college-in-presidential-votes.html.

344 *Carter v the Electoral College, Chicago Tribune*, Mar. 24, 1977, sec. 3, page 2.

345 John Koza, Barry Fadem, Mark Grueskin, Michael Mandell, Robert Richie, and Joseph Zimmerman, *Every Vote Equal: A State-Based Plan for Electing the President by National Popular Vote,* 4th Edition, February 2013, https://www.every-vote-equal.com/.

346 John Koza, Barry Fadem, Mark Grueskin, Michael Mandell, Robert Richie, and Joseph Zimmerman, *Every Vote Equal: A State-Based Plan for Electing the President by National Popular Vote,* 4th Edition, February 2013, https://www.every-vote-equal.com/.

347 Stephen J. Wayne, *The Road to the White House 1996: the Politics of Presidential Elections,* Palgrave Macmillan Publishing, Jan. 1, 1995, https://www.thriftbooks.com/w/the-road-to-the-white-house-1996-the-politics-of-presidential-elections_wayne/2426929/#edition=45810193&idiq=40691269.

348 Stephen J. Wayne, *The Road to the White House 1996: the Politics of Presidential Elections,* Palgrave Macmillan Publishing, Jan. 1, 1995, https://www.thriftbooks.com/w/the-road-to-the-white-house-1996-the-politics-of-presidential-elections_wayne/2426929/#edition=45810193&idiq=40691269.

349 Jocelyn Kelly, *Majority of Americans Continue to Favor Moving Away from the Electoral College,* Pew Research Center, September 25, 2023, https://www.pewresearch.org/short-reads/2023/09/25/majority-of-americans-continue-to-favor-moving-away-from-electoral-college/.

350 John Koza, Barry Fadem, Mark Grueskin, Michael Mandell, Robert Richie, and Joseph Zimmerman, *Every Vote Equal: A State-Based*

Plan for Electing the President by National Popular Vote, 4th Edition, February 2013, https://www.every-vote-equal.com/.

351 Keyssar, Alexander, *The Whole Number Proportional Method of Awarding Electoral Votes,* National Popular Election of the President, May 1, 2021, https://www.nationalpopularvote.com/sites/default/files/memo-whole-number-proportional-v7-2021-5-1.pdf.

352 John Koza, Barry Fadem, Mark Grueskin, Michael Mandell, Robert Richie, and Joseph Zimmerman, *Every Vote Equal: A State-Based Plan for Electing the President by National Popular Vote,* 4th Edition, February 2013, https://www.every-vote-equal.com/.

353 Keyssar, Alexander, *The Whole-Number Proportional Method of Awarding Electoral Votes,* National Popular Election of the President, May 1, 2021, https://www.nationalpopularvote.com/sites/default/files/memo-whole-number-proportional-v7-2021-5-1.pdf.

354 Fair Vote, "Past Attempts at Reform," https://fairvote.org/archives/the_electoral_college-past_attempts_at_reform/.

355 Keyssar, Alexander, *The Whole-Number Proportional Method of Awarding Electoral Votes,* National Popular Election of the President, May 1, 2021, https://www.nationalpopularvote.com/sites/default/files/memo-whole-number-proportional-v7-2021-5-1.pdf.

356 John Koza, Barry Fadem, Mark Grueskin, Michael Mandell, Robert Richie, and Joseph Zimmerman, *Every Vote Equal: A State-Based Plan for Electing the President by National Popular Vote,* 4th Edition, February 2013, https://www.every-vote-equal.com/.

Chapter 7: Why 435? The Reapportionment Act of 1929

357 Thirty-Thousand.org, "Return the House of Representatives to the People;" Article updated on Mar. 21, 2022, https://thirty-thousand.org/article-the-first-of-the-bill-of-rights/.

358 United States Census Bureau, "Apportionment Legislation 1790–1830," https://www.census.gov/history/www/reference/apportionment/apportionment_legislation_1790_-_1830.html.

359 United States Census Bureau, "Apportionment Legislation 1790–
     1830," https://www.census.gov/history/www/reference/apportionment/
     apportionment_legislation_1790_-_1830.html.

360 Bradley Smith and Daniel Tokaji, Interactive Constitution by the
     National Constitution Center, *Matters of Debate: The Common
     Interpretation of Article 1, Section 2, the House of Representatives,*
     https://constitutioncenter.org/the-constitution/articles/article-i#article-
     section-2 and https://constitutioncenter.org/the-constitution/articles/
     article-i/clauses/762.

361 United States Census Bureau, "Apportionment Legislation 1790–
     1830," https://www.census.gov/history/www/reference/apportionment/
     apportionment_legislation_1790_-_1830.html.

362 Wikipedia, "United States Electoral College 1788–2024," https://
     en.wikipedia.org/wiki/United_States_Electoral_College.

363 United States Census Bureau, "Apportionment Legislation 1840–
     1880," https://www.census.gov/history/www/reference/apportionment/
     apportionment_legislation_1840_-_1880.html.

364 United States Census Bureau, "Apportionment Legislation
     1890–Present," https://www.census.gov/history/www/reference/
     apportionment/apportionment_legislation_1890_-_present.html.

365 United States Census Bureau, "Apportionment Legislation
     1890–Present," https://www.census.gov/history/www/reference/
     apportionment/apportionment_legislation_1890_-_present.html.

366 United States Census Bureau, "Apportionment Legislation
     1890-Present," https://www.census.gov/history/www/reference/
     apportionment/apportionment_legislation_1890_-_present.html.

367 United States Census Bureau, "Apportionment Legislation
     1890–Present," https://www.census.gov/history/www/reference/
     apportionment/apportionment_legislation_1890_-_present.html.

368 History.com Editors, April 14, 2010, "The Roaring Twenties: the
     Politics of the 1920s," https://www.history.com/topics/roaring-twenties/
     roaring-twenties-history#immigration-and-racism-in-the-1920s.

369 Ron Elving, NPR, July 10, 2019. "Cities and Immigrants
     Drove Census Controversy 100 Years Ago," https://www.npr.

org/2019/07/10/738111496/cities-and-immigrants-drove-census-controversy-100-years-ago#:~:text=The%20special%20case%20of%20the%201920%20census&text=The%20problem%20was%20that%20the,in%20towns%20smaller%20than%202%2C500.

370 Ron Elving, NPR, July 10, 2019. "Cities and Immigrants Drove Census Controversy 100 Years Ago," https://www.npr.org/2019/07/10/738111496/cities-and-immigrants-drove-census-controversy-100-years-ago#:~:text=The%20special%20case%20of%20the%201920%20census&text=The%20problem%20was%20that%20the,in%20towns%20smaller%20than%202%2C500.

371 United States Census Bureau, "Reapportionment and Census Act of 1929 (June 18, 1929) and the Act Providing for the Fifteenth Census and for the Apportionment of Representatives in Congress," https://www.census.gov/history/pdf/ApportionmentInformation-1930Census.pdf.

372 Wikipedia, "Reapportionment Act of 1929," https://en.wikipedia.org/wiki/Reapportionment_ Act_ of_ 1929#:~:text=The%20Reapportionment%20Act%20of%201929,Representatives%20according%20to%20each%20census.

373 United States Census Bureau, "Reapportionment and Census Act of 1929 (June 18, 1929) and the Act Providing for the Fifteenth Census and for the Apportionment of Representatives in Congress," https://www.census.gov/history/pdf/ApportionmentInformation-1930Census.pdf.

374 Thirty-Thoousand.org, "Return the House of Representatives to the People: Restore the People's House," https://thirty-thousand.org/overview/.

375 The American Academy of Arts and Sciences, The Case for Enlarging the House of Representatives, an *"Our Common Purpose,"* report (Dec. 2021), https://www.amacad.org/ourcommonpurpose/enlarging-the-house.

376 Nicholas G. Napolio and Jeffrey J. Jenkins, *Conflict over Congressional Reapportionment: The Deadlock of the 1920s,* https://www.cambridge.org/core/journals/journal-of-policy-history/article/conflict-over-congressional-reapportionment-the-deadlock-of-the-1920s/EF7DC3467A2812EEA2490EF2239DC499.

377   Michael Balinski and H. Peyton Young, *Fair Representation Meeting the Ideal of One Man One Vote,* the Yale University Press, 1982, https://repository.law.umich.edu/cgi/viewcontent.cgi?article=3532&context=mlr.

378   Wikipedia, "Urbanization in the United States," https://en.wikipedia.org/wiki/Urbanization_in_the_United_States.

379   Nicholas G. Napolio and Jeffrey J. Jenkins, *Conflict over Congressional Reapportionment: The Deadlock of the 1920s,* https://www.cambridge.org/core/journals/journal-of-policy-history/article/conflict-over-congressional-reapportionment-the-deadlock-of-the-1920s/EF7DC3467A2812EEA2490EF2239DC499.

380   Grant Tudor and Beau Tremitiere, *Toward Proportional Representation for the U.S. House: Amending the Uniform Congressional District Act,* March 2023, Protect Democracy and Unite America, https://protectdemocracy.org/work/proportional-representation-uniform-congressional-district-act/.

381   Nicholas G. Napolio and Jeffrey J. Jenkins, *Conflict over Congressional Reapportionment: The Deadlock of the 1920s,* https://www.cambridge.org/core/journals/journal-of-policy-history/article/conflict-over-congressional-reapportionment-the-deadlock-of-the-1920s/EF7DC3467A2812EEA2490EF2239DC499.

382   Grant Tudor and Beau Tremitiere, *Toward Proportional Representation for the U.S. House: Amending the Uniform Congressional District Act,* March 2023, Protect Democracy and Unite America, https://protectdemocracy.org/work/proportional-representation-uniform-congressional-district-act/.

383   Tom Murse as updated on February 12, 2020, ThoughtCo., "How Many Members Are in the House of Representative?" https://www.thoughtco.com/members-in-the-house-of-representatives-3368242

384   Robert Longley, ThoughtCo, Sept. 1, 2022, "Apportionment and the US Census," https://www.thoughtco.com/apportionment-and-the-us-census-3320967.

385   Kristen Koslap, "How Apportionment Is Calculated," United States Census Bureau, April 26, 2021, https://www.census.gov/newsroom/

blogs/random-samplings/2021/04/how-apportionment-is-calculated. html#:~:text=Mathematically%20speaking%2C%20the%20goal%20 of,per%20representative)%20among%20the%20states.

386 Lee Drutman, Jonathan Cohen, Yuval Levin, and Norman Ornstein, *The Case for Enlarging the House of Representatives, Recommendation 1.1,* American Academy of Arts and Sciences, 2021, https://www. amacad.org/ourcommonpurpose/recommendation-1-1.

387 Robert Longley, ThoughtCo, Sept. 1, 2022, "Apportionment and the US Census," https://www.thoughtco.com/apportionment-and-the-us-census-3320967.

388 Robert Longley, ThoughtCo, Sept. 1, 2022 "Apportionment and the US Census," https://www.thoughtco.com/apportionment-and-the-us-census-3320967.

389 Thirty-Thoousand.org, *Restore the People's House,* The American Academy of Arts and Sciences, *The Case for Enlarging the House of Representatives, an "Our Common Purpose"* report (Dec. 2021), https://thirty-thousand.org/overview/.

390 Tom Murse as updated on February 12, 2020, ThoughtCo., "How Many Members Are in the House of Representative?" https://www.thoughtco. com/members-in-the-house-of-representatives-3368242.

391 Alexander Hamilton and James Madison, *Federalist Papers: No.55, the Total number of the House of Representatives,* Yale Law School Lillian Goldman Law Library: The Avalon Project: Federalist No 55 from the New York Packet, Friday, Feb. 15, 1788, https://avalon.law. yale.edu/18th_century/fed55.asp.

392 Thirty-thousand.org, March 21, 2022, "Return the House of Representatives to the People: Section Two: Article of the First of the Bill of Rights," https://thirty-thousand.org/article-the-first-of-the-bill-of-rights/.

393 Tom Murse as updated on February 12, 2020, ThoughtCo., "How Many Members Are in the House of Representative?" https://www.thoughtco. com/members-in-the-house-of-representatives-3368242.

394 Tom Murse as updated on February 12, 2020, ThoughtCo., "How Many Members Are in the House of Representative?" https://www.thoughtco. com/members-in-the-house-of-representatives-3368242.

395 Tom Murse as updated on February 12, 2020, ThoughtCo., "How Many Members Are in the House of Representative?" https://www.thoughtco.com/members-in-the-house-of-representatives-3368242.

396 James Wilson, one of the signatories of the Constitution, speaking at the Pennsylvania ratification convention. See: Farrand's Records, Volume 3, pages 159–160, November 30, 1787, https://thirty-thousand.org/article-the-first-of-the-bill-of-rights/.

397 Alexander Hamilton and James Madison, *Federalist Papers: No.55, the Total number of the House of Representatives,* Yale Law School Lillian Goldman Law Library: The Avalon Project: Federalist No 55 from the New York Packet, Friday, Feb. 15, 1788, https://avalon.law.yale.edu/18th_century/fed55.asp.

398 Thity-thousand.org, "Replace Career Politicians with Citizen Legislators and Return the House of Representatives to the People," https://thirty-thousand.org/overview/.

399 Thirty-thousand.org., March 21, 2022, "Return the House of Representatives to the People: Section Two: Article of the First of the Bill of Rights," https://thirty-thousand.org/article-the-first-of-the-bill-of-rights/.

400 Lee Drutman, Jonathan Cohen, Yuval Levin, and Norman Ornstein, *The Case for Enlarging the House of Representatives, Recommendation 1.1,* American Academy of Arts and Sciences, 2021, https://www.amacad.org/ourcommonpurpose/recommendation-1-1.

401 Our Common Purpose, *The Case for Enlarging the House of Representatives—Part II: The House and Representative Democracy,* https://www.amacad.org/ourcommonpurpose/enlarging-the-house/section/3.

Chapter 8: Today's Effects of the Winner-Take-All Electoral College

402 Ballotpedia, 270 to Win.com, "Electoral College in the 2024 Presidential Election," April 26,2021, https://ballotpedia.org/Electoral_College_in_the_2024_presidential_election.

403 Fair Vote, "How the Electoral Vote Became Winner-Take-All," August 21, 2012, https://fairvote.org/how-the-electoral-college-became-winner-take-all/.

404 John Koza, Barry Fadem, Mark Grueskin, Michael Mandell, Robert Richie, and Joseph Zimmerman, *Every Vote Equal: A State-Based Plan for Electing the President by National Popular Vote,* 4th Edition, February 2013, https://www.every-vote-equal.com/.

405 Fair Vote, "How the Electoral Vote Became Winner-Take-All," August 21, 2012, https://fairvote.org/how-the-electoral-college-became-winner-take-all/.

406 Jesse Wegman (with Sam Kolitch), *Examining the Electoral College: An Interview with Jese Wegman,* December 7, 2020, the Brown Political Review, https://brownpoliticalreview.org/2020/12/let-the-people-pick-the-president-bpr-interviews-jesse-wegman/.

407 Nate Cohn, *The Winner-Take-All Electoral College Isn't In the Constitution,* Taegan Goddards Electoral Vote Map, https://electoralvotemap.com/winner-take-all-electoral-college/.

408 Andrew Chung and Lawrence Hurley, "US Supreme Court Curbs Faithless Electors in Presidential Voting," Reuters, July 6, 2020 (updated from 2016), https://www.reuters.com/article/idUSKBN2472Q0/.

409 Nate Cohn, *The Winner-Take-All Electoral College Isn't In the Constitution,* Taegan Goddards Electoral Vote Map, https://electoralvotemap.com/winner-take-all-electoral-college/.

410 Nate Cohn, *The Winner-Take-All Electoral College Isn't In the Constitution,* Taegan Goddards Electoral Vote Map, https://electoralvotemap.com/winner-take-all-electoral-college/.

411 Wikipedia, per 2020 US Census Bureau, "List of US States and Territories by Population," https://en.wikipedia.org/wiki/List_of_U.S._states_and_territories_by_population#References.

412 Wikipedia, per 2020 U.S. Census Bureau, "List of US States and Territories by Population," https://en.wikipedia.org/wiki/List_of_U.S._states_and_territories_by_population#References.

413 Ballotpedia, 270 to Win.com, "Electoral College in the 2024 Presidential Election," April 26, 2021, https://ballotpedia.org/Electoral_College_in_the_2024_presidential_election.

414 Tara Ross, *Founders Created the Electoral College as a Check to Tyranny,* *The Washington Times,* Feb. 2, 2021, https://www.washingtontimes.com/news/2021/feb/2/tara-ross-founders-created-electoral-college-check/.

415 Jesse Wegman (with Sam Kolitch), *Examining the Electoral College: An Interview with Jese Wegman,* December 7, 2020, the Brown Political Review, https://brownpoliticalreview.org/2020/12/let-the-people-pick-the-president-bpr-interviews-jesse-wegman/.

416 Jason Harrow, Opinion Contributor, "The Winner-Take-All Presidential System Is Unconstitutional. We're Taking It to Court," USA Today, March 8, 2018, https://www.usatoday.com/story/opinion/2018/03/08/winner-take-all-presidential-system-unconstitutional-court-challenge-jason-harrow-column/398742002/.

417 Tara Ross, *The Indispensable Electoral College: How the Founders Plan Saves Our Country from Mob Rule,* Regnery Gateway, 2004, https://www.taraross.com/product-page/the-indispensable-electoral-college-how-the-founders-plan-saves-our-country-from-mob-rule.

418 Jason Harrow, Opinion Contributor, "The Winner-Take-All Presidential System Is Unconstitutional. We're Taking It to Court," USA Today, March 8, 2018, https://www.usatoday.com/story/opinion/2018/03/08/winner-take-all-presidential-system-unconstitutional-court-challenge-jason-harrow-column/398742002/.

419 John Koza, Barry Fadem, Mark Grueskin, Michael Mandell, Robert Richie, and Joseph Zimmerman, *Every Vote Equal: A State-Based Plan for Electing the President by National Popular Vote,* 4th Edition, February 2013, https://www.every-vote-equal.com/.

420 John Koza, Barry Fadem, Mark Grueskin, Michael Mandell, Robert Richie, and Joseph Zimmerman, *Every Vote Equal: A State-Based Plan for Electing the President by National Popular Vote,* 4th Edition, February 2013, https://www.every-vote-equal.com/.

421 Alexander Belensky, *Electoral College in the Two-Party System. Mathematical and Computer Modeling Presidential Elections,* pages 716–717, *Every Vote Equal: A State-Based Plan for Electing the President by National Popular Vote,* https://www.every-vote-equal.com/.

422 Jesse Wegman, *Let the People Pick the President: the Case for Abolishing the Electoral College.* St. Martins Press, https://us.macmillan.com/books/9781250221971/letthepeoplepickthepresident.

423 Jesse Wegman, *Let the People Pick the President: the Case for Abolishing the Electoral College,* St. Martins Press, https://us.macmillan.com/books/9781250221971/letthepeoplepickthepresident.

424 Jesse Wegman (with Sam Kolitch), "Examining the Electoral College: An Interview with Jese Wegman," December 7, 2020, the Brown Political Review, https://brownpoliticalreview.org/2020/12/let-the-people-pick-the-president-bpr-interviews-jesse-wegman/.

425 Phillip Bump, "The Two States that Almost Always Predicts Which Candidate is Headed for Defeat," *The Washington Post*, September 7, 2016, https://www.washingtonpost.com/news/the-fix/wp/2016/09/07/the-two-states-that-almost-always-predict-which-candidate-is-headed-for-defeat/.

426 270towiin.com, *Historical Presidential Elections,* https://www.270towin.com/historical-presidential-elections/.

Chapter 9: Analyzing False Myths

427 John Koza, Barry Fadem, Mark Grueskin, Michael Mandell, Robert Richie, and Joseph Zimmerman, Every Vote Equal: A State-Based Plan for Electing the President by National Popular Vote: Chapter 9.17.1-Myth: A National Vote Would Be Mob Rule, 4th Edition, February 2013, https://www.nationalpopularvote.com/section_9.1.

428 Patrick Rosenstiel, "Dispelling National Popular Vote Myths," Savanah Morning News, March 3, 2019, https://www.savannahnow.com/story/opinion/columns/2019/03/03/patrick-rosenstiel-column-reform-vote-with-national-popular-vote-compact/53215068007/.

429 John Koza, Barry Fadem, Mark Grueskin, Michael Mandell, Robert Richie, and Joseph Zimmerman, *Every Vote Equal: A State-Based Plan for Electing the President by National Popular Vote: Chapter 9.17.1-Myth: A National Vote Would Be Mob Rule,* 4th Edition, February 2013, https://www.nationalpopularvote.com/section_9.1.

430 National Constitution Center, "Article 2, Section 1, Executive Branch," https://constitutioncenter.org/the-constitution/articles/article-ii#article-section-1.

431 Jesse Wegman, *Let the People Pick the President: the Case for Abolishing the Electoral College,* St. Martins Press, https://us.macmillan.com/books/9781250221971/letthepeoplepickthepresident.

432 John Koza, Barry Fadem, Mark Grueskin, Michael Mandell, Robert Richie, and Joseph Zimmerman, *Every Vote Equal: A State-Based Plan for Electing the President by National Popular Vote: Chapter 9.17.1-Myth: A National Vote Would Be Mob Rule,* 4th Edition, February 2013, https://www.nationalpopularvote.com/section_9.17.

433 John Koza, Barry Fadem, Mark Grueskin, Michael Mandell, Robert Richie, and Joseph Zimmerman, *Every Vote Equal: A State-Based Plan for Electing the President by National Popular Vote: Chapter 9.17.1-Myth: A National Vote Would Be Mob Rule,* 4th Edition, February 2013, https://www.nationalpopularvote.com/section_9.3.

434 John Koza, Barry Fadem, Mark Grueskin, Michael Mandell, Robert Richie, and Joseph Zimmerman, *Every Vote Equal: A State-Based Plan for Electing the President by National Popular Vote: Chapter 9.17.1-Myth: A National Vote Would Be Mob Rule,* 4th Edition, February 2013, https://www.nationalpopularvote.com/section_9.3.

435 John Koza, Barry Fadem, Mark Grueskin, Michael Mandell, Robert Richie, and Joseph Zimmerman, *Every Vote Equal: A State-Based Plan for Electing the President by National Popular Vote: Chapter 9.17.1-Myth: A National Vote Would Be Mob Rule,"* 4th Edition, February 2013, https://www.nationalpopularvote.com/section_9.31.1.

436 Wikipedia, "List of United States Presidential Elections by Popular Vote Margins," https://en.wikipedia.org/wiki/List_of_United_States_presidential_elections_by_popular_vote_margin.

437 Jesse Wegman, *Let the People Pick the President: the Case for Abolishing the Electoral College,* St. Martins Press, https://us.macmillan.com/books/9781250221971/letthepeoplepickthepresident.

[438] Wikipedia, "List of United States Presidential Elections by Popular Vote Margins," https://en.wikipedia.org/wiki/List_of_United_States_presidential_elections_by_popular_vote_margin.

[439] Wikipedia, "List of Third-Party and Independent Performances in United States Presidential Elections," https://en.wikipedia.org/wiki/List_of_third-party_and_independent_performances_in_United_States_presidential_elections.

[440] Jesse Wegman, *Let the People Pick the President: the Case for Abolishing the Electoral College,* St. Martins Press, https://us.macmillan.com/books/9781250221971/letthepeoplepickthepresident.

[441] Joscelyn Kiley, "Majority of Americans Continue to Favor Moving Away from the Electoral College," September 25, 2023, https://www.pewresearch.org/short-reads/2023/09/25/majority-of-americans-continue-to-favor-moving-away-from-electoral-college/.

[442] The White House, "From the President to the Vice President to the Cabinet, learn more about the Executive Branch of the Government of the United States," WH.gov, the White House, 2024, https://www.whitehouse.gov/about-the-white-house/our-government/the-executive-branch/.

[443] Tara Ross, *The Indispensable Electoral College: How the Founders' Plan Saves Our Country from Mob Rule,* Regnery Gateway Publishing, https://www.taraross.com/product-page/the-indispensable-electoral-college-how-the-founders-plan-saves-our-country-fr.

[444] John Koza, Barry Fadem, Mark Grueskin, Michael Mandell, Robert Richie, and Joseph Zimmerman, *Every Vote Equal: A State-Based Plan for Electing the President by National Popular Vote: Chapter 9.17.1-Myth: A National Vote Would Be Mob Rule,* 4th Edition, February 2013, https://www.nationalpopularvote.com/section_9.7.3.

[445] Jesse Wegman, *Let the People Pick the President: the Case for Abolishing the Electoral College,* St. Martins Press, https://us.macmillan.com/books/9781250221971/letthepeoplepickthepresident.

[446] Jesse Wegman, *Let the People Pick the President: the Case for Abolishing the Electoral College,* St. Martins Press, https://us.macmillan.com/books/9781250221971/letthepeoplepickthepresident.

447   Merrill Matthews, *Third-Party Presidential Candidates Who Changed American History,* The Hill, August 1, 2023, https://thehill.com/opinion/white-house/4130884-third-party-presidential-candidates-who-changed-american-history/.

448   Merrill Matthews, *Third-Party Presidential Candidates Who Changed American History,* The Hill, August 1, 2023, https://thehill.com/opinion/white-house/4130884-third-party-presidential-candidates-who-changed-american-history/.

449   Jesse Wegman, *Let the People Pick the President: the Case for Abolishing the Electoral College,* St. Martins Press, https://us.macmillan.com/books/9781250221971/letthepeoplepickthepresident.

450   Merrill Matthews, *Third-Party Presidential Candidates Who Changed American History,* The Hill, August 1, 2023, https://thehill.com/opinion/white-house/4130884-third-party-presidential-candidates-who-changed-american-history/.

451   Jesse Wegman, *Let the People Pick the President: the Case for Abolishing the Electoral College,* St Martins Press, https://us.macmillan.com/books/9781250221971/letthepeoplepickthepresident.

452   Merrill Matthews, *Third-Party Presidential Candidates Who Changed American History,* The Hill, August 1, 2023, https://thehill.com/opinion/white-house/4130884-third-party-presidential-candidates-who-changed-american-history/.

453   Merrill Matthews, *Third-Party Presidential Candidates Who Changed American History,* The Hill, August 1, 2023, https://thehill.com/opinion/white-house/4130884-third-party-presidential-candidates-who-changed-american-history/.

454   Patrick Rosenstiel, *Dispelling National Popular Vote Myths,* Savanah Morning News, March 3, 2019, https://www.savannahnow.com/story/opinion/columns/2019/03/03/patrick-rosenstiel-column-reform-vote-with-national-popular-vote-compact/532215068007/.

Chapter 10: Enlarging the House and Expanding the Electoral College

455 Thirty-thousand.org, "Return the House of Representatives to the People: Replace Career Politicians with Citizen Legislators," https://thirty-thousand.org/overview/.

456 James Ceasar and Jamin Raskin, "Common Interpretation of Article 2, Section 1 of the Constitution," National Constitution Center, https://constitutioncenter.org/the-constitution/articles/article-ii/clauses/350.

457 Thirty-thousand.org, March 21, 2022, "Return the House of Representatives to the People: Section Two: Article of the First of the Bill of Rights," https://thirty-thousand.org/article-the-first-of-the-bill-of-rights/.

458 Thirty-thousand.org, March 21, 2022, "Return the House of Representatives to the People: Section Two: Article of the First of the Bill of Rights," https://thirty-thousand.org/article-the-first-of-the-bill-of-rights/.

459 Alexander Hamilton and James Madison, *Federalist Papers: No.55, the Total number of the House of Representatives,* Yale Law School Lillian Goldman Law Library: The Avalon Project: Federalist No 55 from the New York Packet, Friday, Feb. 15, 1788, https://avalon.law.yale.edu/18th_century/fed55.asp.

460 Danielle Allen, "Just How Big Should the House Be? Let's Do the Math," *The Washington Post,* March 28, 2023, https://www.washingtonpost.com/opinions/2023/03/28/danielle-allen-democracy-reform-house-representatives-districts/.

461 American Academy of Arts and Sciences, *The Case for Enlarging the House of Representatives – Part IV: Alternative Proposals for House Enlargement,* 2021, https://www.amacad.org/sites/default/files/publication/downloads/2021_Enlarging-the-House.pdf.

462 United States Census Bureau, "Apportionment Legislation 1890–Present," Census.gov, History, Apportionment, https://www.census.gov/history/www/reference/apportionment/apportionment_legislation_1890_-_present.html.

463 Robert Longley, ThoughtCo, Sept. 1, 2022, "Apportionment and the U.S. Census" https://www.thoughtco.com/apportionment-and-the-us-census-3320967.

464 Tom Murse as updated on February 12, 2020, ThoughtCo., "How Many Members Are in the House of Representative?" https://www.thoughtco.com/members-in-the-house-of-representatives-3368242.

465 United States Census Bureau, "Reapportionment and Census Act of 1929 (June 18, 1929) and the Act Providing for the Fifteenth Census and for the Apportionment of Representatives in Congress," https://www.census.gov/history/pdf/ApportionmentInformation-1930Census.pdf.

466 History.com Editors, April 14, 2010, "The Roaring Twenties: the Politics of the 1920s," https://www.history.com/topics/roaring-twenties/roaring-twenties-history#immigration-and-racism-in-the-1920s.

467 United States Census Bureau, "Apportionment Legislation 1890-Present," Census.gov, History, Apportionment, https://www.census.gov/history/www/reference/apportionment/apportionment_legislation_1890_-_present.html.

468 Thirty-thousand.org, "Return the House of Representatives to the People: Replace Career Politicians with Citizen Legislators," https://thirty-thousand.org/overview/.

469 United States Census Bureau, "Apportionment Legislation 1890–Present," https://www.census.gov/history/www/reference/apportionment/apportionment_legislation_1890_-_present.html.

470 Bradley Smith and Daniel Tokaji, "The United States Constitution: Article 2," National Constitution Center, https://constitutioncenter.org/the-constitution/articles/article-i/clauses/762.

471 Bradley Smith and Daniel Tokaji, "The United States Constitution: Article 2," National Constitution Center, https://constitutioncenter.org/the-constitution/articles/article-i/clauses/762.

472 Thirty-thousand.org, "Return the House of Representatives to the People: Replace Career Politicians with Citizen Legislators," https://thirty-thousand.org/overview/.

473 Kristen Koslap, Senior Technical Expert for Apportionment, Population Division, and Steven Wilson, Chief, Population and Housing Programs

Brach, Population Division, United States Census Bureau, "How Apportionment Is Calculated," https://www.census.gov/newsroom/blogs/random-samplings/2021/04/how-apportionment-is-calculated.html#:~:text=Mathematically%20speaking%2C%20the%20goal%20of,per%20representative)%20among%20the%20states.

[474] Watson Davis, Science, Vol. 93, No. 2411, Mar. 14, 1941, *The 1941 Apportionment Bill,* https://www.science.org/doi/10.1126/science.93.2411.6.s.

[475] National Archives, *Constitutional Amendment Process,* Office of the Federal Register (OFR), August 15, 2016, https://www.archives.gov/federal-register/constitution.

[476] 270 to Win, *Historical Presidential Elections,* 270towin.com, https://www.270towin.com/historical-presidential-elections/.

[477] Sean Trende, *It's Time to Increase the Size of the House,* Sabato's Crytal Ball, UVA-Center for Politics, March 6, 2014, https://centerforpolitics.org/crystalball/articles/its-time-to-increase-the-size-of-the-house/.

[478] Lee Drutman, Jonathan Cohen, Yuval Levin, and Norman Ornstein, *The Case for Enlarging the House of Representatives – Part IV: Alternative Proposals for House Enlargement,* 2021, American Academy of Arts and Sciences, https://www.amacad.org/ourcommonpurpose/enlarging-the-house/section/5_and_https://www.amacad.org/sites/default/files/publication/downloads/2021_Enlarging-the-House.pdf.

[479] James Madison, *Federalist 55 (1788),* National Constitution Center, Historic Documents, https://constitutioncenter.org/the-constitution/historic-document-library/detail/james-madison-federalist-no-55-1788#:~:text=In%20Federalist%2055%2C%20Madison%20addressed,importance%20of%20civic%20republican%20virtue.

[480] Sean Trende, *It's Time to Increase the Size of the House,* Sabato's Crytal Ball UVA-Center for Politics, March 6, 2014, https://centerforpolitics.org/crystalball/articles/its-time-to-increase-the-size-of-the-house/.

[481] Lee Drutman, Jonathan Cohen, Yuval Levin, and Norman Ornstein, *The Case for Enlarging the House of Representatives – Part IV: Alternative Proposals for House Enlargement,* 2021, American Academy of Arts and Sciences, https://www.amacad.org/ourcommonpurpose/

enlarging-the-house/section/5 and_https://www.amacad.org/sites/default/files/publication/downloads/2021_Enlarging-the-House.pdf.

[482] Lee Drutman, Jonathan Cohen, Yuval Levin, and Norman Ornstein. *The Case for Enlarging the House of Representatives – Part IV: Alternative Proposals for House Enlargement,* 2021, American Academy of Arts and Sciences, https://www.amacad.org/ourcommonpurpose/enlarging-the-house/section/5 and_https://www.amacad.org/sites/default/files/publication/downloads/2021_Enlarging-the-House.pdf.

[483] Lee Drutman, Jonathan Cohen, Yuval Levin, and Norman Ornstein. *The Case for Enlarging the House of Representatives – Part IV: Alternative Proposals for House Enlargement,* 2021, American Academy of Arts and Sciences, https://www.amacad.org/sites/default/files/publication/downloads/2021_Enlarging-the-House.pdf.

[484] Danielle Allen, *"Just How Big Should The House Be? Let's Do the Math,"* *The Washington Post*, March 28, 2023, https://www.washingtonpost.com/opinions/2023/03/28/danielle-allen-democracy-reform-house-representatives-districts/.

[485] Statista Research Department, *Population Projections for the United States from 2015 to 2060,* Statista, Dec. 31, 2014, https://www.statista.com/statistics/183481/united-states-population-projection/.

Chapter 11: What Is the Wyoming Rule and the Cubic Root Rule

[486] Thirty-thousand.org, "Return the House of Representatives to the People," https://thirty-thousand.org/overview/.

[487] Thirty-thousand.org, "Return the House of Representatives to the People," https://thirty-thousand.org/overview/.

[488] National Archives, Office of the Federal Register (OFR), *Constitutional Amendment Process,* https://www.archives.gov/federal-register/constitution.

[489] Dennis Negron, *The Different Ways of Expanding the House,* Sabato's Crystal Ball, UVA – Center for Politics, May 18, 2021,

https://centerforpolitics.org/crystalball/articles/the-different-ways-of-expanding-the-house/.

490   Our Common Purpose, *The Case for Enlarging the House of Representative, Part IV: Alternative Proposals for House Enlargement,* American Academy of Arts and Sciences, https://www.amacad.org/ourcommonpurpose/enlarging-the-house/section/5.

491   Dennis Negron, *The Different Ways of Expanding the House,* Sabato's Crystal Ball, UVA – Center for Politics, May 18, 2021,. https://centerforpolitics.org/crystalball/articles/the-different-ways-of-expanding-the-house/.

492   Danielle Allen, "Just How Big Should the House Be? Let's Do the Math," *The Washington Post*, March 28, 2023, https://www.washingtonpost.com/opinions/2023/03/28/danielle-allen-democracy-reform-house-representatives-districts/.

493   Godzoriz Community, *Implementing the Wyoming Rule,* Daily Kos, July 5, 2018, https://www.dailykos.com/stories/2018/7/5/1778149/-Implementing-the-Wyoming-Rule.

494   Dennis Negron, *The Different Ways of Expanding the House,* Sabato's Crystal Ball, UVA – Center for Politics, May 18, 2021. https://centerforpolitics.org/crystalball/articles/the-different-ways-of-expanding-the-house/.

495   Dennis Negron, *The Different Ways of Expanding the House,* Sabato's Crystal Ball, UVA – Center for Politics, May 18, 2021, https://centerforpolitics.org/crystalball/articles/the-different-ways-of-expanding-the-house/.

496   United States Census Bureau, "2020 Census Apportionment Results Delivered to the President" Archived from April 26, 2021, https://www.census.gov/newsroom/press-releases/2021/2020-census-apportionment-results.html.

497   Dennis Negron, *The Different Ways of Expanding the House,* Sabato's Crystal Ball, UVA – Center for Politics, May 18, 2021, https://centerforpolitics.org/crystalball/articles/the-different-ways-of-expanding-the-house/.

[498] Fair Vote, "Why 435? How We Can Change the Size of the House of Representatives," October 12, 2017, https://fairvote.org/how_we_can_change_the_size_of_the_house_of_representatives/.

[499] United States Census, "Apportionment Legislation 1890–Present," https://www.census.gov/history/www/reference/apportionment/apportionment_legislation_1890_-_present.html.

[500] Wikipedia, "Increase the Size of the House via the Wyoming Rule," January 25, 2005, and Steve Taylor, "Representation in the House: the Wyoming Rule," https://en.wikipedia.org/wiki/Wyoming_Rule.

[501] Fair Vote, "Why 435? How We Can Change the Size of the House of Representatives," October 12, 2017, https://fairvote.org/how_we_can_change_the_size_of_the_house_of_representatives/.

[502] Thirty-thousand.org, "The Wyoming and Cubic Root Rules Are Ineffectual Proposals," https://thirty-thousand.org/blog/the-wyoming-and-cube-root-rules/.

[503] Godzoriz Community, *Implementing the Wyoming Rule,* Daily Kos, July 5, 2018, https://www.dailykos.com/stories/2018/7/5/1778149/-Implementing-the-Wyoming-Rule.

[504] American Academy of Arts and Sciences, *The Case for Enlarging the House of Representatives – Part IV: Alternative Proposals for House Enlargement,* 2021, https://www.amacad.org/ourcommonpurpose/enlarging-the-house/section/5.

[505] Alexander Kirk, *The Electoral College: Size Really Does Matter, The Wyoming Rule,* Wikiwand 2020. https://www.wikiwand.com/en/Wyoming_Rule.

[506] Wikipedia, "Wyoming Rule," Published 2024, https://en.wikipedia.org/wiki/Wyoming_Rule#:~:text=The%20Wyoming%20Rule%20is%20a,state%2C%20which%20is%20currently%20Wyoming.

[507] Da Fireball of Daily Kos, *Let's Cube Root … North Dakota and South Dakota,* Daily Kos, September 19, 2014, https://www.dailykos.com/stories/2014/12/19/1352973/-Let-s-Cube-Root-North-Dakota-and-South-Dakota.

508   Rein Taagepera, *The Size of National Assemblies,* Social Science Research and the UV Irvine Published Works, 1972. https://escholarship.org/uc/item/45g370k4.

509   Cuemath, *What Is Cube Root,* https://www.cuemath.com/algebra/cubes-and-cube-roots/#.

510   Rein Taagepera, *The Size of National Assemblies,* Social Science Research and the UV Irvine Published Works, 1972, https://escholarship.org/uc/item/45g370k4.

511   Fair Vote, "Why 435? How We Can Change the Size of the House of Representatives," October 12, 2017, https://fairvote.org/how_we_can_change_the_size_of_the_house_of_representatives/.

512   Fair Vote, "Why 435? How We Can Change the Size of the House of Representatives," October 12, 2017, https://fairvote.org/how_we_can_change_the_size_of_the_house_of_representatives/.

513   Thirty-thousand.org, *Commentaries on Representation using the Wyoming and Cube Root Rules,* https://thirty-thousand.org/blog/the-wyoming-and-cube-root-rules/.

514   Lee Drutman, Jonathan Cohen, Yuval Levin, and Norman Ornstein, *The Case for Enlarging the House of Representatives – Part IV: Alternative Proposals for House Enlargement,* 2021, American Academy of Arts and Sciences, https://www.amacad.org/ourcommonpurpose/enlarging-the-house/section/5.

515   Thirty-thousand.org, "Commentaries on Representation Using the Wyoming and Cube Root Rules," https://thirty-thousand.org/blog/the-wyoming-and-cube-root-rules/.

516   Lee Drutman, Jonathan Cohen, Yuval Levin, and Norman Ornstein, *The Case for Enlarging the House of Representatives – Part IV: Alternative Proposals for House Enlargement,* 2021, American Academy of Arts and Sciences, https://www.amacad.org/ourcommonpurpose/enlarging-the-house/section/5.

517   Lucas Vaughn, "Opinion: The Cube Root Rule Would Change United States Politics for the Better," The Fayetteville Observer, June 18, 2020, https://www.fayobserver.com/story/opinion/columns/2020/06/18/

opinion-lsquocube-root-rulersquo-would-change-us-politics-for-better/41747965/.

518 Lucas Vaughn, "Opinion: The Cube Root Rule Would Change United States Politics for the Better," The Fayetteville Observer, June 18, 2020, https://www.fayobserver.com/story/opinion/columns/2020/06/18/opinion-lsquocube-root-rulersquo-would-change-us-politics-for-better/41747965/.

519 Lucas Vaughn, "Opinion: The Cube Root Rule Would Change United States Politics for the Better," The Fayetteville Observer, June 18, 2020, https://www.fayobserver.com/story/opinion/columns/2020/06/18/opinion-lsquocube-root-rulersquo-would-change-us-politics-for-better/41747965/.

520 Thirty-thousand.org, "Commentaries on Representation Using the Wyoming and Cube Root Rules," https://thirty-thousand.org/blog/the-wyoming-and-cube-root-rules/.

Chapter 12: The National Popular Vote Plan for the Future

521 Jesse Wegman, Let the People Pick the President: the Case for Abolishing the Electoral College, St. Martins Press, https://us.macmillan.com/books/9781250221971/letthepeoplepickthepresident.

522 NCSL – National Conference of State Legislatures, *National Popular Vote,* Updated December 7, 2023, https://www.ncsl.org/elections-and-campaigns/national-popular-vote.

523 Dale Read Jr., *Direct Election of the President Without a Constitutional Amendment: A Call to State Action,* Washington Law Review, vol. 51, https://digitalcommons.law.uw.edu/cgi/viewcontent.cgi?article=2019&context=wlr.

524 Robert Bennett, *Popular Election of the President without a Constitutional Amendment,* The Green Bag, from the original on August 14, 2019, http://www.greenbag.org/v4n3/v4n3_articles_bennett.pdf.

525 Akhil Amar and Vikram Amar, "How to Achieve Direct National Election of the President without Amending the Constitution, a Three-Part Series on the 2000 Election," Find Law, December 28, 2001, https://supreme.findlaw.com/legal-commentary/how-to-achieve-direct-national-election-of-the-president-without-amending-the-constitution.html.

526 Akhil Reed Amar and Vikram David Amar, "How to Achieve Direct National Election of the President without Amending the Constitution," FindLaw, Dec. 28, 2001, https://supreme.findlaw.com/legal-commentary/how-to-achieve-direct-national-election-of-the-president-without-amending-the-constitution.html.

527 Jesse Wegman, *Let the People Pick the President: the Case for Abolishing the Electoral College,* St. Martins Press, https://us.macmillan.com/books/9781250221971/letthepeoplepickthepresident.

528 John Koza, Barry Fadem, Mark Grueskin, Michael Mandell, Robert Richie, and Joseph Zimmerman, *Every Vote Equal: A State-Based Plan for Electing the President by National Popular Vote,* 4th Edition, February 2013, https://www.every-vote-equal.com/.

529 Thomas Neale and Andrew Nolan, *The National Popular Vote (NPV) Initiative: Direct Election of the President by Interstate Compact,* Congressional Research Service, Nov. 10, 2019. https://crsreports.congress.gov/product/pdf/R/R43823/9.

530 Jesse Wegman, *Let the People Pick the President: the Case for Abolishing the Electoral College,* St. Martins Press, https://us.macmillan.com/books/9781250221971/letthepeoplepickthepresident.

531 Jesse Wegman, *Let the People Pick the President: the Case for Abolishing the Electoral College,* St. Martins Press, https://us.macmillan.com/books/9781250221971/letthepeoplepickthepresident.

532 Elliot Ramos, "There's a Plan Afoot to Replace the Electoral College and You State May Already Be Part of It," NBC News, Nov. 10, 2020, https://www.nbcnews.com/politics/2020-election/map-national-popular-vote-plan-replace-electoral-college-n1247159?cid=eml_nbn_20201110.

533 Jesse Wegman, *Let the People Pick the President: the Case for Abolishing the Electoral College,* St. Martins Press, https://us.macmillan.com/books/9781250221971/letthepeoplepickthepresident.

534 Jesse Wegman (with Sam Kolitch), *Examining the Electoral College: An Interview with Jese Wegman,* December 7, 2020, the Brown Political Review, https://brownpoliticalreview.org/2020/12/let-the-people-pick-the-president-bpr-interviews-jesse-wegman/.

535 Jesse Wegman, *Let the People Pick the President: the Case for Abolishing the Electoral College,* St. Martins Press, https://us.macmillan.com/books/9781250221971/letthepeoplepickthepresident.

536 Elliot Ramos, "There's a Plan Afoot to Replace the Electoral College and You State May Already Be Part of It," NBC News, Nov. 10, 2020, https://www.nbcnews.com/politics/2020-election/map-national-popular-vote-plan-replace-electoral-college-n1247159?cid=eml_nbn_20201110.

537 Elliot Ramos, "There's a Plan Afoot to Replace the Electoral College and You State May Already Be Part of It," NBC News, Nov. 10, 2020, https://www.nbcnews.com/politics/2020-election/map-national-popular-vote-plan-replace-electoral-college-n1247159?cid=eml_nbn_20201110.

538 Alex Cohen, *The National Popular Vote Explained,* Brennan Center for Justice, Dec. 8, 2020, https://www.brennancenter.org/our-work/research-reports/national-popular-vote-explained.

539 Taegan Goddard, "The Winner-Take-All Electoral College Isn't in the Constitution," Electoral Vote Map, https://electoralvotemap.com/winner-take-all-electoral-college/.

540 National Popular Vote, "Agreement among the States to Elect the President by National Popular Vote," March 5, 2024, https://www.nationalpopularvote.com/sites/default/files/1-pager-npv-v232-2024-3-5.pdf.

541 National Popular Vote, "Agreement among the States to Elect the President by National Popular Vote," March 5, 2024, https://www.nationalpopularvote.com/sites/default/files/1-pager-npv-v232-2024-3-5.pdf.

542 National Popular Vote, "Agreement among the States to Elect the President by National Popular Vote," March 5, 2024, https://www.nationalpopularvote.com/sites/default/files/1-pager-npv-v232-2024-3-5.pdf.

543 John Koza, Barry Fadem, Mark Grueskin, Michael Mandell, Robert Richie. and Joseph Zimmerman, *Every Vote Equal: A State-Based Plan for Electing the President by National Popular Vote,* 4th Edition, February 2013, https://www.every-vote-equal.com/.

544 John Koza, Barry Fadem, Mark Grueskin, Michael Mandell, Robert Richie, and Joseph Zimmerman, *Every Vote Equal: A State-Based Plan for Electing the President by National Popular Vote,* 4th Edition, February 2013, https://www.every-vote-equal.com/.

545 Tara Ross, *The State of Minnesota Senate Elections Committee, an Act Relating to the Elections Sec 80, the National Popular Vote Compact,* March 16, 2023, https://assets.senate.mn/committees/2023-2024/3121_Committee_on_Elections/Ross%20Testimony.pdf.

546 Alexandra Orbuch, *National Popular Vote Circumvents the United States Constitution,* Princeton Legal Journal (PJL), May 2021, https://legaljournal.princeton.edu/national-popular-vote-circumventing-the-united-states-constitution/.

547 Norman Williams, *The Danger of the National Popular Vote Compact,* Harvard Law Review, March 13, 2019. https://harvardlawreview.org/blog/2019/03/the-danger-of-the-national-popular-vote-compact/.

548 Norman Williams, *The Danger of the National Popular Vote Compact,* Harvard Law Review, March 13, 2019, https://harvardlawreview.org/blog/2019/03/the-danger-of-the-national-popular-vote-compact/.

549 Norman Williams, *The Danger of the National Popular Vote Compact,* Harvard Law Review, March 13, 2019, https://harvardlawreview.org/blog/2019/03/the-danger-of-the-national-popular-vote-compact/.

550 Norman Williams, *The Danger of the National Popular Vote Compact,* Harvard Law Review, March 13, 2019, https://harvardlawreview.org/blog/2019/03/the-danger-of-the-national-popular-vote-compact/.

551 National Archives, the Office of the Federal Register (OFR), "Constitutional Amendment Process," August 15, 2016. https://www.archives.gov/federal-register/constitution

552 Akhil Amar and Vikram Amar, *How to Achieve Direct National Election of the President without Amending the Constitution, a Three-Part Series on the 2000 Election,* Find Law, December 28, 2001, https://supreme.findlaw.com/legal-commentary/how-to-achieve-direct-national-election-of-the-president-without-amending-the-constitution.html.

553 Jesse Wegman, *Let the People Pick the President: the Case for Abolishing the Electoral College,* St. Martins Press, https://us.macmillan.com/books/9781250221971/letthepeoplepickthepresident.

554 Jesse Wegman, *Let the People Pick the President: the Case for Abolishing the Electoral College.* St. Martins Press, https://us.macmillan.com/books/9781250221971/letthepeoplepickthepresident.

555 Jesse Wegman, *Let the People Pick the President: the Case for Abolishing the Electoral College,* St. Martins Press, https://us.macmillan.com/books/9781250221971/letthepeoplepickthepresident.

556 Jesse Wegman, *Let the People Pick the President: the Case for Abolishing the Electoral College,* St. Martins Press, https://us.macmillan.com/books/9781250221971/letthepeoplepickthepresident.

557 Jesse Wegman, *Let the People Pick the President: the Case for Abolishing the Electoral College,* St. Martins Press, https://us.macmillan.com/books/9781250221971/letthepeoplepickthepresident.

Chapter 13: One Person, One Vote: Making Every Vote Equal

558 Library of Congress, Text of Gettysburg Address Delivered at Gettysburg, PA, November 19, 1863, https://www.loc.gov/resource/rbpe.24404500/?st=text.

559 Wikipedia, "One Man, One Vote or One Person, One Vote," https://en.wikipedia.org/wiki/One_man,_one_vote#:~:text=%22One%20

man%2C%20one%20vote%22,universal%20suffrage%20and%20 proportional%20representation.

560 Lawrence Lessig and Adam Eichen, *Equal Votes—Our Fight to Fix the Electoral College—Winner-Take-All Is Unfair,* Equal Citizens, https:// equalcitizens.us/equal-votes/.

561 Mark Dimondstein, "Democracy: Of, By, and For the People," APWU, September 3, 2021, https://apwu.org/news/democracy-and-people.

562 League of Women Voters, "What Is One Person, One Vote?" LWV Blog, May 4, 2023, https://www.lwv.org/blog/what-one-person-one-vote.

563 Brennan Center for Justice, "Supreme Court Upholds One Person, One Vote," "Evenwel v Abbott," https://www.brennancenter.org/our-work/ analysis-opinion/supreme-court-upholds-one-person-one-vote.

564 National Constitution Center, *The United States Constitution-Article II— The Executive Branch,* https://constitutioncenter.org/the-constitution/ articles/article-ii.

565 Jesse Wegman, *Let the People Pick the President: the Case for Abolishing the Electoral College,* St. Martins Press, https://us.macmillan. com/books/9781250221971/letthepeoplepickthepresident.

566 Elizabeth Rusch, *You Call This Democracy? How to Fix our Government and Deliver Power to the People,* Houghton Mifflin Harcourt, 2020, https://books.google.com/books?id=IWOdD wAAQBAJ&printsec=frontcover&source=gbs_ ge_ summary_ r&cad=0#v=onepage&q&f=false.

567 Elizabeth Rusch, *You Call This Democracy? How to Fix our Government and Deliver Power to the People,* Houghton Mifflin Harcourt, 2020, https://books.google.com/books?id=IWOdDwAAQBAJ&print sec=frontcover&source=gbs_ge_summary_r&cad=0#v=onepage&q& f=false.

568 Will Wilder and Stuart Baum, "Five Egregious Voter Suppression Laws from 2021," Brennan Center for Justice, January 31, 2022, https:// www.brennancenter.org/our-work/analysis-opinion/5-egregious- voter-suppression-laws-2021.

569   Brennan Center for Justice, "Voting Laws Roundup: December 2022," February 1, 2023, https://www.brennancenter.org/our-work/research-reports/voting-laws-roundup-december-2022.

570   Brennan Center for Justice, "Voting Laws Roundup: June 2023," June 14, 2023, https://www.brennancenter.org/our-work/research-reports/voting-laws-roundup-june-2023.

571   Mark Dimondstein, "Democracy: Of, By and For the People," APWU, September 3, 2021, https://apwu.org/news/democracy-and-people.

572   Will Wilder and Stuart Baum, "Five Egregious Voter Suppression Laws from 2021," Brennan Center for Justice, January 31, 2022, https://www.brennancenter.org/our-work/analysis-opinion/5-egregious-voter-suppression-laws-2021.

573   Will Wilder and Stuart Baum, "Five Egregious Voter Suppression Laws from 2021," Brennan Center for Justice, January 31, 2022, https://www.brennancenter.org/our-work/analysis-opinion/5-egregious-voter-suppression-laws-2021.

574   Will Wilder and Stuart Baum, "Five Egregious Voter Suppression Laws from 2021," Brennan Center for Justice, January 31, 2022, https://www.brennancenter.org/our-work/analysis-opinion/5-egregious-voter-suppression-laws-2021

575   Will Wilder and Stuart Baum, "Five Egregious Voter Suppression Laws from 2021," Brennan Center for Justice, January 31, 2022, https://www.brennancenter.org/our-work/analysis-opinion/5-egregious-voter-suppression-laws-2021.

576   Will Wilder and Stuart Baum, "Five Egregious Voter Suppression Laws from 2021," Brennan Center for Justice, January 31, 2022, https://www.brennancenter.org/our-work/analysis-opinion/5-egregious-voter-suppression-laws-2021.

577   Brennan Center for Justice, "Voting Laws Roundup: June 2023," June 14, 2023, https://www.brennancenter.org/our-work/research-reports/voting-laws-roundup-june-2023.

578   Jason Harrow, "The Winner-Take-All Presidential System Is Unconstitutional and We Are Taking It to Court," USA Today Opinion Editorial Contributor, March 8, 2018, https://www.usatoday.com/

story/opinion/2018/03/08/winner-take-all-presidential-system-unconstitutional-court-challenge-jason-harrow-column/398742002/.

579 Jason Harrow, "The Winner-Take-All Presidential System Is Unconstitutional and We Are Taking It to Court," USA Today Opinion Editorial Contributor, March 8, 2018, https://www.usatoday.com/story/opinion/2018/03/08/winner-take-all-presidential-system-unconstitutional-court-challenge-jason-harrow-column/398742002/.

580 Lawrence Lessig, "The Equal Protection Argument against Winner-Take-All in the Electoral College," Equal Citizens, Dec. 4, 2016, https://medium.com/equal-citizens/the-equal-protection-argument-against-winner-take-all-in-the-electoral-college.

581 Lawrence Lessig and Adam Eichen, "Equal Votes—Our Fight to Fix the Electoral College—Winner-Take-All is Unfair," Equal Citizens, https://equalcitizens.us/equal-votes/.

582 Office of Communications, Federal Election Commission, *Official 2016 Presidential General Election Results,* from state elections offices, Jan. 30, 2017, https://transition.fee.gov/pubrec/fe2016/2016pregeresults.pdf.

583 Jerry Sims, as quoted to Lawrence Lessig, "The Equal Protection Argument against Winner-Take-All in the Electoral College," Equal Citizens, Dec 4, 2016, https://medium.com/equal-citizens/the-equal-protection-argument-against-winner-take-all-in-the-electoral-college.

584 Jesse Wegman, *Let the People Pick the President: the Case for Abolishing the Electoral College,* The Martin Press, First Edition, Copyright 2020, https://us.macmillan.com/books/9781250221971/letthepeoplepickthepresident.

585 Lawrence Lessig, "The Equal Protection Argument against Winner-Take-All in the Electoral College," Equal Citizens, Dec. 4, 2016, https://medium.com/equal-citizens/the-equal-protection-argument-against-winner-take-all-in-the-electoral-college.

586 Lawrence Lessig and Adam Eichen, "Equal Votes—Our Fight to Fix the Electoral College—Winner-Take-All Is Unfair," Equal Citizens, https://equalcitizens.us/equal-votes/.

587 David Abbott and James Levine, *Wrong Winner: The Coming Debacle in the Electoral College,* Praeger Publishers and the Library of Congress – 1991, https://books.google.com/books/about/Wrong_Winner.html?id=boe0YZ57v_kC.

588 Thirty-thousand.org, "How Small Congressional Districts Virtually Eliminate Gerrymandering," https://thirty-thousand.org/end-gerrymandering/.

589 Thirty-thousand.org, "How Small Congressional Districts Virtually Eliminate Gerrymandering," https://thirty-thousand.org/end-gerrymandering/.

Chapter 14: The Final Word

590 The American Presidency Project, "Keynote Address at the 2004 Democratic National Convention," July 27, 2004, https://www.presidency.ucsb.edu/documents/keynote-address-the-2004-democratic-national-convention.

591 Thirty-Thousand.org, "Return the House of Representatives to the People," Article updated Mar. 21, 2022, https://thirty-thousand.org/article-the-first-of-the-bill-of-rights/.

592 Thirty-Thousand.org, "Return the House of Representatives to the People," Article updated Mar. 21, 2022, https://thirty-thousand.org/article-the-first-of-the-bill-of-rights/.

593 United States Census Bureau, "Apportionment Legislation 1790–1830," https://www.census.gov/history/www/reference/apportionment/apportionment_legislation_1790_-_1830.html

594 United States Census Bureau, "Apportionment Legislation 1840–1880," https://www.census.gov/history/www/reference/apportionment/apportionment_legislation_1840_-_1880.html.

595 United States Census Bureau, "Apportionment Legislation 1890–Present," https://www.census.gov/history/www/reference/apportionment/apportionment_legislation_1890_-_present.html.

596 Wikipedia, "Apportionment Act of 1911," https://en.wikipedia.org/wiki/Apportionment_Act_of_1911#References.

597 Wikipedia, "Apportionment Paradox," https://en.wikipedia.org/wiki/Apportionment_paradox.

598 United States Census Bureau, "Apportionment Legislation 1890–Present," https://www.census.gov/history/www/reference/apportionment/apportionment_legislation_1890_-_present.html.

599

600 United States Census Bureau, "Apportionment Legislation: 1890–Present," https://www.census.gov/history/www/reference/apportionment/apportionment_legislation_1890_-_present.html.

601 Lee Drutman, Jonathan Cohen, Yuval Levin, and Norman Ornstein, *The Case for Enlarging the House of Representatives – Part IV: Alternative Proposals for House Enlargement,* 2021, American Academy of Arts and Sciences, https://www.amacad.org/ourcommonpurpose/enlarging-the-house/section/5 and_https://www.amacad.org/sites/default/files/publication/downloads/2021_Enlarging-the-House.pdf.

602 National Constitution Center, "The United States Constitution-Article II—the Executive Branch," https://constitutioncenter.org/the-constitution/articles/article-ii.

603 American Oversight, *The January 6 Attack on the US Capital,* September 26, 2023, American Oversight: An Informed Public to Strengthen Democracy, https://www.americanoversight.org/investigation/the-january-6-attack-on-the-u-s-capitol.

604 American Oversight, *The January 6 Attack on the US Capital,* September 26, 2023, American Oversight: An Informed Public to Strengthen Democracy, https://www.americanoversight.org/investigation/the-january-6-attack-on-the-u-s-capitol.

605 Wendy Underhill, "What the Electoral Count Reform Act Means for States," NCSL (National Conference of State Legislatures), Jan. 16, 2023, https://www.ncsl.org/resources/details/what-the-electoral-count-reform-act-means-for-states.

606 Tara Ross, *The Indispensable Electoral College: How the Founders' Plan Saves Our Country from Mob Rule,* Regnery Gateway Publishers, 2017, https://www.taraross.com/product-page/the-indispensable-electoral-college-how-the-founders-plan-saves-our-country-fr.

[607] David Ross, *How the Electoral College Was Nearly Abolished in 1970*, History published by A&E Television Networks, Aug. 3, 2020, https://www.history.com/news/electoral-college-nearly-abolished-thurmond.

[608] Joscelyn Kiley, "Majority of Americans Continue to Favor Moving Away from the Electoral College," September 25, 2023, https://www.pewresearch.org/short-reads/2023/09/25/majority-of-americans-continue-to-favor-moving-away-from-electoral-college/.

[609] Joscelyn Kiley, "Majority of Americans Continue to Favor Moving Away from the Electoral College," September 25, 2023, https://www.pewresearch.org/short-reads/2023/09/25/majority-of-americans-continue-to-favor-moving-away-from-electoral-college/.

[610] John Koza, Barry Fadem, Mark Grueskin, Michael Mandell, Robert Richie, and Joseph Zimmerman, *Every Vote Equal: A State-Based Plan for Electing the President by National Popular Vote,* 4th Edition, February 2013, https://www.every-vote-equal.com/.

[611] National Archives, *The Constitution of the United States: A Transcription,* America's Founding Documents, https://www.archives.gov/founding-docs/constitution-transcript#2.